D0258115

RICHARD HOGGART

To my grandchildren, Sasha, Harriet, Louisa, Kit, Millie and Daniel:
users of literacy

RICHARD HOGGART

Virtue and Reward

FRED INGLIS

polity

First published in 2014 by Polity Press

Polity Press
65 Bridge Street
Cambridge CB2 1UR, UK

Polity Press
350 Main Street
Malden, MA 02148, USA

ISBN-13: 978-0-7456-5171-2 (hardback)

A catalogue record for this book is available from the British Library.

Typeset in 10.5 on 12 pt Sabon by
Servis Filmsetting Ltd, Stockport, Cheshire
Printed and bound in Great Britain by
Berforts Information Press Ltd, Stevenage, Hertfordshire

For further information on Polity, visit our website: www.politybooks.com

CONTENTS

ACKNOWLEDGEMENTS

It is usual and proper for a biography such as this only to be published after the subject's death. But as I write, Richard Hoggart, though naturally much reduced by time at the age of 94, is still here and, on occasions, able to reminisce with his faithful family, while for the author of his biography, who met his subject in 1969 and is turned 75, it's getting late, and it will be just as well to complete the thing while he can.

Since that date, visiting him once or twice every year, I have come to know Richard Hoggart fairly well and always to hold him in strong affection as well as awkward reverence. When, some ten years ago, I dedicated my *People's Witness: The Journalist in Modern Politics* to him, he was typically cordial and warmhearted in his approval and so, when in 2005 I wrote, with well-merited diffidence, to ask if I might be his biographer, it was a source of keen pride as well as pleasure when he sent back one of his rapidly written postcards saying simply, 'I can think of no one better.'[1]

I was at the time just beginning a biography of the philosopher R. G. Collingwood, later published by Princeton as *History Man,* and I conceived of a Hoggart biography as standing in an essential continuity of social thought. Research for the Collingwood biography had been handsomely supported by the Leverhulme Foundation, but by the time I resolved to begin the present book in 2010 the great crash had happened, and research funds for elderly biographers were much harder to come by.

In the event, there was to hand the ready and plentiful help provided by Hoggart's three children and their spouses: Simon, Paul and

---

[1] Correspondence now among the Hoggart Papers at the University of Sheffield.

his wife Elizabeth, Nicola and her husband Richard; and, of course, by the incomparable archivist, Jackie Hodgson at the University of Sheffield, where the copious Hoggart papers were lodged after the University awarded him an Honorary Doctorate in 2000. These papers had been carefully retained by Hoggart all the way from his early school reports to personal notes and memoranda from his years as Warden of Goldsmiths.

Family help and the Sheffield archive apart, I am also grateful for generous help of many kinds from all of the following (one thing that struck me whenever I asked for such help was the warmth with which people expressed their interest, and the pleasure they felt that the man who had written what had been for them a life-changing book was to have that life celebrated in a biography).

So, my great gratitude once more to the Hoggart family, and to Deyola Adekunle for her help at UNESCO Headquarters in Paris; Lois Aitkenhead for consistent encouragement; Michael Bailey for the indispensable gift of his two collections of essays about my subject and for cordial letters; Richard Beck for useful criticism and his hospitality; Hilary Britland, as before, for her accomplishments with camera and keyboard; Dennis and Mary Butts, as so often, for critical reading and their plumbing science; James Curran, old friend, for his detailed information about his time at Goldsmiths while Hoggart was Warden; Andrew Davies, former colleague, for a helpful conversation about his screenplay for the 2006 BBC production of *The Chatterley Affair*; Stuart Hall for his reminiscences (a few years ago now) of the Birmingham Centre for Contemporary Cultural Studies, and Chelly Halsey for the same; Lord Peter Hennessey, for recollections of his long friendship with Richard Hoggart; the late David Holbrook for his familiarity with Hoggart's work; Eric Hoyle, for appreciative reading and knowledge of Potternewton; David Howe, for reminiscences of Leicester University when he was Hoggart's student; Jean Humphreys, though I have never met her, for her so very affecting two letters about Hoggart's autobiography; David Lodge, much-respected novelist, for his recollections of his time as colleague and longstanding friend of Hoggart's; Krishan Kumar, a dear friend since we first met at the 1969 CCCS potlatch, for many acute and sympathetic readings of Hoggart's work; Pat Loughrey, present Warden of Goldsmiths, for help with the history of his institution and his generous hospitality; Sue Owen, custodian of Hoggart's studies, for her invitation to me to present a paper at her Sheffield Conference in 2006, the first shaping of the present book (the last such occasion, I think, which Hoggart himself attended); Major David Ryan, for military-historical help with the Pantelleria operation; Greg Sporton, prompt, caustic and loyal as always, sometime Head of Research at the Laban Institute, for his thorough account of Hoggart's complicated dealings with that recalcitrant body; Laurie Taylor, for encouragement and his blithe recollections of the Video Appeals Committee.

Lastly, this is a deliberately short biography. A convention has grown up over the last several decades whereby biographies swell to ponderous and very portly sizes. I have kept this book to the shape in which it may still be held easily and finished – for naturally I hope it will grip its readers tight – within a day or two. Accordingly, I have cut out minor details and extended reviews of each and every book in order to make it above all a good read, taking for granted that that is the best way to vivify and honour my great subject.

PREFACE BY PAUL HOGGART

As I write this my parents, both aged 94, are living together in a care home near my house. Both suffer from advanced dementia. The loving father his three children have known all our lives remains, as does his sense of humour, for he still laughs happily if I tease him in the old way. Occasionally memories of his mother, grandmother or brother Tom well up and threaten to overwhelm him, but most of his working life has vanished in the fog of memory-loss.

This is particularly poignant because this generous, evocative and insightful biography is part of a recent revival of interest in his work, which has brought new books, conferences and appreciative assessments in radio and television documentaries of which Dad is only dimly aware. He listened with pleasure when I read him drafts of the early chapters, however, saying they created 'vivid pictures' in his mind. After decades when his ideas had become unfashionable, this rediscovery has been gratifying for his children. Our lives have been punctuated by approaches, often from complete strangers, eager to tell us how much his work meant to them. Dad himself has had countless letters to that effect.

The Uses of Literacy, it seems, has spoken to successive generations. In 1957 the bold assertion that the culture and values of working people needed to be understood on their own terms and merited serious analysis caught a changing national mood, but it was the story of the scholarship boy's conflicted transition from one social stratum to another which seems to have struck deeper personal chords.

As children we lived with that unfolding story, and it is fascinating to see it here through the eyes of a sympathetic, though not uncritical, chronicler. Shielded from the more vituperative attacks (I did not learn of the post Chatterley trial dog-mess through our letterbox until years later), our own lives became richer and more interesting as Dad's fame grew. Few small boys get to kick a ball about with the England football captain in their own back garden.

As a father he could not have been more devoted. In a typical example, when, in my mid-thirties I was in hospital for several weeks with cancer, he insisted on driving with my mother from Farnham to London to see me every single day. He would have done the same for any of us. We have always talked a lot. When I was a boy, he read me Dickens novels at bedtime. On family walks he would recount the plots of Victorian novels, and he never lost his belief in the enlightening power of literature. In the 1990s he astonished me by revealing that he felt a failure because he had never written fiction. 'I wanted to be the next Hardy or Lawrence', he said. After retirement, an Indian summer writing autobiographies and reflective social commentaries brought some compensation for that.

In my early teens we would go for evening walks around the suburbs of Birmingham. He would linger too long looking through front windows, fascinated by the furnishings and décor as I tugged anxiously at his sleeve. This unselfconsciousness sometimes made us cringe when he made amused 'sociological observations' about fellow diners in cafes and restaurants, barely lowering his voice.

In later life he would relieve the tensions of work with detailed accounts of battles with UNESCO bureaucrats or Senate House mandarins. He always seemed to feel a need to fight harder to compensate for his origins and his non-Oxbridge education. He remained unusually sensitive to slights and simply could not bear to feel he might be in the wrong. This could make him vehemently dogmatic at home and, I gather, at work. Doubtless due to his puritanical upbringing, arguments, whether about the cynicism of commercial culture or the status of Goldsmiths College, always had a fierce moral edge for Dad.

He was always driven. Long after retirement he was up by 6.00, putting in an hour or two before breakfast. After family supper he would retire to his study until bedtime, though his door was always open, and he liked us to wander in for a chat. On holidays with the extended family, he would sip wine on French terraces, reading and scribbling notes on scrap paper held on a battered old clip-board with rubber bands.

Even in his current confusion he remains utterly devoted to my mother. In his prime he was charismatic, witty and energetic. I once asked if any of the women he met had ever shown flirtatious interest. 'Not really', he laughed. 'I think I had an invisible *Keep Off the Grass!* sign.' He was indignant when a colleague's wife once accused him of having a patriarchal marriage. In fact he would have been happy for Mum to continue her wartime teaching career. She herself decided she should be at home with her children. Years later she told me that she had indeed feared patriarchal disapproval, not from Dad, but from her own father.

But Dad's punishing work ethic could blind him occasionally. After the move to UNESCO in 1970, Mum, recently bereaved of her mother, uprooted, with an 'empty nest' and feeling dowdy and over-weight among the chic Parisiennes, teetered on the brink of serious depression. Dad, more embattled than ever, seemed oblivious. Then an unfocused and feckless student, I summoned my meagre reserves of moral courage and took him to task about it. 'I never discuss my marriage with anyone!' he told me tight-lipped. Gradually Dad relaxed, Mum recovered and they became as inseparable as ever.

I often wonder what would have happened if he had not left for Paris and a career as an administrator. Before he left Birmingham, *Cultural Studies* had begun its passionate affair with continental cultural theory, quite alien to his attitudes and instincts. Would he have become a 'fellow-traveller' and interpreter like Raymond Williams? Or angrily rejected it all like E. P. Thompson? Neither, I suspect, but I am sure of one thing: he would have insisted that the discipline remained accessibly engaged with public debates in a way that reso-nated clearly beyond academia.

His work has never been easy to categorize. Over the years he has been accused of being theoretically naive, patronizing, a Maoist (absurdly) and an elitist. But as these pages make clear, always at the core was a fierce belief that ordinary people should not be under-estimated culturally or, in a favourite phrase, 'sold short'. That is as relevant today as it was in 1957.

Paul Hoggart

PROLOGUE: THE CONDITION OF ENGLAND

I

Richard Hoggart was born in 1918, a short time before the war to end all wars came to a brief stop before resuming, in China, Abyssinia, Spain and then the whole world, twenty years later. For a working life which stretched over seven decades, from the small jobs he took while still a schoolboy to the publication of his last book at the age of 86, it is fair to say that his preoccupation was never smaller than the condition of England.

The so-called 'condition of England' debate was initiated by assorted commentators, essayists and intellectuals towards the middle of the nineteenth century and remained in currency as token of an unresolvable altercation not only about English imperial might as opposed to national squalor, hideous inequality and gross philistinism, but also about that always elusive and collective formation, 'the English temper'. It was Matthew Arnold, perhaps the best-known, as well as with John Ruskin and William Morris, the best-equipped of those bold intelligences fluently ready to speak to the nation for the nation's good, who identified the dire cultural properties and emotional thicknesses which characterized the three social classes, 'Populace', 'Philistines' and 'Barbarians'. A century later Hoggart himself entitled one of his own books *An English Temper*.

Few things are less plausible or more exigent than generalizing about the state of a nation. It has to be done; it can't be done. Politicians must attempt the task in order to win over an electorate to their leadership and Party; they must aim to tell sufficient truths to the people about the people such that a majority believe themselves to be *recognized* for what they are and hope for, and feeling themselves

1

recognized, extend recognition and support to the man or woman who names them so.

There again, this is also the artist's and the thinker's duty and purpose. The painter, supremely the landscape painter, paints a picture of the place he or she belongs to: its hills and houses, a view from a window, a bunch of flowers, a letterbox. The picture is a recognition looking for recognition in return, and it is a judgement. So, too, the composer. When Vaughan Williams adorns his theme from Thomas Tallis or summons the ghosts of Wenlock Edge, he gives musical body to the places and the hold they have on him, for better and worse. When D. H. Lawrence utters his memorable curse over the ugliness of the Nottinghamshire townscape as Lady Chatterley drives through it in 1928, his anger and detestation are the obverse of his longing that his country be a beautiful place to live and that the society which is settled there be as good as may be. Patriotism is the powerful emotion which takes the measure of the distance between how things are and how they ought to be. If the gap is wide, patriotism comes out as baffled rage and wretchedness; if the gap is narrow, patriotism issues as pride and admiration.

According to this rather partisan view, all art is an essay in home-making, and every narrative an attempt to imagine the finest life one can think of. So a novel or a biography or a movie, even one picturing lives of quiet desperation or shocking ugliness, should be written in such a way as to check what it tells against the best way of life the author might fashion for the people in the tale.

These imperatives are all the stronger for those writers turning to the very facts of life in front of them, and arranging them for the readers' benefit as both recognition and representation of how things really are or were in the society to hand. At this point a writer such as Richard Hoggart is working very close to the novelists, but what he says must not be fiction; his truths are harder to fix and tell, for he cannot reply to his critics by saying, 'this is how life *might* be represented', for they will retort, quite rightly, 'But you said you would tell us how life truly was and *is*.' Hoggart stands in a great tradition of English, Scots, Welsh and Irish social commentary and representation, peopled by those already mentioned – Ruskin, Morris, Arnold and dozens more, among the throng such honoured names as John Stuart Mill, William Cobbett, Friedrich Engels, George Eliot, Robin Collingwood, Beatrice Webb, Edwin Muir, R. H. Tawney, George Orwell, F. R. Leavis, let alone Hoggart's great contemporaries E. P. Thompson and Raymond Williams.

I let drop this little shower of names briefly to recall the truism that a book such as this, a biography of a splendid man, can only take shape within the frame of a tradition, a concept which needs constantly to be wrestled out of the hands of the political Right and returned to our common intellectual vocabulary, as designating the necessary formations of our every waking thought and feeling. Without a tradition, without, that is, a mobile but holistic ambience of ways of thought, modes of speech, forms of argument, a characteristic idiom *and* a shelf of classic texts by venerable ancestors, no one can think, write or even perceive what there is to see and interpret.

Reporting the world of homemaking and homewrecking is therefore no slight matter, quite apart from its being the civic duty of us all. Of course, it is the daily stock-in-trade of the middle pages of the once broadsheet newspapers and even today, for the rapidly diminishing numbers of their readers, opinionators report, as calmly as they can in the hothouse hysteria of the struggle for circulation sales, on the imminent end of British civilization set against a sky darkened by the storms of climate change, currency collapses and the smoke of war. A life spent, between 1918 and the present, looking for truths about the condition of England, of Britain, of the world itself, and setting down the truths in twenty or so books, takes more than sheer nerve to sustain. It takes extraordinary resolution, coolness and poise also, let alone the hearty catchall, *experience*, which is to say the conscious and protracted transformation of mere eventuality into the passages of significant living and intelligible history.

Effecting that transformation in a way that experience of such a kind as attracts the adjective 'personal' can then adequately stand for the condition of a nation requires all those formidable qualities I have named. But it also requires a particular intelligence, a gift amounting to genius for living forcefully in the actual present while separating that forceful life from another zone of the self where different emotions and the thoughts they direct sort, retain, describe and evaluate the facts, the acts of daily doing. If this turns out to mean that all such thinking, and the writing it may give rise to, is autobiographical, then that is no more than to say that history can only be grasped as a process of self-knowledge, but that this knowing of the self is a fractional discovery in a collective act. It was Hegel who, two hundred years ago and in exceptionally difficult, even tortured prose, first taught the lesson that only from our history can we find out what on earth is going on, so the making of that history had better be the product of the best that has been known and thought, and then retrieved and restated by the best individuals we can appoint.

To say so, so blithely and roundly, is to give that 'we' enormous force and simplicity. For it is obvious that 'we' quite fail to decide what is best about the past and who are the best people to have and to hold the best. The terrific cacophony of the argument about best and worst is what we call our politics. For all that 'politics' is a word from which, in the rich and self-regarding nations of the world, so many people recoil in ignorant revulsion, politics is only another name for the self-knowledge deposited like veins of energy in our history, which it needs to be our common pursuit to discharge as energy into the present.

II

The whole point of this book is to nominate its subject as someone who has met the moral duty of the citizen to look out hard for the best parts of our history and has sought to make them tell in later generations. The subject being Hoggart, this is an easy claim to vindicate. His memorials in the social history of the twentieth century are many and, in Britain at least, as well as not least in the offices of the hopefully titled United Nations, where he spent a few years, prominent enough and often revisited.

The most accessible of the memorials are books, naturally, but it will be a main contention of the narrative which follows that the books cannot be understood as separate from the life. The textbook designation 'life and work' is only any good to us if we take the two as much more intimately imbricated than is usual. People are quick to pounce on biographers with the old injunction coined by D. H. Lawrence, 'Never trust the teller, trust the tale.' More technical objections are also made deploying the 'intentional fallacy'[1] which rebukes those who look for explanations of what a writer meant by identifying his or her intentions and motives. That mischievous goblin of deconstruction, Jacques Derrida, destroyed many careers by advising everybody that the thing simply could not be done.

R. G. Collingwood,[2] on the other hand, said firmly and, to my mind, rightly, that

> ... you cannot find out what a man means by simply studying his spoken or written statements, even though he has spoken or written with perfect command of language and perfectly truthful intention. In

---

[1] W. K. Wimsatt and M. C. Beardsley, 'The Intentional Fallacy', *Sewanee Review*, 54, 1946.
[2] R. G. Collingwood, *An Autobiography*, Oxford: Clarendon Press, 1938, pp. 28–9.

order to find out his meaning you must also know what the question was (a question in his own mind, and presumed by him to be in yours) to which the thing he has said or written was meant as an answer.

A person's thoughts over a lifetime, tabulated, as in Hoggart's works, in a long series of books aspire (this is true of all human beings in all their unwritten narratives) to the condition of art. That is to say, the thinker searches for the words which best express the thought he or she is trying to discover. That thought is only known at its best when the words deployed are right. We are all well aware of this, which is why we say, when the words are wrong, 'No, no, that's not what I mean.' Of course, the thinker, whether writing or speaking, may sometimes say, 'Oh, well, that'll have to do', but on such occasions there remains a dissatisfaction, a sense that truth itself has been disfigured, for the best thoughts demand, as a necessary condition of their discovery, the best and therefore most beautiful expression. Art speech is the only speech.

Every human being thinks. 'Thinker' is not a grand or exclusive term. Rodin's great statue might be of anyone. Human thought transpires from the individual's engagement with a subject or topic. Wallace Stevens describes the activity of thought at its highest pitch like this:

> Three times the concentred self takes hold, three times
> The thrice concentred self, having possessed
> The object, grips it in savage scrutiny,
> Once to make captive, once to subjugate
> Or yield to subjugation, once to proclaim
> The meaning of the capture, this hard prize,
> Fully made, fully apparent, fully found.[3]

This *is* high-pitched but it is also everyday. Any serious person will recognize the descriptions of the effort of hard thought, the discipline of it and the quiet jubilation of the capture of the discovery when it is, however rarely, fully made, apparent, found. If little of our thoughts is so hard won, the struggle for such victories is common human endeavour whether the subject-and-object of thought is ordinary domestic life or the tungsten topics of physics or philosophy.

Wherever one's thoughtful attention is directed, towards the immovably commonplace or unfathomably profound, thought and feeling are inseparable. To say so is to flout the ancient principle

---

[3] Wallace Stevens, 'Credences of Summer' in *Collected Poems*, New York: Vintage Books, 1982, p. 376.

that reason and emotion are forever at odds and clear, truthful and beautiful thought can only be attained by the exercise of pure reason, unpolluted by the passions.

No one doubts that passion may prevent one's thinking clearly, but neither does anyone doubt that feelings shape the intrinsic lines and directions of thought. These bromides take us to the heart of moral understanding, and their relevance just now is that for us to understand the stature and the significance of the thinker-about-society who is our great subject in this biography, we must learn from him to direct the right, the best feelings of which we are capable (and of which we are made the more capable by reading him, thinking and feeling through his words) towards the subject-matter he has chosen, and which has chosen him.

This little detour into what Adam Smith, 250 years ago, called 'a theory of the moral sentiments' returns us to the purpose of this prologue, placed as it is as a gateway to a life-history. That purpose, in this one modest enough volume, is to argue by example against some of the toughest conventions of contemporary intellectual life, especially those which counterpose subjective to objective, fact to value, quantitative to qualitative inquiry.

If I am right about the mutual shaping and intercalation of thought and feeling, the practice of all human inquiry simply cannot purport the separation of subject from object, the effortful putting down of what is called the 'personal' in order to treat things-out-there as if they were detached from human interests.[4] Language itself won't permit it. Even science, in its long, successful endeavour to master the natural world and its cosmic enormousness, selects the facts according to its humanly ordered values. (The fact, for instance, that phenomena may be lethal to humans is hardly independent of the value of remaining alive.)

For our immediate purposes, now and as is more motivated by courtesy than philosophical rigour, let us accept the conventional distinction as between the natural and the human sciences. Then let us say that in our inquiries into human quiddity and its always *historical* making, we seek to summon up and shape those feelings which most

---

[4] Here I gesture towards an extensive critique in the human sciences conducted over the past half-century, the ambitions of which have been precisely to oppose the antinomies I have named between subjective and objective and so forth. See as a beginning, Richard Bernstein, *The Restructuring of Social and Political Theory*, Philadelphia: University of Pennsylvania Press, 1978; Charles Taylor, *Human Agency and Language: Philosophical Papers*, vol. 1, Cambridge: Cambridge University Press, 1985; Jurgen Habermas, *Knowledge and Human Interests*, London: Heinemann Educational Books, 1972.

conduce to the right kinds of interpretation and judgement of the subject-matter before us.

This is not a matter of piously arranging feelings in a mush of amiability. Right feeling, as we shall see in Hoggart's case, may at times certainly start from anger – the anger of a generous-hearted man at the way people disgrace themselves, and defile their own humanity. Right feeling is a product of moral sympathy which is in turn a function of a strong imagination. (These complex movements of mind, body and spirit are very difficult to arrange in a causal order; that is no reason for not naming them, or not using the words as readily as we do in normal conversation.) As a common principle of inquiry into any human dealings, whether the day-to-day business of, on a grand scale, politics, or the day-to-day business of a school or a hospital, a bank or a department store, we learn from example (Hoggart the example to hand), as well as by bringing to the inquiry our own best self, how judicious objectivity and loving kindness (harsh if it has to be) become synonymous. When this happens, keen moral sympathy dissolves into historical understanding.

So a brief opening attempt at an essay on the condition of England is as comparative as, indeed, this whole book is to be. Comparativism is a working method. It jolts or disconcerts us into seeing how things might be otherwise than as they are. It forces on our attention 'how other people's creations can be so utterly their own and so deeply part of us'.[5] There is always the danger that George Santayana pointed out when he said that people compare when they can't get to the root of the matter. But if the root of the matter is made visible then comparison brings into relief the different particularities of each side of what is being compared. Then one can see the sharp, living particularity of each, and what each is worth.

In the study of a life's work, one is comparing how things were with how things are. One is making the very idea of 'progress' work for its living. One is also comparing the person – this writer, this thinker – with how he was and how he appears decades later. With that, we arrive at full justification of biographical writing. A biography, insofar as it is any good (and an unhappy consequence of the happy fact that biography is so thriving a genre is that lots of biographies are awful tat) dramatizes a life and in doing so actualizes a period of history, or rather, that sliver of history illuminated by that single life. With the much-to-be-welcomed demise of Grand Theories of both

---

[5] Clifford Geertz, *Local Knowledge: Essays in Interpretive Anthropology*, New York: Basic Books, 1983, p. 54.

7

historical movement (Marxism, neoliberalism, postmodernism) and of intellectual method (structuralism, discourse theory, imperializing psychoanalysis, postcolonialism) the small tenacious form of biography proves as good a way as any of grasping fragments of the times.

III

Hoggart's life-work was, like that of all great writers, to live, with his kind of vitality and vigour alongside his careful detachment, in the main currents of the historical river. Only by so doing could he find the direction of change, feel its earlier origins, judge it for temperature, volume, for the sheer variety of the waters which composed the flood of time, their thickness, thinness, saltiness and taste. He elected to do this not as novelist but as man of action.

This is rare in British life. American, or Russian, or French political history all have notable figures who were both prominent actors in their epoch as well as its intellectual commentators. The accidents and conventions of British history have tended to separate, as it were, executive from judicial agents. Hoggart brought them together and this placed on him the exceptional strain of being utterly true to the facts of cultural and political life in his writing and of maintaining full responsibility for his actions and decisions as these affected those facts of life. To take two of the most prominent moments of his career, in his strong influence on the Pilkington Committee and his brief, dramatic intervention in the Chatterley trial, he had to make the judgements he did swiftly and in collaboration with an unusual assortment of other people, and he had to be right.

This is to say that he had to have an unusually fine and acute response to the combined mysteries of common sentiment, of popular mood and meaning, of domestic practices and beliefs, all those commonplace oddities which we generalize as culture and which impel the surges and stagnations of a nation's life. Every op-ed journalist or television reporter makes, of necessity, a stab at such an evaluation any week of the year, but the results are rarely either accurate or percipient. They rest on vague notions of mood and impressions of the feelings they guess to be present in a motley succession of individuals the journalists themselves have spoken to or known about. If there is a crowd in the action, then that too will have its temperature taken on the evidence of its collective conduct, a few sudden episodes (violent for preference), its applause for a leader, its banners, T-shirts and heroes. In grosser instances, a journalist will make appeal to such elusive quantities as 'a sense of optimism', 'a feeling of wellbeing', 'a large proportion of pessimists among those I spoke to' and wait to be vindicated by events.

This is not to deride such spokespeople. We need them to give some intelligible shape to the world's news, and to reassure us that the present will lead controllably out of the past into the future. But even the most sensitive and percipient of television's daily storytellers – the John Coles and Walter Cronkites of its great days – have to work from scraps and fragments of evidence while being at once tentative and firm.

This is a long way from the kind of thing Hoggart and the tradition in which he stood were attempting. Now to attempt, as I shall, to compare the huge fresco of working-class culture which he finished in 1957 with a hasty drypoint of the same colossal subject fifty-odd years later is to do no less than draw a moral horizon against which to set this book and the life-story it contains.

To say this is to take for granted that Hoggart's most important book is *The Uses of Literacy*. For my purpose, I would rather say that it presages the shape and significance of the life. After all, its author wasn't yet forty when the book came out; there was a lot of public life as well as published pages to come. Rather, the classic work indicates a strikingly consistent way of life, which is why I contend that the life *is* the work, the one only to be understood as the other. *The Uses of Literacy* teaches us to understand this paradox.

After all, Hoggart is perfectly plain about the necessary restrictions of his vision. In the first half of the book he is recreating the southern parts of working-class Leeds between 1925 and 1936, when he went to university. He then offers to connect these years with the continuities he detects as still alive and strong in 1957. As we shall see in detail in chapter 7, he was repudiating those aspects of his intellectual tradition which had moved against the moral and cultural continuities Hoggart himself so convinces us were still thriving as he wrote. He returned to the content of their culture what he knew and saw to be such strong parts of working-class life as its family solidarity, the great but living archetype of its matriarch, its 'good table' and the 'tastiness' of its tinned food (salmon, pineapple), the swell of feeling accompanying the songs at the club. He found not a brutal, lost proletariat but a thick-textured, active culture, carried by the old big words, for sure – solidarity, neighbourliness, community – but also by its jokes, its tiny gestures, its biking excursions and seaside outings, its downright bloodymindedness before the dreadful creepiness of status and snobbery.

9

Without blinking at the nastier parts of working-class life, its some-time cruelties of men to women, their intermittent drunkenness, their physical cruelty, by playing down the political radicalism Hoggart reports as true only of a minority, noting the trivial sentimentality of much childcare and most ornaments, he reverses the downward inflection of so much of the social commentary he inherited.

At the halfway mark the book, famously, changes. 'Unbending the springs of action' tells us of the softening of old resilience and uncov-ers on the page a new literacy of reflex cynicism. Hoggart takes a grim but minutely careful rollcall of an imaginative class life nourished by a corrupt and phoney matiness in its daily and weekly papers, and distracted from boredom by the deathly fictions of brutal punch-ups and panting, pointless sexual sadism.

If the people's narratives are indeed one moral measure of 'the condition of England', then the ghastly thrillers Hoggart so faithfully mimicked in the book have become by now nursery school trifles, compared with the images of shocking violence easily available on the dozens of television's digital channels, let alone the officially more genteel storybooks of the BBC and other terrestrials. As each evening advances so the tales of murder and rape become more explicit and protracted. It is as though, in Hoggart's own graphic metaphor, a fingernail is drawn down one's opened nerve-endings with a fierce thrill of pain indistinguishable from pleasure. Even mainline series, mostly shipped over from the USA, about cops and robbers in the terrifying outreaches of Baltimore, Detroit and Los Angeles, a heavy succession of socially purposeful and aesthetically serious dramas, all deploying the conventions of the genre as formally as Jacobean melodrama, but all taking for granted an explicitness of violent action and luscious atrocity, plunge into much lower depths than could have been plumbed in 1957.

Are these abominable things measures of a nation's soul? That same nation, according to its state tabulators,[6] watches more than 27 hours per week of television, not including DVD, Blu-ray and – so far unmentioned as well as unmentionable – video games. Much of this latter is the stuff of thrillers such as Hoggart names but, as I say, vastly more explicit, brutal and extended.

The deep puzzle is then to determine what these desperate legends do to us as well as to decide who the 'we' are to whom whatever it is is duly done. There can be no doubting Hoggart's conclusion to his book as a prophecy fulfilled since he ended it in the way he did.

---

[6] *British Audience Research Board*, London: HMSO, 2012.

Again, to define the limits of freedom in any single case is, I have admitted, extremely difficult. But many of us seem so anxious to avoid the charge of authoritarianism that we will think hardly at all about the problem of definition. Meanwhile, the freedom from official interference enjoyed in this kind of society, coupled with the tolerance we ourselves are so happy to show, seems to be allowing cultural developments as dangerous in their own way as those we are shocked at in totalitarian societies.[7]

He has plotted the move from a class to a mass culture. His contention was, even more than fifty years ago, that although the exploitation of some of the dismal aspects of contemporary humankind is plain as day to see, that exploitation is not irresistible and that the idea of free and open choices by freely choosing individuals is not completely vacuous. The heaps of malodorous garbage peddled on TV and DVD along with the worked-up frenzies of a revolting yellow press (to which we shall return) penetrate only a little way into many spirits, into many others not at all. That much is plain from the continuing kindliness of everyday street conduct – the helpful attention certain to be given at a road accident, say, or to a lost child in a playground, amiable greetings at the supermarket checkout (even if all part of the training), the friendliness of policewomen, the brisk accessibility of hospital nurses . . . these gestures give the lie to the supposition that doses of television horrors or the ludicrous bawling of the tabloids make the language of everyday ethics – 'decent', 'healthy', serious', 'valuable', 'poor', 'weakening', 'hollow', 'trivial'[8] – unusable and inaccurate.

What one can surely say is that, as the shaping spirit of class-consciousness has been relaxed by the dissolution of class membership in the sexual divisions of heavy industrial labour – coal, steel, ships, docks, chemicals, warfare – a different kind of free-and-easiness has fashioned itself out of mass culture. Now that not so very many people go hungry within the nation (though the numbers are rising), now the people have thrown off patched and re-stitched and cast-off clothing and can dress freshly and comfortably most of the time, now the action and iconography of class confrontation – long strikes, pickets, lockouts, factory gates – has dimmed for a season, a different kind of popular self-determination is devising a new guise for the citizen.

This character takes liberty for granted. In politics, for most people

---

[7] Richard Hoggart, *The Uses of Literacy*, Harmondsworth: Penguin, 1958, pp. 344–5.
[8] Hoggart (1958), p. 344.

never a social or intellectual category of great importance, there is a not-so-new dismissal of *all* politicians as 'just in it for themselves'. In the now-notorious expenses scandal of 2008 when a number of members of Parliament were discovered to have over-claimed thousands of pounds for subsistence, not so much criminally as in a lax atmosphere of over-permissiveness, the common reaction of most people was no doubt contemptuous but also indifferent – 'what do you expect?' In an attitude almost universal towards state institutions, people commended and felt warmth towards the local MP who had, as most do, given conscientious help when asked for it, but waved away all other MPs of whom they knew nothing as mere politicians, self-seeking and irrelevant. They were perfectly well aware that Britain is a much less uncorrupt country than it was in 1960 – there are far more tax-dodgers, the excessively rich are far less public-spirited and responsible, toadying and time-serving among the powerful much more common, everyday dishonesty taken-for-granted. But rottenness of this kind is tolerated as being beyond reach. Home is where you live and the rich are somewhere else.

This strong localism goes back deep into the soil of the old working class. It transpires in the way people refer admiringly enough to the schools their own children attend, and praise in passing that majority of teachers who do a decent job. It certainly issues in the trust placed in family doctors, direct social exchanges with whom have in so many urban instances done much to mitigate the mild, casual racism of English culture.

Indeed that last point, to my mind, admits of bolder generalization about the moral condition of the country. Perhaps the biggest change in the culture and customs of the country since the *Empire Windrush* arrived in 1948 has been the arrival and settlement of large numbers of mostly black immigrants from the sometime colonies and dominions of the Empire. They arrived with their rights to do so intact from India, Pakistan, Kenya, Uganda, Tanzania, South Africa and the constituent islands of the West Indies. They had been preceded of course by many tens of thousands of white and therefore invisible Australians, Canadians, New Zealanders, but the black arrivals were pretty new, and they came for the money, for the chances, for the homes, and they came to stay, even if that wasn't what they first intended.

What is more, they did their own colonization such that Bradford, a few miles up the road from Hoggart's Leeds, is now almost a majority black city, Birmingham is surrounded by black, once white working-class neighbourhoods, London, especially in the east, is thronged with black faces, and so too is a host of the biggest cities – Bristol, Manchester, Liverpool. There are third and fourth black generations now long-standingly English (not to go west to Cardiff and Tiger Bay nor north to Glasgow), and one may readily detect as active forces in their formation some of those antique decencies which found their predecessors in the old working class.

IV

What calls for celebration in Hoggartian language, however, is the slow, uncertain, sometimes grudging accommodation of the English people to the human facts of immigration. In a way exceptional on the globe, an unignorable quantity of black newcomers have had ceded and have won for themselves a recognized new home, have largely overcome gross prejudice, have proved indispensable to the domestic economy. The passable open-mindedness of the old democracy, a culture which, grotesque disparities in wealth notwithstanding, struggles to honour the idea of equality, has brought off – a race riot or two aside – the peaceable provision of home and membership to a large number of black people formerly treated for half a millennium and worldwide as either subhuman or stripped of rights and freedom and fit only for slavery.

That massive achievement itself bears witness to the continuities Hoggart affirmed and may be counted one big sign of good health in the condition of uncertain unity among the four nations of Britain. Even if senior politicians on the political Right will beat from time to time the old, vicious drum against immigration, their targets are these days more likely to be from Latvia or Romania than the Caribbean.

This rather abstract even if commonly known and felt victory over human meanness gives us some reassurance that there remains an old acceptance of things still playing its ground bass in *British* culture, that 'live and let live' retains its benignant and bracing force, that 'the immediate, the present and the cheerful', in Hoggart's words, still find their happy and glorious expression in everyday life. But another unmistakably huge cultural change may at this distance also be understood as expression of these same tolerant and understanding habits of moral vocabulary. That change, which so casually and explicitly marked the whole society after precisely 1963 when the contraceptive pill became publicly available, was the quite sudden concessiveness agreed upon as to sexual permission and conduct. Probably this delicate ground had been prepared by the loosening of

13

moral vocabulary permitted (and quite right too) by the conditions of warfare, but pharmacology was the real authority. Yet credit may as well be given to the moral language of those classes who found, for by and large generous and genial reasons, that sex could be given a more playful arena in cultural life than had been counted safe before, and thereby initiated a quiet upheaval in social habits which may be allowed, by subsequent history, to be emancipatory and enlarging of human happiness.

Today no one can doubt the losses in cultural life caused by the disappearance of the strong (and killing) disciplines of physical labour, the manly pride taken in the many crafts of that labour, at the ship's hull, at the coalface, in the foundry or beside the blast furnace. By the same token, the loss of the powerful, kindly, portly matriarch as well as of a calmly authoritative father, seen only after work, away at the football or the club on Saturdays, collarless, shirtsleeved, self-confident, this loss is keen and painful. George Orwell wrote in a similar vein of feeling in 1937:

> In a working-class home – I am not thinking at the moment of the unemployed, but of comparatively prosperous homes – you breathe a warm, decent, deeply human atmosphere which it is not so easy to find elsewhere. I should say that a manual worker, if he is in steady work and drawing good wages – an 'if' which gets bigger and bigger – has a better chance of being happy than an 'educated' man. His home life seems to fall more naturally into a sane and comely shape. I have often been struck by the peculiar easy completeness, the perfect symmetry as it were, of a working-class interior at its best. Especially on winter evenings after tea, when the fire glows in the open range and dances mirrored in the steel fender, when Father, in shirt-sleeves, sits in the rocking chair at one side of the fire reading the racing finals, and Mother sits on the other with her sewing, and the children are happy with a pennorth of mint humbugs, and the dog lolls roasting himself on the rag mat – it is a good place to be in, provided that you can be not only in it but sufficiently *of* it to be taken for granted.[9]

There is a wistful though not a sentimental note here, and Orwell himself says that he is recollecting homes seen in his childhood before 1914; visions of the good society are mostly set by the almost-elderly in order to bring into focus the time when the promise of happiness could be kept to the children who heard it made.

[9] George Orwell, *The Road to Wigan Pier*, London: Secker and Warburg, 1937 and 1959, pp. 117–18. I also realize that I am much more blithe and indiscriminate about these matters than Krishan Kumar in his admirable *The Making of English National Identity*, Cambridge: Cambridge University Press, 2003.

But many, very many of the promises of, say, 1945, when Hoggart and his contemporaries took off their uniforms, have indeed been amply kept. Some homes may be hellish, but 'home' remains the richest value in ordinary vocabulary. It is gathered into a nexus of warm, strong sentiments which nowadays find their most vital manifestations in the art of the small garden which the vast extension of social emancipation over our timespan has brought to millions. The allotment is far from vanished,[10] of course, but the sweeping enlargement of home ownership has brought gardening to the back door for a majority of homes. It seems to me that the pleasant, leisurely busyness of the Sunday afternoon garden centre is one of the best tokens of the present day, as well as a repeated episode in national life which speaks well for health and decency and all such durable words.

The same sort of encouragement about, in Hoggart's confident phrase, 'the full rich life', is similarly to be found among all those countless hosts of picnickers, ramblers, bicyclists, drivers and paddlers dispersed in kindly, mutual indifference across the national parks and in the prospects of the so happily named National Trust every weekend. Saturdays and Sundays, having largely lost religious enforcement but still sanctified as 'free' and 'leisure' time, have been filled by now for over two lifetimes by an agreeable and restorative metaphysics. The subject of the art forms of popular culture is town-and-landscape. On postcards, placemats, Christmas cards, good and bad reproductions on sitting room and kitchen walls, inside millions of photograph albums and millions more in the storage capacity of digital hand cameras, in amateur painting classes and junior school classrooms, a whole society learns a correspondence between the forms of its feeling and the beauty of a natural landscape humanly refashioned over the past 700 years or so.

If much in both the pictures and the response is cliché, much is not, and in any case the clichés of ritual and litany are the necessary vehicles of proper piety and devout feeling. So I suggest that some of Hoggart's 'springs of action' have taken on renewed elasticity, given wiriness by no less a powerful cliché than a return to nature.

Moreover, loving worship does not stop there, in these commonplace acts of expressiveness, self-repair (loss of self, more like) and decoration. A great communal act of pedestrian devotion also takes place on any sunny Sunday of the summer, when the car-owning majority piles into the automobile and, weaving around the cyclists,

---

[10] I commend to the reader *The Allotment: Its Landscape and Culture* by David Crouch and John Ward, London: Faber, 1988.

15

takes itself off for the day in the country, at the seashore, at the wild-life park, in the national park, going round the stately home. Similar respects are paid to art, as the steady streams of visitors to the city and metropolitan galleries testify (more in total, if you include the stately homes, than attend football matches – a statistic worth italicizing), as well as queues, as often as not, on the Bank holidays, waiting to troop, reverently enough, round the mightiest cathedrals: Durham, York, Lincoln, Winchester, Tewkesbury.

Each member of these families, according to his or her lights, is joining in a short, sprawling, friendly and unritualized act of worship in the great cathedral of Art and Nature which the Romantic painters, poets and composers built between about 1770 (the birth of Wordsworth) and the publication of the fifth volume of John Ruskin's *Modern Painters* in honour of Turner in 1860.

These absorbed and absorbing social practices speak up eloquently for the lastingness of so many qualities deep in the culture Hoggart described in *The Uses of Literacy* and now finding easier fulfilment in the far less creaky bodies of the later generations and the well-enough dressed, pinker-cheeked, stronger-boned bodies of their children and grandchildren.

Seeing these triumphs of emancipation, seeing men and women of 50 and 60 looking twenty years younger than their parents at the same age, living twenty years longer what's more, takes some of the confidence out of threnodies sung, accurately enough, over the losses of neighbourhood, community, solidarity and so forth. Even the devastation of Northern England, from Hoggart's Hunslet to my own home county of Durham, the population of which, after Mrs Thatcher's *Blitzkrieg* during the 1980s, was left unemployable, unregarded, unpaid or rather paid off for a generation as long as North Sea oil lasted, even there the cities have sprung forth in an aesthetic, economic resurrection. The great Victorian metropoles – Newcastle, Leeds, Manchester, Liverpool – have emerged from underneath the filthy deposits of black smoke and sooty fog cleansed, restored, freshly painted, the lime-and-gritstone gleaming at times pinkly, the main streets washed and unlittered, fine new trams in some places, the desolation of the dispossessed far out on the ring roads or huddled invisibly well out of sight.

There has been a sort of reconciliation between classes. For nowadays, a sullen bell tolls, signalling, as seems likely, a hiatus in history, perhaps the end of an era. Once the promises of socialism became, for a long historical season, unfulfillable, what was called neoliberalism dressed capital up in bewitching new colours and roared away until, in 2008, it drove itself over a cliff edge. People scrambled out of the smashed-up wreck and looked, those who could, beadily for their own means of escape. Governments, bound fast to the electoral cycle of hope and disappointment, punishment and popularity, obeyed the deep ruling which conjures all the political formations to fight to the end to reconstruct the old social and economic order now on its last legs. So a ruling managerial class, with the never full-hearted support of a people, aiming always to re-establish an imaginary past, moves deeper all the time, through crisis after crisis, in an impossible attempt to restore the old, familiar illusions.

That is the political realm of our history, and our present hero only occasionally enters political argument in a direct way. But at the beginning of his intellectual career he warned, in tones of grim realism, what might happen to a class culture as it became transformed into a mass culture. He saw, none clearer, those masses as being in thrall to commodities, to the crazy rout of acquisition, as well as to the emotional poverty so well reflected in *EastEnders*, or the desperately phoney matiness and sincere insincerity of the quiz shows and unreal reality TV.

By the time we reach the present, having already passed the comprehensive, unacknowledged hiatus in our social progress of the 2008 crash, the question is compelled upon us: what will become of a culture – of the essential life of a still stouthearted civilization which is so besotted by commodities, mesmerized by money, so often foolish and trivial in its life-choices?

V

One might fashion the beginnings of a reply by excusing 'the people' (to keep on using that vague referent) as, in three-quarters of their number, they so delighted, for the first time in their class history, in plenty: plenty of food, plenty of (unexhausted) leisure, of fair health (and free doctors), of easy, even foreign travel, a plenitude of the dizzy varieties of narrative effortlessly available on television. Is it merely curmudgeonly to begrudge a two-generations-long indulgence in the cornucopia of consumption?

But, 'the words of Mercury after the songs of Apollo'; Hoggart did justice to both, but he ended his books in the sombre, prosaic accents of Mercury. Anyone now reckoning up that inheritance will find it hard to make up new songs of hope.

The narratives on screen which have replaced the dismal

17

sex-and-violence thrillers which served as symptoms of the 1950s have plunged far deeper than those originals into expertly rendered cruelty and desolation. The most ordinary of home-grown police serials on terrestrial television presents with irresistible vividness a world at the edge of industrial wastelands, where victims are tied to chains in echoing warehouses and steadily mutilated, while decentish police, judiciously balanced as to gender, drive screeching to a rescue likely to come too late.

These repetitive scenes are the stock-in-trade of endless hours of television; their worst and most lethal efficacity is the toneless killing of time. The time would have died anyway. Maybe if leisure is to be thought of as lethal, maybe better to fill it with the awful vanities of quiz shows whose professionalized merriment and suspense holds an audience in something like a human connection? Maybe the ghastly recriminations of arbitrary incarceration, in return for the cheque, with people whom in real life one would go miles to avoid, all as played out according to *Big Brother*'s reality TV, can just about be forced to declare a bit of moral sympathy.

One has only to put the supposition, to put it down. If this is the imaginative cultural life of millions and if, as the philosopher said, 'the natural wakeful life of the ego is a perceiving', then imagination and perception are joined in the making of a dismal nothingness. And yet. And yet. Prolific among the dreadful plenty of reality TV and its other side, police horror stories, are the many, many programmes leading those who choose them towards high art, practical archaeology, first-class opera, distant anthropologies, the history and geography of the homeland, coastline, Lakeland, waterways, underground.

If therefore one is, tentatively enough, addressing the condition of England, and doing so by way of evaluation of the imaginative life of its subordinate classes, one can only come up, in detail, with even-handed judgements: much is awful, enough is good. If one turns to those areas of expressive culture which provided *The Uses of Literacy* with some of its finest and most moving passages – tasty food indeed, the longed-for homeliness of home, the normal, brisk kindliness of institutions – the health centre, the primary school, Sainsbury's, Boots and, by and large, the office, the garage, the building site – if one turns to these, one comes away restored in one's sense of the continuities of decency, of commonsensible practicality, of loving kindness.

Some such social vision is then less of the keenness of loss than of historical momentum. Neighbourhoods have dislimned into separate households, lifelong employment into restless mobility in search of durable work, the determinate roles of husband and father, wife and mother, become far more provisional and soluble, and past decades of marital misery swept away in the process. So what can we include by way of opening, in this chapter, the story of England and its contradictory contexts? Hoggart ladled out to himself generous helpings of poetry. Eliot's *Sweeney Agonistes* serves for a gloomy conclusion, its mad comicality and utter bleakness:

> I tell you again it don't apply
> Death or life or life or death
> Death is life and life is death
> I gotta use words when I talk to you
> But if we understand or if you don't
> That's nothing to me and nothing to you
> We all gotta do what we gotta do
> We're gona sit here and drink this booze
> We're gona sit here and have a tune
> We're gona stay and we're gona go
> And somebody's gotta pay the rent[11]

We could however turn elsewhere in Eliot, or to the pages of W. H. Auden, the subject of Hoggart's first book, for more encouraging support and a cheerier outlook as the present generation treks away from progress. 'To make an end is to make a beginning.' 'We shall not cease from exploration.' 'Time will say nothing but I told you so.'[12] But the cultural condition of Hoggart's country and mine is perhaps best served by looking out for versions of those characters and dispositions on whom Hoggart, with a due irony, places responsibility for the future. The 'saving remnant' and 'the earnest minority', 'these dissatisfied romantics'[13] are in some cases vitiated by such self-doubt and diffidence that they render themselves ineffectual. 'We would rather be ruined than changed': Hoggart levels Auden at them. But plenty of them had then and retain now a potent significance.

He found them in WEA classes, in the old Working Men's Institutes, in Do-It-Yourself and the huge omnipresence of domestic clubs and societies holding effortlessly up the big tent of cultural busyness, carpentry, photography, water-colouring, dog, cat, fish and pigeon care, cycling, chess, bridge, gardening, shooting, scrambling, biking and motorbiking, ballroom dancing . . . the list is endless. George Orwell spotted all this on the road to Wigan Pier, but he thought it all betokened the *privateness* of English life as well as noting that 'in

---

[11] T. S. Eliot, *Complete Poems and Plays*, London: Faber and Faber, 1969, p. 125.
[12] W. H. Auden, *Collected Poems*, E. Mandelson ed., New York: Vintage edn, 1976, p. 314.
[13] Hoggart (1958), pp. 318, 322, 315.

all societies the common people must live to some extent *against* the existing order'.[14]

The last remark is surely true, but living in such a way is (surely?) better thought of not as an expression of privateness but of mutuality, fraternity, communality. These strong and rational practices are possessed in common. They cannot be turned to governmental or ruling class purposes, for that would be to take away their intrinsic resistance.

Culture is as much a way of struggle as a way of life. One can see this in one of the noblest innovations ever dreamed up by the roaming intellectuals of the British Labour Party, its Open University, so often celebrated by Hoggart. Since its inception it has been testament to the desire of thousands to cultivate the life of the mind and to win true education from fresh study and self-knowledge. At the same time it has been used as a training instrument for re-employment and bent thereby to the service of a national economy taking precedence over everything else in national life.

Some such struggle on behalf of the old big slogans – freedom, equality in education, disinterested judgement of oneself and others, historical direction, national will and hopefulness, unaffected happiness – makes the very shape of the life of Richard Hoggart; his heart kept time to that marching drum. Sure, he was *against* all that opposed or manipulated those mighty freedoms and fulfilments; but it was by being *for* that the life and the work found their magnificence. The words of Matthew Arnold, always such a source of inspiration, define the meaning of my tale which follows.

> He has not won his political battles; he has not carried his main points, he has not stopped his adversaries' advance, he has not marched victoriously with the modern world; but he has told silently upon the mind of the country, he has prepared currents of feeling which sap his adversaries' position when it seems gained, he has kept up his communication with the future.[15]

[14] George Orwell, *The Lion and the Unicorn*, Harmondsworth: Penguin, 1982, pp. 39, 40.
[15] Matthew Arnold, *Essays Literary and Critical*, London: Dent, 1906, pp. 43, 44.

— 1 —

THE STONES OF LEEDS

I

In 1855, when Mrs Elizabeth Gaskell published her novel *North and South*, it was already commonplace to talk of England as divided into two nations at the boundary of Yorkshire. In 1918 this was no less true, and the Great North Road, prouder in name than in width or surface, unrolled itself out of London and trailed smoothly away towards the mighty metropolis of the foreign lands heralded, indeed, by a great road sign, big as a man, announcing 'The North'. Leeds was one of the mightiest cities in the province, cooked black by the soot of ages falling from the mills, the railways, their trains always visible not only as the rushing expresses on their way to Scotland, but from the little chuffing freight trains busy on every one of the dozens of branch lines circling the city and coiling thickly through the packed, dilapidated terraces separating heavy industry from green suburb.

Leeds is pretty flat, but the 'close-ribbed streets', in one dead end of which the Hoggart family were crowded into a tiny, two-bedroomed terrace house, nonetheless they

> . . . rise and fall
> like a great sigh out of the last century.

'Back to backs' they were called, and were, each with a short yard criss-crossed with washing lines, a high wall at the back irresistible to boys to sit on and outrage passers-by in the blank, walled, cobbled street below.

I say 'cobbled' but in truth the surfaces were laid with slightly curved, black stone blocks about 15 inches square, smooth to walk

21

on, just ridged enough for heavy-laden horses and donkeys to find a grip and heave up the slope. There were no cars in 1918, none parked in North Leeds until after the second war. Street traffic was slow and intermittent. In the early morning, the horse and cart of the milkman clopped slowly around the narrow roads; the milkman sometimes doubled as greengrocer. A chatty little queue of local housewives would form, their hair folded inside a neat scarf headdress, most of them in pinafore aprons, each holding a big jug into which the milkman would pour out a quart from a metal dipper with a long handle. During the morning the rag and bone man would make his slow traverse of every street, his long mournful cry of 'J-i-i-ingle' tolling his unbroken passage, and one or two people would labour out with antique articles – an old tin scouring board on which to scrub the washing, a much-refilled pillow, its ticking worn gossamer-thin, a broken saw, every object much repaired, reluctantly scrapped.

After the traders in poverty, the handcarts, variously laden with domestic bits and pieces, some of them surprisingly bulky – a vast old armchair, a wardrobe, I once saw a whole three-door cast iron oven – being moved across a dozen streets, a main road, up and down two steep hills, for the benefit of family or friends elsewhere in the neighbourhood.

The habits of thrift, of making-do-and-mend, of household tools and utensils which nowadays would have been chucked out a decade earlier, betokened a necessity, a dogged definition of utility and indeed of passive endurance which characterized the English working class between, let us say, 1920, by which time the big northern cities had each passed a population total of 250,000, and the moments at which the unprecedented tides of prosperity began to flow across three-quarters of the country after 1960 or so.

When Seebohm Rowntree and Charles Booth set themselves towards the end of the nineteenth century to investigate and measure poverty in, respectively, York and London, Booth found 30 per cent of the capital living close to destitution, and Rowntree, scion of the Quaker philanthropist family whose chocolate factory was, with the church, source of the city's wealth, found 43 per cent in the same circumstances.[1] In 1899 Rowntree estimated that an individual family needed £100 a year to edge above the poverty line.

Thirty-seven years later, in a show of remarkable stamina, Rowntree found, with more precise statistical instruments, 31 per cent of York's

---

[1] Figures summarized by Peter Laslett, *The World We Have Lost*, London: Methuen, 1965, chapter 9.

22

population still in the same battered boat. But as Laslett points out on Rowntree's behalf,[2] the cause of destitution in 1899 was pitifully low wages; the cause in 1936, however, was unemployment. Over the years of Richard Hoggart's boyhood, the British welfare state was brought parsimoniously to birth. From Lloyd George's introduction of national insurance and old age pension in 1908 and 1911 to the Beveridge Report and the great work of Richard Titmuss in preparation for the National Health Service and family allowances between 1943 and 1946, the huge trawler of 'cradle to grave' support and protection against accident, sudden incapacity or loss of a job, together with provision for the everyday rearing of children, was massively constructed.

Those years more or less see the three Hoggart siblings from birth to settlement in adult life, in and out of military uniform, then, for the two boys at least, if not sister Molly, securely in a lifetime's well-regarded employment. Their mother, shadowy heroine of their early years, Adeline Emma ('Addie') was child of a respectable shopkeeper in Liverpool, a slim, pretty woman with soft wavy dark hair and the dash and spirit to leave home in 1915, get a job serving in the canteen at the Light Infantry Brigade headquarters at Strensall Camp a few miles out of York, where she met Tom Hoggart who had served in the Boer War, been in and out of the army since, enlisted in 1914, married Addie in 1915 and fathered son Tom two years later, Richard, for many years known by his first name as 'Bert' (like the D. H. Lawrence Richard came later so much to admire) in 1918, Molly in 1920.

Then, abruptly and in his early forties, Tom Hoggart Senior died of brucellosis, caught from drinking contaminated milk, a fierce bacterial fever at that date, untouchable by the antibiotics which by 1945 would have rendered the illness negligible. But in 1920 the life expectation of very poor British males at birth was 43, although soldiers were well enough fed, and indeed weight and height increases among conscripts after 1915 were famously remarkable. But earlyish paternal death among the poorer classes was common enough, as was more than one death among the children of families averaging nine or ten until the steep falls in mortal demography beginning among the middle classes in the 1920s.

To begin with, there were the three Hoggart children, and Addie. She had little to do with her relations in Liverpool but although her husband Tom had left her well ringed with relations in Leeds, as

---

[2] Laslett (1965), p. 207.

we shall see, until death struck again in 1926 the four of them lived in a tight little island of their own, succoured only by the narrow exigence of the Guardians, their State protectors, the last trace of the father of the family a medal reading 'the Great War for Civilization 1914–1919' and a *Book of Common Prayer* inscribed to Tom by Addie, 'May God watch over you and keep you safe.'

The Board of Guardians was then the source of all public assistance, and its officials made a tight enough estimate of what was due to a mother of three children far too small to permit her going to find work in a Leeds garment maker's on tiny wages. So the Guardians provided about a pound a week, mostly in food coupons realizable only at certain grocers, for the Hoggarts the Maypole chain, and they paid the weekly rent of four shillings.

Four bob paid for the little cottage in Potternewton. It was a minute remnant of a hamlet engulfed by the flood of housing which cascaded outwards from the rambling city spread roughly along the river Aire, and then beside its squalid and jostling partner and thoroughfare, the Aire and Calder Navigation canal. The mountains of wool spun in the north of the county poured into Leeds and the country's clothing was stitched together by tens of thousands of women hired by a few hundred men, large numbers of them Jewish émigrés from Central European pogroms and prejudices, assembling a respectable family pile before moving to the grand suburbs in the north of the city and building the dignified synagogues of Lidgett Park and Moor Allerton.

Potternewton had been a rural hamlet long before all this massive building and displacement. Then the black industry swept in, the clothiers accompanied by the loom-makers, the sewing machine manufacturers, the warehouse construction industry, the barge-builders, and everywhere the railway engine builders, the parallel metal lines, the black trains, the heavy black smoke, the specks of soot, blobs of the stuff sometimes an inch wide, covering over the once green wolds, turning the mighty new city into one of the greatest in the country, known across the Empire, one fifth of the globe.

Leeds Grammar School long predated the high peak of Victorian production and naturally became the forcing house of the city's newish ruling class.[3] One John Heaton, doctor, social reformer and city spokesman, returned from the Grand Tour alight with admiration for Florence and Siena, as well as for the great woollen Guild Halls

---

[3] I follow Tristram Hunt's *Building Jerusalem: The Rise and Fall of the Victorian City*, New York: Henry Holt Books, 2005, as well as Asa Briggs's classic, *Victorian Cities*, Harmondsworth: Penguin, 1957.

of Bruges and Ghent. He enjoined his fellow-citizens to build, in his own words, 'a noble municipal palace . . . to be erected in the middle of their hitherto squalid and unbeautiful town',[4] the *Leeds Mercury* chimed in to the effect that Leeds needed a beautiful tower to 'adorn this great seat of industry with buildings worthy of the people of Leeds and of their country', and largely thanks to Heaton the grandest and most expensive town hall outside the capital, its tower 90 feet high, was opened by the Queen herself in 1858. Outside and in, the splendid building still speaks eloquently of how Yorkshire's wealth, its sense of civic pride as well as its self-made and boastful vainglory, displayed itself to the nation and its narrative.

Potternewton, only a couple of miles up the slope from the Town Hall, was in a different country. Not just in terms of wealth or civic awareness, but in the merest dispositions of space and district. The Hoggart cottage, built of stone, was huddled round by later, tight little blackened brick terraces, tucked in at the end of a short courtyard where no vehicle could reach, and the recollection of the peasant dwelling it once was, was still made visible in the 1920s by willowherb and dandelions growing between the cobbles. Modernity stopped up at the end of the street in Potternewton Lane, where the tramlines ran and the heavy trams rumbled into the depot, to be swung round on a turntable and pointed back to the city centre.

In the corner of the courtyard stood a wooden, crudely built privy shared by the three houses, discharging into a cesspool periodically emptied into a horse-drawn collection trolley, when the always detectable odour became very strong. The plank door opened straight into the only living room. The deep cast-iron fireplace was surrounded by and heated by an iron range with two ovens on each side, the whole thing kept clean and dull-surfaced with blackleading. In front of the range lay a clip (or proggle, or clootie) rug made from little multicoloured rectangles of rag and worsted pushed thickly through the hessian underlay, probably an old sack. Such a rug set off every working-class fireplace in the land, substituting for a carpet, a metaphor for more broadcast and deep pile underfoot. Behind the living room was a small scullery or washroom, with running water taking a bit of heat from the fire, a flagged floor, a hip bath, a scouring board for the laundry, a hand-turned mangle, a low window. From the living-room a short stair led to one very small and one slightly larger bedroom, the two beds shared by the foursome family.

Hoggart's own recollections of his eight or so years of life before his

---

[4] Hunt (2005), p. 248.

mother's death are inevitably thin, but it is clear that the family stood always at the very edge of destitution, of unfed, unclothed extremity, and were kept back from that edge only by the unyielding watchfulness of a mother not at all brought up on such short commons, and minutely attentive to the arithmetic of necessity as well as to the no less tiny details of status, accomplishment, demeanour and apparel, which would set her own children on the long path out of poverty.

One aspect of the new condition of England is a habitual deprecation of the struggle for status, although of course in innumerable ways the struggle goes on. What is insufficiently honoured is Addie Hoggart's kind of fighting stand – though the fight was with the invisible weapons of anxious protectiveness, stressful providence, loving kindness and principled gentility – on behalf of children for whom she was utterly determined that they should find an easier, happier, more fulfilled future.

Hoggart himself was – need one say? – blessed with a naturally happy nature. He recalled being greeted, at about the age of five, by the amiable old lady with a large mole on her chin, who kept the small bakery at the corner of their entry, as 'Sunny Jim, always cheerful.' The original Sunny Jim first appeared on the back of a breakfast cereal called *Force* in 1902:

> High o'er the fence leaps Sunny Jim,
> *Force* is the food which raises him.

Sunny Jim himself was a regency buck in scarlet tails and natty pumps, but the appellation was common for eighty-odd years. Hoggart took it as a compliment but also as an accurate enough description of what he was like, made it into a small discovery of selfhood, of there being an 'I' about whom he could think of while separating himself from himself, the ego become an object of thought. Probably this is the earliest motion of the mind intrinsic to all those becoming capable of moral introspection and self-aware self-criticism. No inevitable salvation in that of course; but it's a help.

His mother's courageous gentility and the Guardians' close-fisted assistance could not, however, keep up her health against the relentless battering of poverty, shortage in her diet, Yorkshire cold and Leeds smoke, and the ceaseless care and chattering demands of small children. One day she brought back from the Maypole grocery shop, with its marble walls and tiled floor, its glassed-in, appetizing display counters, a couple of slices of boiled ham, not shiny and wafer-thin as it would be today, but cut thick and firm from the bone. Threepennyworth perhaps, the money eked out onto a narrow margin, away from daily necessity. The ham was for her, a solitary treat. The children besieged her for it, like quarrelsome and insistent baby starlings. She had to give way, give it away. Her whole life-habit, her tight and tense lovingness insisted, yet again, on self-denial. The children snaffled her share. She resented it, even bitterly. It had been her treat, in a life without a single person who might be counted on for the very occasional such afterthought. The odd neighbour might call with a little something spare from her own hard calculations, but rarely. The ham was the product of strict forbearance. Its loss was sharp, ragged also; it drew a grated edge across a sensibility for which no adult, not one, could have a tender touch.

Hers was a life lived always on the edge of a steep downward slope into irretrievable loss: loss of balance, of respectability, of provision, always straining upwards against the terrific pull of social gravity, never a moment off guard or off duty. Once upon a time, her son recalled a sixpenny bit lost between shops, one fortieth of the week's income, and saw his mother's face as she struggled to compose herself, to recalculate her sums without panic, saw the tears well up and fill her eyes without quite brimming over, the jaw clenched, her grip maintained.

Holding onto 'respectability' – that all-powerful and pervasive principle – wasn't something as nowadays to be scoffed at by the *bien-pensants*, as part of a social class system now happily superseded by a genial egalitarianism. It was less a single principle than a whole frame of being, one which bolted together duty and self-esteem, responsibility and satisfied relief, loving care and moral judgement, all into a daily way of life. Necessarily comparative – 'I'm not going to live like *that*' – it was not the vehicle of snobbery but the guide to demeanour, the code of propriety, the measure of a good life. The loss of the value of respectability – and the loss in present-day Britain is almost complete – betokens a society some of whose seriousness has drained away, a people no longer as steady as they used to be.

One May day in 1926 Hoggart, then aged eight, walked past the tram depot on Potternewton Lane and saw a group of men standing together by the tramlines. Another boy told him they were on strike, and what that meant, that everyone in the country with a job was on strike, was refusing to work, that it was general over England. The term was wholly new to Hoggart, as well it might be, and there was nothing to see, just a group of rather uncertain-looking men standing about, if a picket then one without self-righteousness or collective anger. He went down the lane and turned into the courtyard from which his watchful, careful mother excluded history, politics, religion,

all that. The world was tiny, geographical and, under mother's jurisdiction, safe. Its space was the still-rural-seeming cottage, the short
lanes and 'ginnels' or 'snickets' all around, narrow, hemmed-in, high-
fenced or high-walled cuts in the dense texture of street and terrace.
They led, by and by, to sudden open ground, rough, unkempt, often
(in the North) called The Moor, the best such sudden expanse, of
green and sun on stone, was the cemetery, its old stones well-spaced,
friendly, familiar, the homely place filled with air.

II

In the dark winter month of February 1927, Herbert Hoggart came
home from school without his brother Tom, then ten, or sister Molly,
then six. He lifted the loud latch on the plank door and, as he pushed
it open, saw by the weak gas light his mother lying before the fire
on the clip-rug, gasping, coughing helplessly, doubled up and on her
side. She was grey with exhaustion, the long-ignored and suppressed
tuberculosis now taking command of a wracked body and a drained
soul. A neighbour was called, the small children stood in numb and
fearful immobility as their mother was taken to hospital, saying to the
two little boys, 'look after your sister', so that they nodded solemnly
and Tom took the hands of his little brother and sister. So she left,
and fought for breath, and died, and they were orphans, a grave word
in the annals of class history.

The mother's family were in Liverpool, and not exactly at the
ready to do familial duties. Father's relatives, the Hoggarts, were to
hand, and the children went by tram and their grandmother met the
sudden expense of the tram tickets to take them the miles across to
the south of the city, to Hunslet where she lived. There was a funeral,
with huddled masses of black-clad womenfolk and the children, lost
and forlorn, at the front of the crowd by the open grave; there was a
funeral tea, with potted meat sandwiches from Dawes the baker on
the main road, an abrupt expense also met by Grandmother from
non-existent reserves.

Inevitably there was a family moot held to decide on the children's
future. Family solidarity and neighbourly communality surged into
the space left by the still-young mother's death, no offer of care
however was forthcoming from Addie's family in Liverpool, the children tensed with fear when someone said that orphanages, a dread
word from nineteenth-century fiction, were 'very good nowadays',
but grandmaternal authority turned the idea away at once. Tom was

Richard Hoggart's grandparents, taken just before his grandmother, who brought him up from the age of eight, was widowed. Unless otherwise noted, photos reproduced from the Hoggart Collection at the University of Sheffield, by kind permission of the Hoggart family.

assigned to Aunt Alice and Uncle Jack's numerous family in Sheffield, where he remained until conscripted fourteen years later, Molly to an elderly and widowed sort-of-aunt a street or two away from the grandmother, and Richard, still 'Bert' to everyone at that date, 'without doubt the luckiest', to his grandmother, there to join two aunts, a female cousin and likeable, feckless Uncle Herbert, always kindly, far too fond of a drink, often unemployed.

So it was a women's world in which Hoggart grew up, Uncle Bert notwithstanding. But that world flourished in Hunslet, a much more thronged, boisterous and dangerous place than the tight little redoubt in Potternewton. Hunslet, long since laid waste by the coming of the M1 in the early 1960s, lay close to the city centre, three miles south of the old home and as distant as a foreign country. It abutted the river, the canals, the big factories of Cross Green and Stourton, the vast sewage plant, the railway marshalling yards. The irresistible plenty of department stores, especially magical Woolworth's and, a bit later, Lewis's Food Basement, was within half an hour's walking

29

distance, the University at Woodhouse a couple of miles north. The streets were a jumbled mixture of domestic housing, ready food, and technicolour local production – the Prince Albert Hotel run by Mr Stockdale at the end of Newport Street, Florrie in the sweet shop, terrible fumes from Nicholson's chemical works, the flames at the forge on Grove Road – Hunslet remained a map of its very earliest industrial days. There was, in easy reach, a boilerworks, two glass works, a tannery, three brickworks, and, up beside the cemetery, Beggars Hill Farm. On Sundays, the children went to the infinitely kind and blind Sunday School teacher (sixty years later Hoggart found her at 90 and put her in a TV programme. She knew his voice at once.)

The grip of the family, in another small house, where at first little Bert shared a bed with Uncle Bert, then maybe in his mid-twenties, remained, as it had to, tight and loving also, in contradictory ways. Grandmother was undisputed monarch of the household; she ruled silently and lovingly, always protective of her grandson, heedful also, unable no doubt to follow the tremendous growth of his intelligence but eager that it should thrive, occasionally taking the boy by the hand and out for a walk, away from the claustrophobic oppression of too many people gathered about a coal fire in the range, one of them the tyrant, Aunt Clara.

Clara's passions dominated the house without shaking Grandmother's rule. She was endlessly liable to launch tirades of voluble abuse, often at the full pitch of excellent lungs, at a wide variety of social targets, frequently her brother Herbert ('Ha! Out drinking again? You pitiful creature, you couldn't hold onto Jean, could you? And who can blame her?'), once into his teens, Bert-becoming-Richard also ('Where've you been? Coming in at this hour? What about your homework? Going down the same staircase as your Uncle Bert, I suppose'). But the human oddities of neighbours, city and nation were all ready targets for Aunt Clara's torrential abuse, whether drink, sexual freedoms ('Filthy, filthy. They can't control themselves'), the commonplace failings or just the ordinary culture of the place ('Common as dirt. Common as dirt. They don't want to work, they don't deserve work, and why anybody pays them when they're out of work I don't know. They'll just sit back and . . . and . . . and').

Aunt Clara slept by herself in a small back room, presumably because she would have started up a quarrel with anybody else during the small hours. She had, it seems, in an intense precipitate boiling away in the bile of her being, the assorted prejudices of those of her class aspiring to gentility, always at the ready, to be spat into the air as rage, hatred, detestation, revulsion. She was compelled by quarrelling. Her nephew saw with complete clarity the driven contortions of her nature, twisted up as it was with love for and pride in his achievements. (At her death in the 1970s there was among her things a scrapbook with cuttings recording the many successes and distinctions of her nephew's life.)

Her vile temper, however, made for great unhappiness on countless occasions, Bert's grandmother sitting through it all in silent misery and, herself offering no reproaches, taking brutal punishment in her turn, Herbert permanently a target, Hoggart himself intermittently so, and the other sister, Aunt Lil, a mild kindly soul, getting her unfair share as well.

There is a striking footnote to add about Clara. Just before the outbreak of war in 1939 Aunt Clara teamed up with a bosom pal, also unmarried, and scarified when Clara deemed it necessary. They left their garment tailoring jobs, eight hours a day on the treadle of the sewing machines, set up their own little bespoke tailoring business, obtained sufficient wartime grants at a time when the government was anxious to keep as many people in production as possible, sold out judiciously as peace broke out, and retired on comfortable profits to a life of genteel recrimination and satisfying malice in one of the redbrick semi-detached houses on the curve of Morecambe Bay.

Clara, you could say, taught young Hoggart about the spite and rancour fizzing off the top of rivalrous gentility. He saw it, recoiled from it, comprehended it. Lil taught him very different moral lessons, taught him the moral tolerance of her class ('Ay, 'e's a man can't say nay to 'is wife', 'Don't be 'ard, live and let live', 'Poor thing, we mun give her a cup of tea'), an acceptance of others' failings – nothing was going to stop Bert senior's slow and drunken decline – taught him the needfulness, from time to time, of softer and more blurred moral judgements than might seem strictly necessary to the sharp confidence of the well-off middle classes. Lil exemplified these strong, soft attitudes, and the boy saw them given life-shaping and decisive force by the careful, worried authority of Grandmother.

Grandmother could do nothing about Clara, and didn't try. She bore the tirades silently but doggedly, sometimes rescuing her grandson by taking him into the urban evening, the city roaring quietly in the distance, for a respite. But she never failed the boy in her selfless love, gave him from a full, speechless heart the lesson of loving kindness he lived by all his life, accommodating it to his own sharp-eyed, talkative, reticent disposition until he found, in his work as in his life, that, as we shall learn time and again from his example, detachment

31

and moral sympathy will at best, dissolve acerbity and indignation, melt into one another and issue as understanding.

I suppose Hoggart was helped in this by the extreme exigence of his early years. To be one of a fatherless three tended by an invalid mother of remarkable courage as well as privacy of nature, to find her dying, to see brother and sister dispatched to different homes, to become the most junior member of a household of four women (including a stray cousin, Ivy, exiled from Sheffield) and one feckless young man, all these presences and absences taught his exceptional intelligence and his happy openness of disposition, a self-protectiveness against slights (but we all have that), a shrewd appraisal of enmity and opportunity (we all need that), happy gratitude for the inadvertent and glowing moments of life (and we all cherish that), and then long-suffering, gentleness, truth . . . and the blessings of a good table.

One of the most endearing aspects of Hoggart's autobiography as well as his many other works of social criticism and celebration is the frequency with which he returns to the subject of food, and his unaffected openmindedness towards its innumerable forms and contents, his excellent preference for tastiness whatever the official class judgements he is always ready to repudiate ('the few times I've eaten at the Athenaeum the food has been nothing to write home about'). The unyielding struggle against destitution of his earliest years taught him keen appreciation of a square meal wherever it was provided, and he never failed to see the human as well as the moral meaning of a good plateful. It was love in action, for sure; it was also a keeping of the fabled promise of happiness, a benignant history and the culture it made finding solid shape, good colour, and tasty mouthfuls there on the plate, to be tucked into and away.

He never lost this ardour for the table, though never in the least gluttonous, spare and stocky all his life. He always spoke – my wife and I both remember it keenly – of his favourite dish as being bacon, sausage, eggs, beans and tomatoes. This, the canonical plateful of the English breakfast, represents the artful shaping of meaty, salty protein, sweetly balanced by the fruity tomatoes and the pungent tang of the world's best-travelled canned food, Heinz beans. The colours too are so appetizing: the shining chestnut and dull carmine of the products of the pig, the scarlet fruit, the golden yolk in its bright white, the beige beans – it is a poem set in the bright middle of the rainbow and one best artwork from the British kitchen.

Hoggart thought so, and me too. But these were foods well out of reach in 1930 for Newport Street, Hunslet. Tastiness there was the product, as Dickens once put it (in *Great Expectations*), 'of those parts of the beast of which the beast, when living, had least reason to be proud': tastiness came from black pudding, liver, cowheel, chitterlings; on a big day, pork pies (Mr Wopsle would have approved); and from the sea, shrimps, cod's roe, orange-brown kippers, cardinal-red salmon, tinned of course (as Hoggart said, 'I still find it far "tastier" than fresh salmon').[5]

These were the dishes of high enough living, the menu for 'high tea' when the family came in from work, restored its energies eating together round the square kitchen table. For 'filling up' hungry children, a slice of white bread would be handed out, to eat on the hoof (this is long before the ready-sliced and wrapped loaf), spread with beef dripping and including, if you were lucky, a blob of meat jelly, all sprinkled with salt, savoury to excess.

The anthropology of meaning has done much this past half-century to return intellectual life to its roots in daily sustenance and domestic conduct. Hoggart has been, in his theoretically untheoretic way, a leading contributor to the cultural turn taken by social thought. But food is a peculiarly forceful item in this change, and Hoggart takes that force to heart at every turn of his life. The art and interest of food is in its taste, for sure; but that taste is inseparable, in satisfaction and in the body's response, from bulk, and its settlement in the stomach. Take and understand the colour, taste, solidity and the cultural history of a plateful, and you are pretty close to the meaning of life. Perhaps it is not too bluff a thing to add, but put sex next to food, as Hoggart often does, and you hold meaning and its secrets together.

Once upon a time when he was aged ten or eleven, little boy Bert wandered into the scullery where his cousin Ivy (the exile from Sheffield) was washing herself comprehensively in the only hot water basin in the house (the water heated in a copper basin from below with coals carried from the fire). She was then a well-built, good-looking girl in her very early twenties, of irreproachable propriety. Turning round to find her cousin unexpectedly a pace or two behind her, she clutched a towel to her 'large, low-swinging breasts like very big King William pears' but not before the boy had fully taken in their 'disturbing beauty', many decades later to compare that early epiphany to the marked disadvantage of other breasts on casual display on the beaches of the Cote d'Azur which merely resembled 'little apples, Cox's orange pippins'.[6]

---

[5] All the details from the table to be found in *The Uses of Literacy*, pp. 37–8.
[6] Hoggart, 1988, p. 69.

III

Working-class heroes, in the mythology of English literature and politics, are affirmatively male. There is every reason why this is so, especially in the north. The classical forms of employment, slung on pulleys from the flanks of great ships, tilting the giant hoppers of red molten steel, or hacking coal from the roof of a tunnel only one foot above your head, stripped to the waist, eyes bright in a blackened face beneath the rakish helmet and its flashlight, these images still beget fresh images of power, heat, dirt and danger a generation after they vanished from the facts of industrial production.

Hoggart's kind of heroism, very like that of the D. H. Lawrence whose novels of the Nottinghamshire coaling villages Hoggart so keenly responded to, was quite a long way from iron and coal. Like Lawrence's, his was a woman's world and it was his good fortune to be formed by the watchful, speechless love of as good a woman as could be found in the three Ridings of Yorkshire, and to have the moral imagination not only to cherish and understand his luck, but also to grasp what there was to learn and live from in the hot virulence of his Aunt Clara and the passive, kindly tolerance of Aunt Lil, let alone his cousin Herbert's pitiful acquiescence in his own failure and cousin Ivy's silent independence and the energy which in time took her away to a quiet marriage and, eventually, a position of family authority just like Grandmother Hoggart's.

It is then our good fortune that this crowded enclave in the little terrace house at 32 Newport Street, Hunslet, compressed, as it did, these dense forces and thick presences into what we have learned from Hoggart and allies in his trade to call a culture. That culture taught, in the heavy atmosphere of home, and taught by way of its table, its timetable, its often maddening crowdedness, its open quarrels and its open restoration of peace, its fierce defence of its respectability, it taught resilience, endurance, pacific tolerance, quiet acceptance, never more so than among its womenfolk. At a lowish level of intensity, it also taught the hopefulness of ambition, of what is now called an 'aspirational' sense of direction. But it must be added that aspiration in the 1930s reached little further than a white collar and a thirty shilling worsted suit.

Bert's elder brother Tom won, for the first time in the family's history, a scholarship to a grammar school soon after the children were split up on their mother's death. But there was no question of his staying on for more education after he had taken his School Certificate at sixteen (two whole years after compulsory schooling ended). 'School Cert' was enough; he had qualified for social promotion. Time for a job.

Richard (as he appointed himself by way of his second name, some short time after accession to grammar school) was spared these compulsions by the extraordinary understanding of his grandmother and her taciturn acceptance of generous advice from his schoolteachers. At seven years old or thereabouts (school attendance was legally required but loosely enforced; the HM Inspectors checked attendance records, but no officers pursued truants) Hoggart had started school, but when he went to Hunslet he started educational life in a much more noisy, rebarbative, tough and punitive institution than ever before. His close, feminized upbringing met the harsher winds and rougher seas of Jack Lane Elementary School.

Cultural folklore has long since instructed posterity in the toughness of such schools, especially one on the edges of the Leeds canal system and its heavy engineering. But there was assured authority in the dark classrooms (the windows set too high to gaze day-dreamingly out of) and their lanes of wooden desks with the seat built into its metal frame, a porcelain inkwell covered with a sliding brass top at the rim of the desk lid. Certainly, there were public thrashings administered to miscreants before the whole school after morning prayers, but maybe these featured more largely in the folk memory than in fact.

Hoggart's headmaster (no 'head teachers' then) confutes the cliché version of the authoritarian sadist with a strong alternative which also has its place in folklore. Mr Harrison looked out conscientiously for boys and girls from very poor homes and, finding a pupil as full of promise as Hoggart, told him often 'You've got to get on, lad', told him so because he was sure the boy *could* and should get on, went out of his way to Newport Street to tell Grandmother of the boy's promise and that he should try for grammar school.

So it was that, in the summer of 1929, Hoggart and a not very big crowd of other eleven-year-old hopefuls, only a couple from Jack Lane, trooped off to Cockburn High School 'to sit for the scholarship', which was to say take largely factual examination papers in arithmetic and in English language drills, and undergo a brief, monosyllabic interview, although among his fellows, 'Oggy' had a high reputation as a clever talker, even if he could only manage 'w' for 'r' (a very commonplace speech defect he corrected in his teens with elocution lessons).

Hoggart's teachers knew that the solemn, unblinking boy, always small for his age, was clever, though it was only Mr Harrison who had any sense of just how clever. It isn't much noticed just how much better educated as well socially more confident and confided-in teachers have become since the profession became all-graduate after 1967 and its wellbeing defended and built upon by university departments of education, professors, research and suchlike. Mr Harrison stood out as exceptional, both in manner and dutifulness; most of his staff emptied what bits of knowledge they had – this is history, that is arithmetic – into the little heads in front of them with not much regard for the consequences, for retention, for *thought* itself.

Mr Harrison did better by the boys and girls. He called on Grandmother and underlined what Miss Jubb, the official from the Board of Guardians who called regularly to make sure, formally but delicately, that the Guardians' money was being spent as it should be on the three children's welfare, had already told the old lady. She too had spotted just how intelligent the boy was. However, the Board school arithmetic he had been taught could not at all cope with the exercises of the scholarship paper, and Hoggart failed.

No child from Jack Lane had ever passed. Hoggart was Mr Harrison's first racing certainty. Others, hardly less distinguished than Hoggart, similarly failed the class test, Sir Roy Shaw and Lord Raymond Plant, still to come in our story, among them. Mr

Richard Hoggart with his class at Jack Lane Elementary School.
Mr Harrison is on the right.

Harrison's sense of social justice and pride in his own judgement were affronted. He took himself to the City Education Authority opposite the colossal ostentation of the Town Hall, armed with an essay written by his fluent pupil. He came back with a place for Hoggart at Cockburn High School.

IV

Leeds is a grand city: 'grand' as in Yorkshire argot, and grand as in the architectural history books. The walk from Newport Street to Cockburn High School was nearly two miles, unthinkable in these days of the school run but no school buses then and fares on the corporation bus to be saved. So Hoggart learned to love the city's grandeur by way of its landmarks on the way to and from school and in all weathers, heavy rain regularly coming down from the eastern slopes of the Pennines.

In Hunslet he passed St Mary's church, solid Victorian black with a good spire, built only fifty years before the boy was born. In Waterloo Road he passed the Wesleyan chapel (his family, not churchgoers, counted themselves Primitive Methodists), a fine brick building with six bay windows and big pediments over the two entrances. As he approached the city – something, as you'd expect, he did rarely until into his teens – he came into Briggate, on to Victoria Square and the tremendous Town Hall, out into Calverley Street and past the Civic Hall, only finished when Hoggart was fifteen and the boastful confidence of Victorian Leeds by then a bit depleted, but still bold enough to hold up a four-column portico before the walker passes the Italianate massiveness of the Education Department where Mr Harrison took Hoggart's essay and which properly declares Leeds's pride in its schools, none prouder than Leeds Grammar School itself, up towards the university. This latter institution had started out in Waterhouse's confident hands in the handsome idiom of Victorian Gothic, and by 1926 thought itself due for a bit of splendour so awarded itself a high tower of no distinction but nonetheless a landmark of the city and, no doubt, already familiar to young Hoggart when he arrived as a student in 1936, to find the university done out in the idiom of Doric revival.

This long perambulation[7] can only conjure up the ghosts of the

---

[7] Guided by Nikolaus Pevsner, *Buildings of England: Yorkshire, West Riding*, Harmondsworth: Penguin, 2nd edn, 1967, pp. 317–38.

landmarks by which the boy came to love and know by heart the mighty commercial metropolis, product of the Victorian boom and its inconceivable medley of production, trains, heavy engineering and assembly, the magnificent warehouses still crammed with wool and worsted material on its way to clothe the country as well as the continent of Europe, and with modifications from Lancashire cotton to match local temperatures, the Empire.

Hoggart's city centre, given its poles by the buildings we have glanced at, took its glamorous inaccessibility from the wealthy shops – Schofield's, Marshall and Snelgrove's – and the several Leeds arcades – Thornton's in high Gothic, the County Arcade opposite with a vast cross axis continued across Queen Victoria Street into Cross Arcade. These were the splendid display windows of the city, amazing monuments to the invention of stress-bearing plate glass in the 1820s. Leeds's arcades seem to me quite to diminish their Parisian origins. Walter Benjamin famously noted how glass architecture presages Utopia,[8] and how the Parisian arcades were appointed the cathedrals of the luxury goods trade, itself a novel product of nineteenth-century capitalism. Leeds brought this new frame for popular art to its most splendid incarnation; for a small boy from a poor household, the most available version of such sheer plenty was Woolworths in its heyday, and its most dazzling display the jewelled shards and tumbling treasures of the pick-and-mix sweets counter.

Colour; noise; plenty; mass; that's what there was to gaze at in downtown Leeds. The festival of such values was the coming of the Fair. The Fair arrived on the date of the Holbeck Feast, and its autumn site was on one of the bare, black, clinkered wastes of open ground still wistfully known as 'the Moor'.

In the autumn a thrilling, seedy caravanserai of garishly painted flats, metal marquees, shooting galleries, steam organs, lurid helter-skelters, arrived on the Moor and in hours transformed itself into a miniature city, bright with thousands of painted lights, deafening with the din of amplified music and the roar of generators behind the dodgem cars, the big wheel, the steam organ, the dignified undulation of the little horses on the yellow, crimson, gold and green merry-go-round.

The Wall of Death was young Hoggart's favourite (and of all the boys on the Moor); they approached it with a terrified mixture of dread and fascination. Inside a large wooden cylinder about twenty-

---

[8] Walter Benjamin, *The Arcades Project*, ed. Eiland and McLaughlin, Cambridge MA: Belknap Press, 1999.

five yards in diameter, young men, muscular and stripped to the waist would, once the audience was assembled, race their bikes around the vertical walls of the drum fast enough to defy gravity, undoubtedly braving danger and serious injury.

The travellers, who brought and built the fairground city, dismantled it and then vanished, were the larger city's most mysterious visitors. The Fair was its most tantalizing and fearsome manifestation. The great city's stolid, exciting busyness arrived at this annual climax and, in doing so, bound its small spectator to the rhythm of its geography and history. That is what a richly creative culture does; from time to time it transforms its landmarks into sites of magical beauty. It shows its children that, at the end of the working day, they will find the promise of happiness, and it will be kept.

— 2 —

BEST BOY: A GRAMMAR SCHOOL
EDUCATION

I

Cockburn High School, to an eleven-year-old in 1929, may not have held out the promise of happiness, but it was replete with momentous possibility and, in spite of brother Tom's prior success in the scholarship exam, young Richard declared by way of insisting on his second name that he saw plainly what the transition to the school, with its unaffordable cap and blazer in chocolate and old gold (coughed up for by the City Education Department), signified for him. He arrived alone – it would not have occurred either to him or his grandmother that it might be otherwise – stomach tense with nervousness and anticipation – and trod his uncertain way along the wide stone corridors past big doorways with heavy wooden doors and high glass windows punctuated with stained glass lozenges, until arriving at his designated classroom, then waiting, trying to remain unobtrusive, until assigned his own desk.

Before puzzling his way to his classroom, however, the new scholar had already been swept into a great wave of the rituals by which the grammar school system of the nation drenched its members with the saturation of membership, distinction and identity. The first such sonorous ritual was the school assembly which opened every morning and was at its most enveloping on the first day of term.

Cockburn took its place – this being England – in a huge, thick-textured hierarchy of national grammar schools, elaborately grouped by prestige, longevity, propinquity to political power and social eminence, national geography, architectural distinction – the list of social class markers was flagrant and endless. Cockburn came well below the senior such establishment in Leeds, Leeds Grammar School

40

itself, but would have outranked brother-establishments with buildings of lesser distinction in towns of junior importance in the region – Dewsbury perhaps, or Castleford. There again, any such ranking would have been fiercely and silently contested.

Class, social class and the cold, hard extrusions it effects on personality is at the heart of all this, and was at the heart also of the banal morning ritual which opened Hoggart's first term. At that date, already at least fifty years old and due to last for the next four decades at least, term began, as each day began, in the grand hall around which the corridors and classrooms were built. The boys clattered in by years, juniors first, seniors last, the rather bundling parade overseen by school prefects, visible as such by trifling variations of uniform – a coloured pullover maybe, brown rather than black shoes, blazer unbuttoned. The girls, one third of the school, kept separate assembly.

Once all the boys, with much scraping of chairs, were seated, with members of staff down the sides of the hall, wearing their academic gown as badge of scholarly office and marking them off from PE instructors in singlets, plimsolls and sweater as well as from the school porter in a shiny blue suit, once the parade was assembled, the headmaster entered and mounted the stage at the further end of the hall.

With a tremendous but subdued rumbling and rustling 300 boys stood respectfully up, the Head surveying his charges from above. Hoggart looked, timidly but curiously, at the black-gowned emblem of the authority which would rule his life for seven years, very gradually opening itself to friendship, and the Michaelmas term was under way.

What one might call,[1] especially with the creator of the discipline of cultural studies at one's elbow, the expressive order of schools like Cockburn was a solid, clinker-built, even a noble thing. Most people nowadays no longer doubt but that the transformation of a national school system from a selective allocation to a comprehensive intake was a just and seemly reform, and certainly the grown-up Hoggart held this view. Indeed, his friends and allies, Jean Floud and Chelly Halsey, conducted the research and wrote the book which changed the old policy and convinced the Labour Party's leading intellectual, Anthony Crosland, then Minister of Education, that the momentous change was indeed just, overdue and in itself affirmative of the grand

---

[1] Following Basil Bernstein, 'Ritual in Education', *Class Codes and Control*, vol. 3, London: Routledge and Kegan Paul, 1975.

41

ideal of equality. As Floud and Halsey showed, the nationwide distribution of grammar schools was such that, for instance, in one local authority in Yorkshire, only 18 per cent of children went to local grammar schools whereas in the two adjacent authorities the proportions were 30 per cent and 35 per cent. It wasn't, for many of the unfortunate, a matter of intelligence but of places in school.

The comprehensive argument clinching the comprehensive school was however the crass partiality of the alternative. Selection by the purportedly objective eleven-plus exam, measuring, it was claimed, only innate ability, was determined overwhelmingly by social class. The social status and wealth of the child's father were what counted. Social class categories I and II in the Registrar-General's *Directory of Employment* outnumbered children from categories IV and V by three to one.[2]

Once the research juggernaut began to roll over the forces of educational reaction, they fairly steamrollered (but never eliminated – look about you) the opposition. It is relevant that the winning argument began to gather its strength at the same time as *The Uses of Literacy* was published. Hoggart came to his views as part of the strong postwar current running along the river of British public sentiment and guiding it towards a little more egalitarianism and justice in its social arrangements. For a season, after 1945, that sentiment speeded up the flow of things towards a more open sea of opportunities, plenty of those who had been under fire or bombs having come to the view that if they had risked their lives for the blessed country, it was more than time the country gave them a bit more in return; specifically, free doctors and their care, a decent pension and the vast enlargement of popular education to which Captain Hoggart was to give his whole life.

So the tributes and affection their former pupils still quite properly give their old grammar schools, held, expressed and confirmed by official associations, honours boards, old school ties, bequests, prizes, reunions, must be placed in this rougher sea. The change welcomed by Old Cockburnian Hoggart to comprehensive education was a part of progress in its strongest sense, progress towards a better because more equal, more expansive, more brightly coloured society, one in which life-chances (as they say) were less chancey and more generous. This optimism, this sense of happier possibilities, has dimmed

---

[2] The canonical research by Jean Floud and A. H. Halsey, *Social Class and Education Opportunity*, London: Routledge and Kegan Paul, 1956 and J. W. B. Douglas, *The Home and the School*, London: Routledge, 1962.

since, let us say, the Baroness Thatcher ended her tyrannical rule and nowhere is the better for it.

The harsh language of class enmity and advantage was not much spoken at Cockburn. The school was comfortably placed in a cohesive neighbourhood, even if it didn't expect to include many boys from Hunslet. When it did, it marked them with the same deep signs and symbols as it did the boys to whom such things came naturally.

So daily assemblies, along with all the many rituals which served to bind pupils old and new into a moral community – football and netball matches, especially against keen rivals, school plays and concerts, carol services, sports days, speech days (an indicative title), uniforms, collective punishments and rewards (prizes) – all these familiar occasions, along with many others inscribed upon every little soul and in minute, repetitive detail the powerful narratives of school membership, as well as membership of the superordinate non-school society and the rules of its most powerful representatives.

School rituals communicate compacted and predictable messages. Commands and assumptions flow from them with a minimum of explicitness. Basil Bernstein, magus of the relevant sociology, who attended at about the same time as Hoggart a London boys' school ritualized much as Cockburn was, calls the old order 'stratified' and the then emerging order of the comprehensive school 'differentiated'. In the stratified school all the rituals worked to affirm common membership, clear roles, distinct seniority and, in those days, strong gender separation.

In the old grammar schools, strong boundaries – between age groups, between those with authority in its variegated forms (prefects, secretaries of societies, captains of sports) and those without (but with strongly instilled ambitions to acquire some), between the very subject-matter of the curriculum and its hierarchy (arts versus science, pure versus applied maths, home economics versus biology and zoology) – all these powerful dividers and clarifiers taught social lessons of tradition, class, discipline and moral conduct all as being fixed and dependable. The new schools of the 1970s made their rituals, for sure, but these were much more permeable and individualized, their expression more uncertain and negotiable, their hierarchies changeful and their symbols temporary.

It is easy to understand, pretty well by definition, why conservatively minded people, especially politicians, hark back so wistfully to the old, secure orders still visible in private schools, although the

43

combination of financial power and prestige makes it much easier for them to match cultural change to social opportunity.

II

Cockburn lived by the totems and taboos of the old grammar school order, but did so with the discretion and delicacy enjoined upon it by its not being Leeds Grammar School whose pupils (all boys) were drawn from the wealthier families of an area stretching way beyond the city, where the parents were sufficiently constrained by income or (just as often) strongly encouraged by their own local feeling of belonging to Yorkshire not to dispatch their sons to the boarding schools of the soft south.

Indeed, in an illuminating detour, we can find bloodstained old history ('All history is the history of class struggle') clearly legible even in the 'poshest' (Hoggart's word) of Yorkshire's grammar schools. For Leeds also took in its scholarship boys, indeed was obliged to, after the 1944 Education Act assigned a 'direct grant' to such schools along with the requirement to allocate a legislated proportion of free places.

One such entrant was the deservedly eminent English poet, Tony Harrison, twenty years Hoggart's junior, who later dedicated a poem to Hoggart, which compressed in bitter, jerky, studiedly *un*poetic speech all his hatred of the old class struggle in the daily classroom. Harrison was assigned in the sixth form to read aloud Keats's *Ode to a Nightingale*. (His being a common surname, Harrison was addressed by the teacher with his initials.)

> 4 words only of 'mi'art aches' and. . . 'Mine's broken,
> you barbarian TW!' *He* was nicely spoken,
> 'Can't have our glorious heritage done to death!'

I played the drunken porter in *Macbeth*.

> Poetry's the speech of kings. You're one of those
> Shakespeare gives the comic bits to: prose!
> All poetry (even Cockney Keats?) you see's been dubbed by [AS] into
> RP.

In the second part of the poem, Harrison turns on his tormentor (this is forty years later: it was no slight slight):

> So right, yer buggers, then! We'll occupy
> your lousy leasehold Poetry.

I chewed up littererchewer and spat the bones
into the lap of dozing Daniel Jones,
dropped the initials I'd been harried as
and used my *name* and own voice: [UZ][UZ][UZ],
ended sentences with by, with, from,
and spoke the language that I spoke at home.[3]

There can be little doubt that at Cockburn 'Received Pronunciation' (in the deadly phrase) was greeted appreciatively, but even less doubt that scarcely any pupil would have spoken it. No teacher would have stopped a boy reading in a broad Yorkshire accent; the class would have been rendered speechless.

So 'Oggie's' schoolboyhood, poor as his family was, would have been much more tolerant than in the posher place, and in any case this was an exceptionally bright student in a school dedicated to discovering and nurturing academic intelligence even at a time when it was able to send so few pupils on to the local university. From the start his school reports fairly glowed – 'a very good beginning' in 1930, 'very hard work and excellent progress' in 1932, 'keen and intelligent' the next year, seven credits in his 1934 School Certificate, more credits in English literature, French, history and Latin in his Higher Certificate two years later. Cockburn and Hoggart did each other proud, and each was.

The very architecture of the school spoke a kindlier, more tolerant Yorkshire idiom than the eponymous original uptown in Moorland Road with its lowering Gothic façade and chapel, its sombre gatehouse. Cockburn's exterior was – they all were – grand enough, with cupolas at each corner in a hushed echo of the chateaux of the Loire. Inside, as Hoggart[4] himself recollected, 'the designers had somehow hit upon dimensions which were human'. Naturally, the corridors were wide, immensely high, tiled, stone-floored, shrilly echoing, there hung everywhere that faint, ineradicable, thick school smell of decades of overboiled vegetables, of hundreds of thriving, heated, growing boys in well-worn jackets and trousers which rarely saw a dry cleaner (there were few such in any case in those days), of hundreds of off-duty cigarettes smoked by staff and caretakers but of course strictly forbidden to the boys. And there was 'a feel, an atmosphere which suggested that they were full of people doing their best

---

[3] Tony Harrison, 'Them and [UZ]' dedicated to Hoggart in *Selected Poems*, Harmondsworth: Penguin, 1984, p. 122.
[4] Richard Hoggart, *A Local Habitation: Life and Times*, vol. 1: 1918–40, London: Chatto and Windus, 1988, p. 157.

to do well by those they were concerned with . . . firmly, responsibly, decently'.[5]

The three adverbs match man to school. There was plenty wrong with the grammar schools of the 1930s, let alone of the 1960s when progressive educationists thought that their day was done. Their main justification was supposed to be the uncovering and then the cultivation of intellectual ability, but in truth they were only assiduous in this task on behalf of their 'top stream' pupils. That is to say, most grammar schools received each year a new intake of about seventy eleven-year-olds who were immediately assigned to one of three ability 'streams' on the basis of their IQ scores in the eleven-plus entry examination (before 1944, in the scholarship exam, the arithmetic paper which brought Hoggart low).

These assignations to stream remained pretty inflexible, however well pupils performed within each stream. Indeed, one strong reason for dissolving grammar into comprehensive schools was just this inflexibility with the always protean development of adolescence. Once you were swimming along in one stream, you stayed there. Rare changes were generally downwards.[6] The more or less acknowledged function of grammar school streaming was to ensure that the boys and girls in the top stream went either to university (the girls to teacher training colleges) or to other points of access to 'professional' lives (accountants, lawyers, senior management); that those in the middle stream went into respectable and probably local employment after taking their Higher School Certificate (civil service, department store managers, on-the-job trainee engineers, armed services – the girls to nursing and inevitably secretarial work), and that the bottom stream, burnishing nonetheless their grammar school credentials, would find (for the boys) settled posts as small businessmen or respectable clerks in the then endless busyness of local productive life relatively untouched by global competition and underpaid overseas labour; the third stream girls would staff the offices and reception desks of companies wanting a bit of flair at the front-of-house, and then get married and raise children.

These were the not-dishonourable, imaginatively narrow, politically docile processes which confirmed the British social system between, say, 1918 and 1968. The top stream at Cockburn stuck more or less together for their seven years in the school, Stanley Binner and

---

[5] Hoggart (1988), p. 157.

[6] As shown by Brian Jackson, in *Streaming: An Education System in Miniature*, London: Routledge and Kegan Paul, 1964.

Freddie Moss Hoggart's closest friends. For a little orphan of eleven from a very poor home, however, holding one's own in tense, explicit competition with other boys and girls less hampered by poverty, by a crazy aunt and a drunken cousin, by the two-mile walk to and from school in all weathers, by booklessness at home, diminutive stature, high anxiety and uncertain knowledge of his own powerful wits, it's no surprise that round about the end of the summer term of 1932 Hoggart gave way to what was then known as a nervous breakdown.

This was how the family's kindly, neighbourly doctor put it. The boy was stuck: tense with apprehension of nameless menaces, rigidly unable to do his (plentiful) homework, frozen into a helplessness he could do nothing to dislodge.

There were folk-diagnoses which helped Grandmother to comprehend her beloved Richard's predicament. Too much brainwork, 'brain-fever', went along not only with knowing a case or two of nervous breakdowns herself but also with her speechless, enfolding love of the boy. The Board of Guardians paid up for a fortnight's convalescence on Yorkshire's beautiful windswept coast, its miles of hard, dark yellow sand and friable cliffs. In the convalescent home there were big windows overlooking the sea, 'a nurse of exceptional sweetness', a couple of bullies and, for Hoggart, recovery.

Perhaps what was happening was Hoggart's early disciplining of his always fine, attenuated sense of the presence and nature of the people around him, and his subjugation of this vivid alertness to the necessity of *work*, the work which would release him into the huge freedoms of intellectual inquiry and the exhilaration of solitary study.

If so, it was also the case that the happy gregariousness of 'Sunny Jim' would always be quick to tie down those flights of speculation to their common human anchorage, to hold tight to the connection between all creative thought and practice and its origins in the endeavours of existence.

It was Coleridge who first theorized the imagination as the prime faculty of mind, and counterposed to it the lesser but still necessary play of fancy, 'a mode of memory emancipated from the order of time and space'.[7] Since the great Romantic's day, the imagination has come to assume a more and more dominant position in pedagogy, and its development thought of as ever more crucial to the educated person. For Coleridge, in exalted mood, the imagination was 'a repetition in the finite mind of the eternal act of creation in the infinite I AM'. Grammar school English teachers in 1935 didn't make much

[7] S. T. Coleridge, *Biographia Literaria*, London: Dent, Everyman edn, p. 167.

play with psychology, but they had their strong and generous pieties, and they believed (as well they might) that it could only be of benefit to their startlingly intelligent (and, they had found, talkative) sixteen-year-old if his obvious delight in words were put to stand below the grandest fountain of language in English, Shakespeare.

Nor was this to be a mere matter of reading-round-the-classroom (though there is nothing wrong with that). Mr Kerry, head of the school English department, knowing how there wasn't a penny to spare at Hoggart's home, had collected from his own and his colleagues the £6 (not at all a small sum at that date, when a working man would rarely take home more than £2 at the end of the week) needed to pay for Hoggart to attend a school camp held in Stratford on Avon in the summer.

The camp was arranged by Flowers, the big brewery in Stratford: bell tents by the river, and three trips to see Shakespeare plays in his new memorial theatre given over almost entirely to Shakespeare productions. He saw *Antony and Cleopatra*, *The Merchant of Venice* and *Henry IV Part 1*, punched, small as he was, a much bigger bully of a boy in the face, and came home with his fancy and imagination much enhanced by brave words and direct action.

Once back at school, his English teacher leaned on him to enter the essay competition open to all who attended the camp. Hoggart entered and won. The sixteen-year-old's prose, allowing for a faint shine of treacle, is, in his first publication, enviably assured and cadenced.

> How dreary is the business of striking camp! It has none of the bright hope, the lively, joyous anticipation of pitching. Yet let us not be ungrateful. We have gathered this week memories and experiences which will cheer us in the days to come and give us 'Roses in December'.[8]

Can there have been many teachers, nationwide, who made collections, unprompted, to send their brightest boy or girl to see Shakespeare? If they weren't politically radical (and until the war came, they weren't), they nonetheless signed up for that enlargement of opportunity, that opening of horizons and of individual sensibilities which was the school's first principle.

That was the best that most grammar schools could do. It wasn't negligible, but nor was it a noble repository of intellectual disinterestedness and cultural sensitivity, as some of its more canting defenders (Secretaries of State among them) have pretended. For the most

---

[8] *The Cockburnian*, 20, Winter edn, 1935, p. 14.

part, the school confirmed the judgements of the entrance exam and assigned, with more or less of docility, its pupils to those categories in social classes A, B and C1 as set out in the infallible *Directory of Employment*, which it was its duty to fill. It did what it could for culture and it put down anarchy. It helped to thicken up local identity, it dignified its habits and rituals as tradition, and in doing so did its important bit for continuity.

Within its tranquil frame and rather washed-out ambitions however, it could make room for one or two rare spirits. Best of all when one such was the Head (it may have been that the struggle to establish girls' education after, say, 1850 or so, as a serious and warrantable activity, has meant that women Heads have, by and large, more fight as well as more imagination than the men).

Hoggart was lucky in having on his side at school, first, Mr Harrison at Jack Lane Elementary School, to go on his behalf to the Education Office in Leeds and come back with a place at Cockburn, and then Mr Norden, the Head at Cockburn who spotted young Hoggart's good wits and scribbled on his end-of-year report in 1934, 'should think of professional life'. When the formidable Miss Jubb, the official visitor on behalf of the Board of Guardians, paid her monthly visit to Newport Street to make sure all was well, Grandmother asked her to explain the Head's note.

'It means he could be a doctor or a parson.' It meant therefore that, equipped with his intelligence and the language it had mastered, he would leave behind his class and number 32 Newport Street and reach much further *upwards*, up and down being the only directions open to social passages.

Grandmother understood at once and, with her usual loving comprehension, forewent the precious wage the boy could otherwise have brought home. He progressed, a year later, into the sixth form, the Guardians raised their weekly contribution to fifteen shillings, and Hoggart became one of the headmaster's favoured pupils.

Round about the age of fourteen, talkative 'Oggie' had discovered Hunslet's public library, then a newish, solid brick building with good stone lintels and stone steps to the entrance. It had an electric fire, padded seats, its shelves were open, it was quiet and its supervisory librarians typically soft-spoken and encouraging. Hoggart called in on his way home, went there if Aunt Clara was in full spate at home, did his homework at times in the useful little study room, prowled the shelves for what he could find.

He found poetry. At school, as in almost every school in the country, the poetry textbook was one edition or another of Francis

Palgrave's *Golden Treasury*, and a treasure house of the very best Victorian taste it is. Jack Lane Elementary had only introduced Hoggart to a lot of Robert Service and a little Kipling, though both had brought him the great pleasures of a firm rhyme scheme, strong rhythms, easily remembered alliteration, four-line stanzas. Palgrave introduced him to poets and to poems and snatches of poems which would lie to hand for the rest of his life. This is what it is to possess a living literary culture; this is what it is for any one of us to be seized by a poem, so to digest it that it becomes, as Coleridge said it would, a shaping spirit, a shaper of one's spirit, a solace, or a disconcerting companion, right up to one's end. A great poem makes each of us a poet.

So Thomas Nashe spoke from Palgrave's pages and told him his antique commonplaces:

> Brightness falls from the air;
> Queens have died young and fair;
> Dust hath closed Helen's eye:
> I am sick, I must die.

There wasn't a lot of poetry read at Cockburn as Hoggart moved through his two years in the sixth form towards his Higher School Certificate. His set texts included Shakespeare, naturally, but in spite of his visit to Stratford, Shakespeare had not yet caught fire for him. There were plenty of novels, however: *The Mayor of Casterbridge*, Scott's *Heart of Midlothian*, *Great Expectations*, and Pip's solitary, put-upon and reflective boyhood tolled many a familiar bell in Hoggart's life. But it was Hardy who, as for so many boys sensing themselves on the move from narrow, unhorizoned localities into something far larger, somewhere exhilarating, for sure, but swept by the winds of agoraphobia as well, who seized his sympathy and carried him forward to the searing recognitions of *Jude the Obscure*. Jude's sudden, horrorstruck and ravishing epiphany of sex, when the good-looking hussy Arabella throws the pig's genitals at him after the slaughter, naturally struck a strong chord in the seventeen-year-old boy who, brought up among women, had never taken a girl out. Jude's vision of the skyline of Oxford, transliterated as Christminster on the edge of peasant Wessex, matched Hoggart's of the black, imposing Parthenon of Leeds University, towery and branchy and river-rounded enough for Yorkshire, on the slope lifting towards Woodhouse.

The school discipline of English, then as now, was divided into the two halves of language and literature. The study of language, derived straight from the Elizabethan curriculum, entailed the endless parsing of the grammatical units of sentences clause by clause: predicate (subject plus verb), object, subordinate clauses (adjectival, adverbial, noun clauses in apposition) as well as the wholly redundant identification of cases (nominative, accusative, genitive, dative, ablative) taken straight from Latin exercises, all these drills and many more (fixed rules, different *from* never *to*, of pronunciation – 'ett' *not* 'ate') filled exercise books and were solemnly marked out of ten. Implicit in many such injunctions were the strict markers of social class; to get one of these rules wrong was to betray one's inferior status. To know the difference between the imperfect and past historic tenses was to be on one's way to linguistic mastery.

It was dry-as-dust also. No wonder that such a boy as Hoggart roamed the shelves at the public library looking for poems which swept him along on the great wave of the pentameter as he found it in Palgrave's pages, found it first and unforgettably in Swinburne, then found it in Sonnet 73:

> That time of year then mayest in me behold,
> When yellow leaves, or none, or few, do hang
> Upon these boughs which shake against the cold,
> Bare, ruin'd choirs where late the sweet birds sang.

The same thrilling effect rolled out from Thomas Gray's wonderful *Elegy*:

> The curfew tolls the knell of parting day,
> The lowing herd winds slowly o'er the lea,
> The ploughman homeward plods his weary way,
> And leaves the world to darkness and to me.

You turn the old pages and you and Hoggart alike irresistibly recall a letter of John Keats, eagerly writing 'How can I help bringing to your mind the line'; then you turn to Keats's own, opulent beatitude:

> Season of mists and mellow fruitfulness,
> Close bosom-friend of the maturing sun;
> Conspiring with him how to load and bless
> With fruit the vines that round the thatch-eaves run . . .

After Keats came Wordsworth as a matter of course, and although Hoggart had never been to Tintern Abbey he had cycled deep into the Yorkshire dales, seen and felt the haunted beauty of Fountains Abbey and wordlessly understood the replenishment of the spirit which Wordsworth named as the gift of the great Cistercian relic.

51

His bike, incidentally, was a present from the volcanic Aunt Clara, and a reward for doing so well at sixteen in his School Certificate. It cost a mammoth five pounds. It carried its rider clean out of so much that trapped, confined or weighed him down: bus fares, sheer distances, clocking-in times, the ponderous heaviness of the rest of the family. With the Salem Chapel cycling club, not all a churchy association, the boy found the happiness of egalitarian companionability. The club members cycled out together, but each of them was free as air. They shared fourpenny pots of tea in the Dales, they stopped together at the best-known views, they made sure no one was left behind.

What is the content of happiness? It is, someone has said,[9] something that opens at the centre of a perfectly unselfinterested experience, one into which one is wholly absorbed, lost to oneself: in front of a painting, gazing at something beautiful, playing a game, hearing music, dissolving into a story. As the moment opens up, 'it gives birth to a happiness instantly recognizable as your own'. The corner of life that you are contemplating appears to have the same proportions as your own life. Cycling, in a group and with friends for sure, but cycling in the free air, moving out of town (but a lot of town to cross first) gave the boyish Hoggart, small, sunny-tempered, sure of himself, exactly that sense of proportion, and the happiness which due proportion brings. The familiarity of the proportions may change, as one's life advances; just as the horizons of the cycling club expanded, so did Hoggart's sense of the shape of his life. As he got older, the misty blue distances came clearer; they turned into the gentleness of Wharfedale, the rolling reach of the moors topping a thousand feet towards Denton, Blubberhouses beyond. These were the proportions his life gradually assumed, plenty of it unknowable naturally, but reached for eagerly as he strained on the bike pedals up some tough hills, letting go recklessly on the downward slopes.

The High School offered, on its good days, something of the same happy proportionality, at least for a boy of Hoggart's gifts and disposition. He may have been small, but he had angrily punched the big bully in the face at the Stratford camp. His pawky independence, his swoops of eager feeling at the poems and music he found, mostly, for himself, his calm appraisal of his teachers, all matched the something homely and kindly he found in the very spaces of the school, its big façade with the shapely cupolas at each end, the wide stone staircases, the high classroom doors and the high windows of the classrooms

[9] John Berger, 'A Field', *About Looking*, London: Writers and Readers, 1980, p. 198.

themselves which in later life always came to mind when he read
Philip Larkin's lovely lines:

> Rather than words comes the thought of high windows:
> The sun-comprehending glass,
> And beyond it, the deep blue air, that shows
> Nothing, and is nowhere, and is endless.[10]

The place *suited* him. It represented grammar school education at its
limited best, local in its purview, decent, properly respectful of the
best intelligences it counted among its pupils but largely disposing
of most of them with a tranquil lack of ambition which perfectly
matched the lowish hopes of the families filling morning assembly
with their children, matching also the unreflective ways the teachers
in their chalk-dusted academic gowns assigned each boy, each girl, to
their futures.

These included in particular Mr Kerry, the English teacher who
organized the collection for Hoggart's trip to see Shakespeare, a
gentle young woman teacher of French from southern England, Miss
Roxburgh, later headmistress in Winchester, and her bow-tied Head
of Department, both of whom grounded the boy well in the French he
would be speaking daily in the Paris offices of UNESCO forty years
later.

These people counted for much in the Cockburnians' formation,
none more so than the head of English, and the headmaster himself,
Clifford Norden. Mr Kerry spotted, of course, what a good pupil he
had, led him carefully and properly as we saw, through Palgrave's
Golden Treasury and the map of English grammar, kept an eye, as he
would for all such pupils, on his progress, pressed him when the time
came to hope for a place at the university ('You'll want to do English,
Hoggart?'), filled in the forms himself, and Grandmother, Miss Jubb
and the Guardians had done the rest.

The headmaster, a cultivated theologian, and the head of English
got on well together and from time to time Norden would take a class
in English, do so without particular preparation and talk genially and
memorably about books to the sixth-formers. Himself a product of
one or other of the two ancient universities, he conducted such sessions much as they were carried on in the undergraduate tutorials for
a couple of students at a time at Oxford and Cambridge. That is, he
talked about the writers the little Arts group, only five or six strong,

---

[10] Philip Larkin, 'High Windows', *Collected Poems*, London: Faber and Faber, 1988,
p. 165.

was studying, connecting writer to circumstance – to place, to friends and family, to fortune, fame and health – in a freewheeling, spacious way which at once gripped and liberated his audience. It was there, in particular his asking of himself as much as of his best pupil, what it was to be 'cultured', as Hoggart had written of Hardy, that you might find the very moment at which Hoggart himself discovered his lifelong vocation to find and hold the manifold meanings of the word 'culture'.

Twenty years or so before Hoggart was listening to Mr Norden thinking aloud about Thomas Hardy, another working-class young man, twenty-nine at the time, was also thinking hard about all that Hardy meant to him. D. H. Lawrence, in a long essay searching out the deepest themes of a literature, said of Hardy,

> There is a lack of sternness, there is a hesitating betwixt life and public opinion, which diminishes the Wessex novels from the rank of pure tragedy. It is not so much the eternal, immutable laws of being which are transgressed, it is not that vital life-forces are set in conflict with each other, bringing almost inevitable tragedy – yet not necessarily death, as we see in the most splendid Aeschylus. It is, in Wessex, that the individual succumbs to what is in its shallowest, public opinion, in its deepest, the human compact by which we live together, to form a community.
>
> Most fascinating in all artists is this antinomy between Law and Love, between the Flesh and the Spirit, between the Father and the Son.[11]

Hoggart lived and wrote at a much less high-pitched level than Lawrence. His Aunt Clara, you might say, tore herself to shreds on the shallow thorns of public opinion. Hoggart found his human compact in the strengths of culture – in manners and morality, for sure, but only in those precepts of morality which led into a territory well beyond poor Clara's vicious snobbery and helpless frustration. For, as Lawrence continues,

> . . . all morality is of temporary value useful to its times. But Art must give a deeper satisfaction. It must give fair play all round.
>
> Yet every work of art adheres to some system of morality. But if it be really a work of art, it must contain the essential criticism of the morality to which it adheres. And hence the antinomy, hence the conflict necessary to every tragic conception.

11 D. H. Lawrence, *Selected Literary Criticism*, ed. A. R. Beal, London: Heinemann, 1955, pp. 184–5.

Like all great novelists, Hardy caught up in the careers of his characters the always imminent tragedy, the lived-in comedy of people's struggle to shake off the deathliness of an old moral, political and economic system, and to catch hold of the truth and vitality in a new one.

Hoggart saw the tragi-comedy played out in Hardy, saw it in Lawrence also, and found its deep correspondence with his own life. Blessed, however, with so capacious and happy a disposition, he transposed their massive music into the serene and cheerful suites of his life and work. Say that the readiest way one may grasp and shape a life in a secular age is to make of it as finished a work of art as one may, then Richard Hoggart made of his life as good such a work as the history of his day would permit. Say also that the tip his headmaster lightly let drop about Thomas Hardy set his fortunate nature on a path on which he would discover how to make life and work accurately intertwine.

— 3 —

A CIVIC EDUCATION: THE UNIVERSITY OF LEEDS

I

It is quite a walk from Hunslet to the university, which since 1967 or so has become a neat little city of its own, tidily ringed as an academic precinct and guarded by the Gatehouse which still admits you, as it has done since 1835, to the Woodhouse cemetery right in the middle of the campus. When Hoggart took the two-mile uphill walk from Newport Street the original buildings had been completed by the great Alfred Waterhouse in 1886 when the place was entitled the Yorkshire College of Science, and intended, in the excellent Victorian way, as a forcing house for industrial and technological innovations to hold off the by then galloping advances of German manufacturing after that country's late-come unification at Bismarck's hands in 1870.

In 1904 the place became a university in its own right, though still very much under the tutelage of London, and after the colossal upheaval of the First World War, the city at large concluded that to hold its own in the new world, its university would have to embody some pretty bold ambitions. So it built high, wide and, for the West Riding, handsome enough, topping things off with a landmark tower visible on the hill to the city below, all in the by then slightly lifeless idiom of the Greek revival but with a Yorkshire massiveness, setting things off with the circular front of the Brotherton Library, just in time for the arrival of the new undergraduate in 1936.

He was just eighteen. The university, small enough then in all conscience – only 1,700 students, two in every seven women (a proportion a good deal higher than at Oxbridge), 80 per cent of them from the West Riding, a tiny handful from India come to study textiles, presaging the day when their country would inherit the world – small as it now seems, a vast agora even to talkative, self-sufficient Hoggart. He looked back fondly at the cupolas of Cockburn and nervously forward at the bulky darkness on University Road and Woodhouse Lane where, pinched a little by the bigness of the Mining and Agricultural buildings, the English department lived a quiet life in a gabled Victorian house round the corner.

It is no great distance from now back to then; merely a lifetime. But it's hard to be exact and vivid about the smallness and privation of the poorer student's domestic life in the years before, indeed, either of the two wars. A generation before Hoggart's, the English novelist, Storm Jameson, left behind a grim enough childhood in Whitby, on the north-east Yorkshire coast, and arrived, with a scholarship award, to read English literature at Leeds.

Coming from a fishing port, she was repelled by 'the ring of steel furnaces and mills belching out smoke by day and flames by night, the ceaseless beat of industry' but, utterly unlike the clichés of 'dreaming spires and fields yellow with buttercups' as it was, she knew that, for young men and women of her class, 'a degree was the only gateway to a tolerable life'.[1] Her threshold of tolerance was a good deal higher than Hoggart's, but her recollections and his are at one in their chronicle of starveling diet, shabby, even sordid terraces, 'a graceless sooty Latin Quarter without benefit of cafés, without a rag of charm' (her words), of digs with no bathroom, of the magical enchantment of time itself provided by the cinema, of a ninepennyworth of fish and chips for a treat.

To begin with, Hoggart lived at home, continued the taken-for-granted and arduous necessity of *walking*, walking to save bus fares of only three pence, walking by dark and in the wet, many miles of walking every week, walking into a kinship with all those characters in Thomas Hardy making their steady, effortful way to the labours awaiting them. Perhaps it was the pedestrian need of students' lives up to, say, 1960 which most marked them off from the taken-for-granted and high-speed mobility of today's undergraduates.

After several months of student life, Hoggart won a happy break from walking to and from Hunslet when he obtained from the always humane Leeds Education Authority an enlargement of his grant big enough to pay for accommodation in a Hall of Residence. The room was always warm, the food was plain but good, and the customs of

[1] Storm Jameson, *Autobiography vol. I: Journey from the North*, London: Virago, 1984, p. 52.

the place, following the conventions of Oxford and Cambridge colleges codified no more than a century earlier as part of a general effort to bring the civilizing process a bit closer to wild students, included a formal evening meal at a fixed time, preceded by a spoken grace and attended by the Warden in charge, a stout, benign Professor of Education called Frank Smith.

Smith was a man of some repute, and indeed the so-called civic universities of the north and midlands – at Liverpool, Manchester, Sheffield, Birmingham, Nottingham, Leicester, Bristol, Glasgow (Durham and St Andrews being much older and therefore differently placed in the hierarchy) – assigned themselves a justified status and dignity. Their departments of science, handsomely endowed by and adjusted to the local industries, matched for distinction anything done at London or Cambridge, and among the professors, of whom there were few, was more than a sprinkling of the names of men (almost always men) of substantial achievement and reputation. They counted for something in local society, they were men of substance, and it is much to be feared that to a twenty-year-old of Hoggart's keen and irreverent eye they were marked by the common class properties of noticeable corpulence, plump features, pinstripe suits and a tremendous manner. The vice-chancellor of the day collected then as now a knighthood, and his senior professors invariably owned large houses with walled gardens in the best districts: Edgbaston in Birmingham, Clifton in Bristol, Woodhouse in Leeds, the New Town in Edinburgh.

So it was a slightly awe-inspiring delight for Hoggart to meet, to be taught by and to befriend Bonamy Dobrée, Professor of English, whose exotic name (inherited from his Channel Islander father) marked him out from his fellows, but the contradictions of whose career made him at once professorial, bohemian and imperial. He was of an impeccably upper-class formation, was sent to Haileybury and Sandhurst, was a regular army officer for three years up to 1913, rejoined instantly when war broke out, had had enough of killing as a profession after the war and, at the age of thirty, went to read English at Cambridge where the new and radical Tripos (three-year degree) in English had been launched in wartime. He had had as a contemporary at Cambridge the man who was most to embody and fight for the significance of the new degree and to dominate its form and content for two generations, F. R. Leavis, but Dobrée, while always respectful of Leavis, took his precepts lightly and went his own way.

That way led him to a Chair in Cairo's English-speaking university where he succeeded Robert Graves 'in the former harem-palace of the

Khedive, built in luscious French style with mirrors and gilding'.[2] He arrived in Leeds only a year before Hoggart, white-haired and military-moustached at forty-six, took to the young man strongly, coached and coaxed him on, found him, as he was, open, ardent, strong in his feelings, in a love of literature, eager to discover whatever intellectual life would bring.

He was the third such presence in Hoggart's life: Mr Harrison, Mr Norden, Professor Dobrée, but he became a friend as well as a guide and protector, and Hoggart never lost an understandable awe of him. Once, in very late age, recollecting, as so often, what Dobrée had meant to him, Hoggart said, 'the daffodils stood to attention when he went by'. Maybe his wartime experience, maybe his patrician inheritance, more likely something generous, freebooting, nonchalant in his nature, led Dobrée to look out for likely lads, to pass them books well away from the syllabus which seemed likely to light them up, to stand by those in trouble with the university, to drink with them in the Students' Union. And he was quick, lively, authoritative with it, told the lads off when it was called for, like Mr Norden at Cockburn ranged freely, with an intellectual dash and recklessness, in his lectures and his conversation, was friends with T. S. Eliot, Edwin Muir, Storm Jameson and Henry Moore.

Every lucky person – and Hoggart was certainly that – has a teacher in their life who changed their life. Dobrée did that for Hoggart. About as unlike each other as people may be and still be of one nation, the older man took to whatever it was in the younger one which was not like he was himself but was so very likeable, was also warmhearted, open, obviously sincere, extremely intelligent (rather than intellectual), staunch as to principle.

There is a wonderful paragraph in *David Copperfield* in which Dickens describes an instantly recognizable human attribute which, I think, Dobrée did share with Hoggart, and which each saw, fondly, in the other.

> I believe the power of observation in numbers of very young children to be quite wonderful for its closeness and accuracy. Indeed, I think that most grown men who are remarkable in this respect, may with greater propriety be said not to have lost the faculty, than to have acquired it; the rather, as I generally observe such men to retain a certain freshness, and gentleness, and capacity of being pleased, which are also an inheritance they have preserved from their childhood.[3]

---

[2] Robert Graves, *Good-bye to All That*, Harmondsworth: Penguin, 1960, p. 266.
[3] Charles Dickens, *David Copperfield*, Harmondsworth: Penguin, 1967, p. 61.

Dickens's childhood was every bit as arduous as Hoggart's, and Hoggart – sagacious always in self-knowledge – attributed not only to the harsh severance from his brother and sister which orphanhood brought to his young life but also to the endless tirades of Aunt Clara a too-tender responsiveness on his part to the slights and rebuffs of ordinary life. No doubt that sensitivity was also due to an intelligent man's lively awareness of the daily offensiveness of English, no, *British* class differences, imprinted on one's soul (often deliberately) by the innumerable details of social organization, by speech and look, by innocence being stripped off and natural courtesy turned to bitter resentment.

Nonetheless, Hoggart determinedly retained his 'freshness and gentleness and capacity of being pleased', and Dobrée fostered these things, became, by his kindness, expansiveness, occasional overbearingness (he arranged, without warning, for Hoggart to be interviewed for a job he didn't want on the *Yorkshire Post*), an ideal father as well as close friend.

By 1936, when Hoggart began his studies, English literature had become the most rigorous, argumentative and exhilarating of the humanities in British universities. At that time, transatlantic influences were much thinner, Parisian fashions scarcely audible. But twentieth-century intellectual life in what a little later the French well named 'the human sciences' is marked by a jostling sort of race between the disciplines in which first one, then another, catches hold of and is braced by a congruence with the passing spirit of the day. In the 1930s – and through to the 1950s when Hoggart himself did so much to relax its grip and change its temper – English was that leading discipline, and took its leadership with a certain *arriviste* lower-class raucousness, offending the old stagers, history and philosophy, by its assertiveness, its disregard for such canonical proprieties as knowledge of the classics or respect for longer-established subjects, its happy violation of disciplinary boundaries and 'keep out' notices warning trespassers off logic, say, or architectural history, flouting the prohibition on politics.

Writing in 1945 while recollecting Oxford in 1923, Evelyn Waugh has an unpleasing character say to his cousin, the freshman hero,

> You're reading history? A perfectly respectable school. The very worst is English literature and the next worst is Modern Greats. You want either a first or a fourth. There is no value in anything between . . .[4]

---

[4] Evelyn Waugh, *Brideshead Revisited*, London: Dent, 1993, p. 21.

We may be sure that Waugh, new literature-maker and reactionary, was thinking of the subject as it was as he wrote, and had been for more than a decade. For English, never more so than at the hands of F. R. Leavis and in the pages of his calm and contentious journal, *Scrutiny* (which began publication in 1932), was committed, by its very method and the stout framework of inquiry which Leavis and his associates constructed, to holding the object of study hard up against the individual's own deep allegiances and moral standards, demanding of him or her an account of just what that strange meeting meant.

Such insistent encounters blew a gusty wind through (as they used to say) the groves of academe, and the winds certainly reached Leeds. There were plenty of members of staff who read *Scrutiny*, for this was still the day of the journal, and among many competitors, Eliot's *Criterion* stood out for its unruffled certainty of doctrine while being flanked by such varied neighbours as the eclectic and cultural *Realist*, the always respectable *Bookman*, and the solidly immortal (still with us) *Times Literary Supplement, New Statesman and Nation* and the *Spectator*.

Dobrée was well known in many of these pages, and his happy combination of Gascon musketeer and Baudelairean *flâneur* meant that his pupils were unlikely to be subject to the sometimes excessive zeal and self-righteousness which touched, even intoxicated, some of Leavis's followers.[5] All the same, students of Hoggart's breadth of reading had all been captured by Robert Graves's autobiography, *Good-bye to All That*, which came out in 1929 to great acclaim; Dobrée had known Graves personally, and in any case with rumours of war in every newspaper, young men wanted to know what war had been like in case things would be like that again.

One delicious little anecdote told by Graves caught the fancy of any pious iconoclast of the old totems of class culture. Graves arrived to read English literature at Oxford in 1919, after three whole years in the trenches.

> At the end of my first term's work, I attended the usual college board to give an account of myself. The spokesman coughed, and said a little stiffly: 'I understand, Mr Graves, that the essays which you write for your English tutor are, shall I say, a trifle temperamental. It appears, indeed, that you prefer some authors to others.'[6]

---

[5] The intellectual climate of Leavis's Cambridge in the 1930s is caught in detail by Ian Mackillop, *F. R. Leavis: A Life in Criticism*, London: Allen Lane, 1995.

[6] Graves (1960), p. 240. Leavis of course later used the extract as an epigraph to his *The Common Pursuit*, London: Chatto and Windus, 1952.

So too did the best of the young men and women of Yorkshire in 1936, and Dobrée certainly wasn't going to stop them. He loaned out specially chosen books to his specially chosen, to Hoggart he gave an odd-looking choice in which to find something of himself reflected. It was *The Education of Henry Adams*, 'quite simply the greatest autobiography of American letters' says the blurb.[7] This, however, was at a time when very little American literature was read at British universities and this was in any case the life-story of a direct descendant of one of the founding fathers of the United States, impeccably élite, Harvard graduate, much travelled in Europe and, not coincidentally, patron of the young Algernon Swinburne, whose poetry so fired young Hoggart in Hunslet library.

Hoggart found in Adams an echo of his own powers of observation and detachment. He found a sympathetic similarity in Adams's fierce self-criticism.

> His work seemed to him thin, commonplace, feeble. At times he felt his own weakness so fatally that he would not go on . . .[8]

Self-belief, as people say nowadays, is to any intelligent person delusive without self-doubt, even moments of self-dislike. Either way, self-possession, so certainly conferred by Harvard, would prove a slippery thing. Hoggart had it, no doubt, but like Adams's version it was always sliding out of his grasp in the face of larger experiences than the self which he possessed at the time could accommodate: like Adams when the sudden epiphany of Beethoven hit him, Hoggart borrowed a set of the fifteen or twenty brittle records of *Traviata* and was swept away by them; they made you, he said in his old aunt's phrase, 'want to give all your money away'.

He listened to them in the company of a pretty young woman in a brown silk dress whom he had – he noticed pretty women all his life – spotted at freshmen registration, but was far too shy to approach. She too was reading English, they were in the same group, she knew, naturally, that the short stocky boy was often looking at her, although she already had a steady admirer on the staff of the Estate Management department. After a term-and-a-half of nervous swallowing, Hoggart found the courage to pause on the steps of the Brotherton Library and invite Mary France to accompany him to the cinema to see *Green Pastures*.

[7] Henry Adams, *The Education of Henry Adams: An Autobiography*, Boston: Houghton Mifflin, 1961.
[8] Adams (1961), p. 66.

Richard and Mary snapped from behind by a friend while at a playreading society meeting at the University of Leeds in 1938.

The movie was just out. It told a succession of Old Testament tales as seen through the eyes of a devout, boisterous and barely literate black American audience. It is very funny, wholly and cheerfully devout, it featured those sound actors Rex Ingram and Oscar Polk, and went down just as well at the Paramount cinema, Leeds, as it had across the Deep South.

Going to the pictures together was as customary a convention with which to begin friendship between the sexes as could be found any time between 1930 and 1970. The evenings were sealed by fish and chips for a shilling and then, if the money ran to it, a bus up to Mary's hall of residence, two miles beyond Devonshire Hall, and then the long walk back with the girl's picture in his head.

They proved a lifelong match in a way less rare than people nowadays suppose. They shared high intelligence, North Country origins, something of the same kind of solitariness, for Mary was the only child of schoolteachers, but also the same kind of cheerfulness, of readiness before life, of toughness under hardship, of unshakable loyalty, and a love of poetry.

Nothing much to add to such qualities except one's admiration.

II

He was made welcome at the Frances' family home in Stalybridge, a little town below the Pennines and across the county boundary, some forty-odd miles south-west towards Manchester. Mother and father were churchgoers, father an elementary school headmaster, Mary was born soon after Harry France came home wounded from the Somme.

It was quickly assumed by the couple and everyone else that Richard and Mary were a permanent couple and, 'spooning' according to the present day's demonstrative affections being strictly forbidden by university regulation, they defied Mrs Grundy by holding hands under the library tables. No wine in student life then, and very little beer; pots of tea after hiking or biking or bussing into the Yorkshire dales or as far as highly respectable Harrogate. They each read D. H. Lawrence's happy and highspirited travel book, *Sea and Sardinia*,[9] and admired the nerve of the Lawrences as, armed with bacon sandwiches and a thermos of tea, they fraternized with Sardinian peasants on the long bus journeys the length of the island.

Hoggart had already had the chance to set off on some such arbitrary journey before the sun is up and when one doesn't really want to launch oneself into the scary unknown, but goes nonetheless, pressed under disinclination by the force of circumstance. For he had been summoned to an audience with the bluff and august Director of Leeds Education Authority which paid his exiguous scholarship. Out of the blue, the great man offered the lad thirty pounds with which to visit 'abroad' if he were to write down in detail how he would spend such a windfall on the other side of the North Sea.

Hoggart returned to tell the Director that he would cycle the 170 miles (!) to Harwich, take the ferry to the Hook of Holland, a train to Cologne, and walk down the Rhine, staying in youth hostels. He would spin out his thirty quid to last a month.

The tale tells us much about the man: the self-sufficiency, the ready acceptance of solitude, the stamina, the undemonstrative eagerness to find and see life, any old life. In the event he found, for the first time in his life, bedbugs in a b-and-b where he shared a bed with a truck-driver. The bed was 'crawling with large black creatures', splashing blobs of his own blood across the dirty sheets when he killed them. When, a couple of years later, Hoggart read the Left Book Club

---

[9] *Sea and Sardinia* came out in 1923, from Martin Secker. The edition used here is from Penguin's *D. H. Lawrence and Italy*, 1985.

edition of Orwell's *Road to Wigan Pier*,[10] he recognized the scenery at once.

> All the windows were kept tight shut, with a red sandbag jammed in the bottom, and in the morning the room stank like a ferret's cage. You did not notice it when you got up, but if you went out of the room and came back, the smell hit you in the face with a smack...
> Partly blocking the door of the larder there was a shapeless sofa upon which Mrs Brooker, our landlady, lay permanently ill, festooned in grimy blankets. She had a big, pale yellow, anxious face. No one knew for certain what was the matter with her; I suspect that her only real trouble was over-eating. In front of the fire there was almost always a line of damp washing, and in the middle of the room was the big kitchen table at which the family and all the lodgers ate. I never saw this table completely uncovered, but I saw its various wrappings at different times. At the bottom there was a layer of old newspaper stained by Worcester Sauce; above that a sheet of sticky white oil-cloth; above that a green serge cloth; above that a coarse linen cloth, never changed and seldom taken off. Generally the crumbs from breakfast were still on the table at supper. I used to get to know individual crumbs by sight and watch their progress up and down the table from day to day.[10]

Hoggart duly reported back to the Director, who didn't forget him. A couple of years later, when he was working for his finals, was expected to get a First and was touched again, although more mildly, by the sort-of-catatonia and depression which struck during his Higher School Certificate, the Director heard from Dobrée of his plight and called him back.

Hoggart emerged with another £30 and permission to spend it going to Venice and back by train in order to see the immortal city and to have a look at Italian Fascism in action. He lived on tinned sardines and figs, and spent the change on the opera. *Il Duce*, with useful timing, exhibited the manners of Italian Fascism by invading the peasants and poverty of Albania while Hoggart was in Venice, and both were rewarded by big headlines.

Politics, in Leeds in the 1930s, was unignorable. It is hard now to recreate the sense of incredulity on the part of the British people who had lived through the frightfulness of the First War as they saw the new menace trundling across the continent towards them, advertised in part by civil war in Russia as well as by Mussolini's and then Hitler's adventures in Abyssinia, Albania, West Africa and, of course,

---

[10] George Orwell, *The Road to Wigan Pier* (1937), here quoted from the Secker and Warburg edn (1959), pp. 8–9.

Spain, all followed by the *Anschluss* and the *Sudetenland* invasions. The yearning for the reassurance of Munich and 'peace in our time' was irrepressible, however much twenty-year-old men like Hoggart, who would have to do the fighting in the end, came home and quarrelled with their Aunt Claras about the disgrace of appeasement and the certainty of war.

Politics wasn't only unignorable on the street, it was everywhere in the then study and the making of English literature. Poetry had always mattered a great deal to Hoggart in his studies both at school and university, and the poetry as well as the novels which were being written in a period of splendid achievement as well as prodigality, during what Eliot later called 'the years of *l'entre deux guerres*', was heavy with politics, a politics of foreboding as well as celebration.

Two poets, ten years apart, dominated poetry, T. S. Eliot and W. H. Auden. Eliot of course, along with his friend and mentor Ezra Pound, had inaugurated modernism in English poetry, given it, as Leavis's famous guide book put it, 'new bearings'.[11] But for all that *Scrutiny* was at such pains to expel from poetry any crude political tub-thumping, no one could doubt the political content of *The Waste Land* or *Hugh Selwyn Mauberley*. When, in 1938, the Professor of Metaphysical Philosophy at Oxford, R. G. Collingwood, wrote as he did of *The Waste Land*, it was plainly a political as much as a moral vision he was endorsing.

> The poem depicts a world where the wholesome flowing water of emotion ... has dried up. Passions that once ran so strongly as to threaten the defeat of prudence, the destruction of human individuality, the wreck of men's little ships, are shrunk to nothing. No one gives; no one will risk himself by sympathizing... We are imprisoned in ourselves, becalmed in a windless selfishness. The only emotion left us is fear: fear of emotion itself, fear of death by drowning in it, fear in a handful of dust.[12]

Wystan Auden was a quite different sort of writer. His poems began to appear in 1928 and his voice – conversational, laconic, resplendent, drily assuming the knowledgeability of his readers as well as the certainty of the readers' ignorance, fluent, startling – spoke piercingly to the many young men and women who shared its inexplicit politics.

> ... The tall unwounded leader
> Of doomed companions, all

[11] F. R. Leavis, *New Bearings in English Poetry*, London: Chatto and Windus, 1932.
[12] R. G. Collingwood, *The Principles of Art*, Oxford: Clarendon Press, 1938, p. 335.

Whose voices in the rock
Are now perpetual,
Fighters for no one's sake,
Who died beyond the border . . .[13]

Auden plays lightly over a featureless landscape spotted with violent
action, perhaps heroic, perhaps obedient, shot with briefly rousing
images ('The tall unwounded leader'), glimpses of movement caught,
as it were, by a sniper:

And the host after waiting
Must quench the lamps and pass
Alike into the house.

Against Eliot's settled pessimism, Auden counterposed the feasibility
of action and his lines, imminent with a bewitching danger, dizzily
non sequitur, etched themselves in one's memory.

Control of the passes was, he saw, the key . . .
It is time for the destruction of error.
The chairs are being brought in from the garden,
The summer talk stopped on that savage coast,
Before the storms, after the guests and birds . . .[14]

Auden shifts so abruptly from an invitation to gaze down on a whole
history to a tiny detail visible from the same vantage point:

Consider this and in our time
As the hawk sees it or the helmeted airman,
The clouds rift suddenly – look there . . .

Then he baffles his readers and enchants them simultaneously with
a villanelle which promises so much before ending on a banal,
unforgettable dictum-pentameter.

Suppose the lions all get up and go,
And all the brooks and soldiers run away;
Will Time say nothing but I told you so?
If I could tell you I would let you know.[15]

Auden in the 1930s, like so many idealistic young men of the day, was
drawn strongly towards Marxism because it had a narrative which
addressed the times, because it forswore Eliot's kind of resigned

---

[13] W. H. Auden, 'Missing' (1929), in *Collected Poems*, E. Mendelson ed., New York:
Vintage, 1976, pp. 30–1.
[14] W. H. Auden, excerpt from E. Mendelson ed., New York: Vintage, 1976.
[15] Auden (1976), p. 314. Poem written in 1940.

pessimism, because it named Fascism for the horrible thing it was, and called its supporters to arms. Auden's armed response to his times was to write his poems. Hoggart at twenty was no Marxist but a straight Labour voter – he knew the life of the proletariat too intimately to suppose that it could provide anything like an adequate dictatorship, and in any case by 1938 quite enough was known about the monstrousness of Stalin's regime for communism to seem irredeemably defiled.

Auden doubtless quickened Hoggart's blood as well as giving him an eye for detail which blended the picturesque and the dangerous, harshness and tenderness, the summons to action and the certainty that action will be ambiguous and may be degrading. So Hoggart could devise an honest Labour socialism in which equality is a prime social value but on a level with the happy fulfilment of whatever individuality you can, more or less peaceably, fashion for yourself. Such a socialism taught him the peculiar rigidity of Britain's class system and quickened in him that lifelong, even-tempered dedication to the enlargement of life-chances – of the chance to live a better life which is not to say merely a better-off life – which is the best aspect of the British Labour Party's long tradition.

In 1938 the political feelings ran high enough to keep such commitments firm, but they coursed through a body politic with a naturally stolid disposition, averse to radicalism of all kinds, gentle enough in those days and maybe these, tranquilly tolerant of the intolerable, and timid towards the worst threats of the time. Such are the intersections of culture and sensibility, those definite but elusive zones of being where a whole social atmosphere, sixteen pounds to the square inch, presses upon a person's carriage, walking through the world, kneads and figures it as that person treads steadily on, gives him or her direction of a kind, mass and energy and character, too. The process is lifelong, yet the result, if one can think of a person's character as a result, is nonetheless something made by that person all by him- or herself. This deepest of all puzzles became the subject and object of Hoggart's lifework. The study of his nation's literary narratives gave him his form, for novels and poems deal intrinsically with the feeling for life even if the stern contemporary proponents of Theory might disavow that way of putting things. Reading the poetry and novels of the 1930s alongside the literary canon prescribed by the syllabus gave the best students of that generation their intellectual lead. Several names to be encountered in a leading part later in these pages and alongside Hoggart – Roy Shaw, Asa Briggs, Andrew Shonfield, Edward Thompson, Raymond Williams, David

Holbrook – made the same sense out of their studies and their lives. For the study of literature, especially as that was given an evangelical light by such as F. R. Leavis and *Scrutiny*, as well as, in his more modest, harlequin way, by Bonamy Dobrée, illuminated plainly how language is the vehicle of civilization, how at that date (and today's date also) civilization was most darkly menaced, and how the giving-and-taking of narratives is the central moral transaction of society, the site on which it uncovers its best and worst values, its form of life.[16]

III

These things being so, the everyday politics of protest in 1938 was coterminous with reading Swift and Blake (Dobrée was an eighteenth-century scholar, though he ranged far beyond this chronological limit). Hoggart read Ignazio Silone's *Fontamara*, the contemporary, vivid tale of desperate poverty and exploitation in southern Italy under Mussolini – it was one of the just-started Penguin publications, sixpence a time – and he read Grassic Gibbon's *Sunset Song*, a cadenced threnody sung over the Scottish peasantry's losing, by 1914, its long-held-onto, poor, beautiful and *local* culture. In both, Hoggart saw Thomas Hardy's thread of life and death continued into the present. In both, he found once more the theme of a life's work, a loving and an acerbic judgement on a whole society as carried and expressed in the details of speech and manners, of domestic rhythms and everyday practices – food, clothing, fidelities, ethics, sex, and imaginative life. He had found in Auden a tone of voice, a *style* (in a very strong sense of the word), rapid, allusive, switching from a view of the political horizon to the immediacy of a choice of action, and adjusted this to his own equable temper and striking powers of detached observation. He found in the novels both of the great tradition (in Leavis's grand phrase) and of the best of contemporary Leftism – Silone, Grassic Gibbon, Orwell, Winifred Holtby, Vera Brittain, Edward Upward – that discovery of value and meaning in the commonplace facts of life which roused D. H. Lawrence to write, in 1925, his essay 'Morality and the Novel', a favourite of Hoggart's.

---

[16] 'Forms of life' is a key phrase of Wittgenstein's in his *Philosophical Investigations*. I add it here partly to counter the canting use of 'values' in political conversation, partly to put values solidly down in a way of life.

Philosophy, religion, science, they are all of them busy nailing things down to get a stable equilibrium . . . they, all of them, all the time, want to nail us on to some tree or other.

But the novel, no. The novel is the highest example of subtle inter-relatedness that man has discovered. Everything is true in its own place, time, circumstance, and untrue outside of its own place, time, circum-stance. If you try to nail anything down, in the novel, either it kills the novel, or the novel gets up and walks away with the nail.[17]

Hoggart's best work, as well as the intellectual discipline he found in the study of literature and transformed into a means – I would say 'method' if that were not a kit for nailing things down – for express-ing and judging the very movement of life, reaffirms Lawrence's anti-precepts.

By definition, however, life was on the move, and full of menace, in 1938. Hoggart went with his friends to lectures and meetings about the gathering storm – with Mary, with Jocelyn Dorian Cooke the vicar's son, and with the beautiful Tom Hodgson, a quiet, courteous poet who died in bomber raids over Germany in 1943 and, older than his fellows, was their unacknowledged legislator.[18] There were Blackshirts on the street in Leeds, and the Communist Party had suf-ficient young members from most social classes to make a show, and while all politics was shot through with a desperate apprehension, it had its own kind of urgency for students in a big industrial city and a university undominated by Oxford or Cambridge.

Auden's way of talking moved well outside the little realm of poetry, was echoed in its way by the work of Mass Observation which was started by Charles Madge and Tom Harrisson in 1937, and dedicated itself to the collection of personal accounts of innumer-able private lives volunteered by hundreds of diary-keepers, letter-writers, unpublished autobiographers, amateur family historians. Still going strong, the organization at its inception was in those two pairs of hands, and the first three volumes, picked up at number three by Allen Lane at Penguin, told an instantaneously large readership an everyday story of the country's folk. When one adds to this the magnificent documentary films made by John Grierson of fishing trawlermen in the North Sea and the romantic journey of the *Night*

---

[17] D. H. Lawrence, 'Morality and the Novel', in his *Selected Literary Criticism*, ed. A. R. Beal, London: Heinemann, 1955, p. 110.

[18] His posthumous collection of poems, *This Life, This Death*, was the first, after Yeats's poem itself, to turn 'An Irish Airman' into a wartime emblem. But see also William Wyler's famous documentary *The Memphis Belle* (1944), and David Puttnam's excellent remake in 1990, for the poem's reappearance.

Mail with Auden's poem written as an accompaniment, then the tradition, form and method of Richard Hoggart's work finds its origins and its cultural context.

He said later of himself that there was 'something fashionable' about many of his interests then, and that they were not 'of the first importance in developing such intellectual grasp as I may have'.[19] It's a tricky thing to dispute a man's formation against his own account of it (though such a trickiness is intrinsic to the art of biography). But surely those novels, that poet, Mass Observation's diaries and letters, Grierson's films, let alone, say, such wideawake movies, also seen in the Paramount, Leeds, as Darryl Zanuck's *The Grapes of Wrath*, just before Hoggart was called up, Renoir's World War One classic of 1937, *La Grande Illusion* at the university's film society, Carol Reed's 1939 *The Stars Look Down*, a great movie of class struggle if ever there was one, *surely* these constitute formative influences on the making of a mind?

'Influence' is much invoked in intellectual history, and impossible to define, or even to be sure of catching in action.[20] Novels and films, nonetheless, pile up in one's recollection, are sorted according to the dominant principles of a life and thicken those up insofar as they are vivid and telling – telling, that is, of ways of life and their keenest moments. Mostly, we reckon up such moments by retelling the story; a novel or a movie has been formative when, reading it or seeing it again, we look out eagerly (may dread it as well) for the moment which tells, and then tell others about it in the hope that they too will come under the influence.

The strongest influence on the life of an impoverished university student in a country still struggling with protracted economic slump was money – hence the power of novels and films to which poverty was centrally painful. The shilling spent at the cinema turnstile didn't come out of the tightly squeezed bursary, it came out of casual earnings in the vacation. Then reading was carried on, as it was for Hoggart, during the long, solitary nights as a warehouse clerk under the railway arches, occasionally clocking in the loads of goods dropped off by long-distance truckers on the 250-mile run from Newcastle to London via Leeds. Twice a night he had to be wide enough awake to ensure that nothing in the load had fallen off the back, check the stuff in and return to his own long-distance reading,

[19] Hoggart (1988), p. 196.
[20] I have in mind Quentin Skinner's essay, 'Meaning and Understanding in the History of Ideas' in his collected essays, vol. 1, *Visions of Politics*, Cambridge: Cambridge University Press, 2002.

71

on that job, *The Iliad*. His only other company was the occasional prostitutes who turned up, not for trade – Hoggart had neither the money nor the inclination – but to warm themselves for a while at the vast, gothic cast-iron stove, when trade was slack.

There had to be many such forays as a casual labourer – helper for lousy pay at a Herne Bay summer camp, free for poor urchins from the East End, helper to the YMCA at the other end of the country at a big TA camp in Ponteland. The hours in Northumberland were interminable, the pay even worse than in Essex; characteristically, Hoggart told them bluntly so, and went home to his Aunt Clara's. His courageous grandmother had died at the end of his first Christmas term in 1936. Aunt Lil had, in her forties and to universal astonishment, married, a little time before, a widower miner, Bill Varley, and become stepmother to his seven children aged between eight and twenty. She made an exemplary wife and parent.

You could say the young student had a full enough life, certainly he made it so. But 'dogged' is a more accurate adjective even though, along with his excellent intelligence and his powers of application, he was blessed with that gift for happiness. Far from everybody is. In his case, along with the high tension which twice tilted him into depression, and along with his sensitiveness to slights, 'sunny Jim's' sunny disposition would always out; it did so all his life.

The three-year round of study, odd jobs, home time, and all he took from Bonamy Dobrée's great generosity of attention brought him up to his final examinations in the summer of 1939. Dobrée knew how good a student Hoggart was, warned him against his working in the library every night until nine when it closed, wangled him the grant for the trip to Venice. When the young man duly got his First Class Honours degree, Dobrée was on hand to find financial help for rapid study towards an MA.

It was summer 1939. Neville Chamberlain made his thin-voiced declaration from 10 Downing Street on 3 September, saying that, since the German government had made no response to his ultimatum that German troops withdraw from Poland, 'consequently this country is at war with Germany'.

Rearming late, hurrying through new measures of military mobilization, the British government had legislated for six months' militia training for all men under thirty. Immediately after the news of Hoggart's First, Dobrée arranged for him to begin the MA. It was to be a study of Swift's satire, for the older man was sure that an academic career of distinction opened the other side of Armageddon, if the lad survived, if the country survived.

Hoggart proved as quick a worker at graduate level as his patron had predicted. By the time Chamberlain made his announcement, the dissertation was well on its way. The army held off until the summer of 1940. Richard, his brother Tom, and Mary went on a happy, laughter-filled, last walking holiday, youth hostelling in the Lake District. They celebrated the award of the MA with a posh hotel three-course lunch at three shillings and sixpence each. The call-up papers arrived in August. They were not for six months by that stage of the war. They were for six years.

— 4 —

A MILITARY EDUCATION IN 'AN INGENIOUS AND CIVILIAN ARMY'

I

The rite of passage from adolescence to manhood for millions of British youths between 1914 and 1960 was conducted in wooden huts and with boot polish and Brasso.

When his call-up papers arrived, Hoggart was sent a railway warrant and orders to present himself at the basic training camp of the Royal Artillery near the town of Oswestry. It was and is a nondescript little place on the borders of Wales and Shropshire, so placed that the gunnery exercises could be carried on athwart the bare and rolling Welsh hills to the west.

Basic training didn't vary much for conscripts in either world war or for the National Servicemen who provided soldiery for the Cold War. Eight weeks of being bawled at and drilled on the parade ground in minor movements of the feet; eight weeks of simple instruction in map-reading, firing portable weapons, setting a map the right way round, daily physical training of a routinized sort – 'touch your toes, and down, down, unroll slowly, head up, relax!' – short movies advising the youngsters on punctual bowel motions, personal cleanliness, the nature of venereal disease; eight weeks, above all, of polishing best boots, or rather caking the toes and heels with a compound of spit and Kiwi boot polish which would then shine like glass and was as brittle, polishing brass buckles, pressing coarse khaki trousers and blouses into razor-sharp creases, scrubbing 'blanco' – a thick greenish paste – into canvas belts and gaiters so that they appeared smooth and unmarked, all this laundering and shining so that on parade every recruit might pass the muster, not be singled out in a shrieking hyperbole as 'filthy, filthy, a disgrace to the regiment' and punished

74

accordingly with 'jankers', a dreadful sequence of compulsory displays of oneself spotlessly turned out any time between reveille and lights out.

For a long time these procedures were part of popular culture, recognizable to every family one of whose members had been in uniform, fondly parodied in innumerable movies for home consumption such as *Private's Progress,* or sternly commended in *Officer and Gentleman* across the Atlantic. What all those noises unmistakably made, was a *culture.* It had its own rich *patois,* its enveloping rituals and customs, a massive continuity affirmed in ensigns, battle honours, folk tales, ceremonies, songs, jokes, gestures, scatology. Most powerful and pervasive of all, it was stratified by class. The strongly marked and bounded differences between ranks – grades of officer, grades of warrant officer, of non-commissioned officers, of other ranks (as the phrase went) – had been in force at least since Wellington's day, and were immediately recognizable to the recruits of 1940 as a hardly exaggerated picture of ordinary society.

All the same, over the next six years these three million or so young men and women changed the Armed Services for the better and for good.

When they arrived at the guard room to check in for the first time, wearing the ordinary civvy clothes of 1940 – lace-up shoes, shapeless and slightly baggy grey trousers, thick shirt and tie, maybe a sleeveless pullover though when Hoggart arrived it was a warm August, tweed jacket or the top half of a suit long separated from its other half – the army had a swift way with them. A punitive haircut on day two, the issue of coarse, hairy battledress, of painfully inflexible boots, the fixity of timetabling, the cheerful egalitarianism of mealtimes, these rough routines rapidly worked upon the young men until, eight weeks later, they were indeed and to all appearances, uniform in their uniform.

But not ultimately. They were conscripts, for sure, but they were also sure that the hideous menace of Fascism must be fought and stopped. They felt themselves, mostly in inarticulate ways, to belong to their country, or those bits they knew by heart and, as they could, loved as their own. They knew its shabby decency and tolerated without much resentment its gross, sometimes cruel injustices. They had come to defend it and to perform, readily enough, those duties which would suffice to do so. The army makes much of the idea of 'duties', but not many of the recruits would have invoked the singular noun to describe the warlike actions they knew as constituting their duty. They also knew perfectly well when duty had been violated, whether by cowardice or crassness or a man's simple failure to come up to scratch. When later a very young officer in Hoggart's battery lost his nerve and ran away under heavy bombardment, no one condemned him. He was slipped quietly into the queue to medical quarters. Everyone knew such conduct must remain an exception and inexcusable; nonetheless they excused it and, in the invaluable, coverall army phrase, carried on.

By 1945 and victory in Europe these five-year irregulars had changed so much in the ways of the Armed Services, had proved themselves so resourceful and creative, transformed time-hallowed ways of doing things, faced and defeated God knows how many pop-eyed and spluttering insistences that things must go on as they always had, that the ingenious civilian army was poised to put its clinching weight behind the British Labour Party's complete and unexpected victory in the general election which followed the end of hostilities.

Just how justified the hopes were for a new Britain in which old social class horribleness would be broken up for ever Hoggart found out when he finally came home after six, not five, years. In wartime, class struggle continued within the rigid rules of military life in wartime, and not infrequently, the right side won, the cast-iron structures were bent apart, ingenuity and insubordination turned into new and improved regulations and ways of doing things.

So he may have consoled himself, not untruthfully, following a wandering path drawn by High Command across Britain between basic training in the autumn of 1940 and sailing for North Africa two years later. Heavy aerial bombing by the German Luftwaffe had begun over London on 8 September 1940, while Hoggart was still square-bashing. Anybody with a degree was immediately marked as OR1 or Potential Officer; somebody as quick and bright as Hoggart was also marked down for the artillery, where a talent for arithmetic and geometry was pertinent, as well as some grasp on tactics, and a readiness to see, by way of the map, where to direct fire and how to con a battlefield.

The same was true of tank troop commanders, and while Hoggart learned gunnery, his later allies and comrades in the intellectual mapping of working-class history and emancipation, Raymond Williams, E. P. Thompson and David Holbrook, were busy learning the same sort of tactical principles for tank movements. This was to be the next, post-14–18 kind of warfare, whereas the poor bloody infantry officers had only to follow the loud gunfire and do as they were told, as they always had.

Tank and gunnery training was much of a muchness (certain makes of tank were designated S-P, or self-propelled, guns). The language of such military training has never been better caught, more drily and affectionately parodied, than by Henry Reed's poems, published soon after the war and cordially welcomed by poetry-reading soldiers. They serve to remind us how much of the patient, tedious waiting, which is so vast a part of wartime life, is filled with laughter at this or that aspect of the military. Hoggart used sometimes to berate himself for lacking the gift of playfulness and no doubt his childhood life had taught him the merit of silent watchfulness. But he had his own characteristic openness to others, his generous warmth, his zestful sense of the ridiculous. So he saw and relished Reed's comedy. It brought keenly back the times when as an Officer Cadet he was learning 'bracketing', directing gunnery fire in response to a forward observation post, bisecting the angles at which his guns pointed, bringing their shells onto target. So it was that he and the other cadets were told

> Not only how far away, but the way you say it
> Is very important. Perhaps you may never get
> The knack of judging a distance, but at least you know
> How to report on a landscape: the central sector,
> The right of arc and that, which we had last Tuesday,
> And at least you know
>
> That maps are of time and place, so far as the Army
> Happens to be concerned, – the reason being
> Is one which need not delay us. Again you know
> There are three kinds of tree, three only, the fir and the poplar,
> And those which have bushy tops to; and lastly
> That things only seem to be things.
>
> A barn is not called a barn, to put it more plainly,
> Or a field in the distance, where sheep may be safely grazing.
> You must never be over-sure. You must say, when reporting:
> At five o'clock in the central sector is a dozen
> Of what appear to be animals; whatever you do,
> Don't call the bleeders *sheep*.[1]

[1] Henry Reed, 'Lessons of the War', in *Collected Poems*, Manchester: Carcanet Press, 2007.

Second Lieutenant Hoggart, 1941.

II

The army fed him, in its coarse, filling way, well. After the privations of university scholarship – scrambled eggs in his room, fish and chips on the way back from the cinema – the energetic busyness, field exercises and long hours of the six-day working military week were replenished by three tasty meals a day. Breakfast: sausages, bacon and eggs, at a time when civilians carried ration books and were allotted three rashers weekly, the army's eggs laid out in vast trays like the massed regiments of yolks; lunch, meaty stew and four kinds of potato – boiled, roast, mashed, chipped, some soldiers took all four – and cabbage and sprouts, apple pie or crumble; high tea, more sausages, vast hoppers full of baked beans, bread and margarine, big eight-pound tins of unrationed jam, limitless strong, sweet tea with condensed milk, poured into the white one-pint mugs which every soldier carried.

The food gave working-class and public-school soldiers alike their sense of home and their stolid morale. Hoggart was grateful for it,

Hoggart (second from left) and comrades, 1942.

as well as liking it anyway. Dispatched, as an officer cadet, to heavy anti-aircraft artillery training some fifty miles due south of Oswestry, to the rather run-down, sometime spa town of Llandrindod Wells, he came home again to the same menu. In more attenuated forms, he was to find it in open warfare in North Africa, and in the occupation of captured enemy territory in Naples. As we saw, one of Hoggart's signal contributions to the theory of culture was the importance he assigned to the class and historical formation of food, and the strong emotional as well as digestive meanings he found in it.

Mary, not yet his wife, was teaching in a boys' school in Ecclesfield near Sheffield, and was long remembered there. Whenever she could, during his two years of waiting and drilling and, occasionally, defending assorted dockyards against the Luftwaffe, she came through the blackout and by interminable train journeys with long detours, unexplained delays, the odd air raid, to find Richard, to stay in a local bed-and-breakfast, and to walk with him into the countryside around whatever town it was.

He was appointed to his commission in late April 1941, and visited his family and Mary's parents in his officer's service dress of quite well-cut and well-figured barathea material and a peaked cap for formal wear. When he saw his sister Molly, now in uniform also, and his brother Tom, he caught up with the news that Tom, long a member of the Peace Pledge Union, was on the long and difficult

79

route to refusing to serve as a combatant. From the start and char-acteristically, Tom had volunteered to serve as a stretcher-bearer, and after appearing before punitive tribunals, carried stretchers as an RAMC sergeant at the D-Day landings in 1944, seeing, as his brother said, 'much more danger than I saw in my longer service'.[2]

Hoggart was dispatched to command a troop of gunners in the 58th heavy anti-aircraft regiment of the Royal Artillery, then at Green Street Green, a couple of miles south of the Thames at Greenhithe in Kent. The German bombers came up the river over Tilbury to attack the docks at Rotherhithe. But the first devastation of London during the *Blitzkrieg* was over, and the regiment was assigned to 'rapid mobility' duties.

These entailed frequent and exhausting exercises in exactly that mobility, whereby the massive guns were rendered mobile by folding back the four three-foot diameter pads which took the heavy recoil of firing the thing and thereby permitted its great wheels to meet the ground. Once the gun was hitched to its huge conveyor truck, the vehicle could move ponderously away, its great bulk loaded with shining 3.7 shells, behind it the gun itself, its four pads pointing upwards on their thick prongs, the long barrel pointing backwards, shining a little in the evening light.

The truck drivers were largely taken from the same civilian profession and had the qualities one might expect from such soli-tary, responsible work. They possessed a solid dependability, made manifest in their settled, heavy posture and physical bulk; they were quiet, resourceful, trustworthy, self-confident. As a young officer of twenty-three, you couldn't want for better men. A gun troop is not like a platoon of infantrymen; the lines of command are thicker and more reciprocal, the duties more technical as well as physically more demanding, the distinctions of rank less simply allocated. By the time you've been in a troop for a few weeks, the army has transformed the troop into a unit, not friends for life, though that happened, but bound together, interdependent, comrades.

For twenty-four months, like hundreds of thousands of civilian soldiers at the time, the 58th heavy ack-ack regiment suffered the usual arbitrary-seeming moves from Kent to Newport in Wales (guarding the docks during air raids), to Barnsley in Yorkshire, to Bovington in Dorset during the bitterest winter for a generation, to Gloucester and Glasgow, and to St Andrews, training on the sacred

---

[2] Richard Hoggart, *A Sort of Clowning: Life and Times 1940–1959*, Oxford: Oxford University Press, 1991, p. 16.

golf links. Meanwhile the battle for the Atlantic was being fought and halfway won, and in December 1941, as the ice thickened in Dorset, Pearl Harbour was attacked, the Americans were in, and the terrible history of the moment brightened a little.

Hoggart's happy disposition and sardonic eye for class absurdity kept him, as one would expect, equable, competent, a bit detached, always friendly. He did a cookery course, then passed out top as a mere lieutenant on a staff college planning course, bought and read Eliot's *Burnt Norton* and *Dry Salvages* when they came out, until in July 1942 he and Mary were married in her home town of Stalybridge as the certainty of moving to a theatre of war loomed very near.

One silent Sunday in late September 1942, as General Montgomery's Eighth Army began its huge build-up at El Alamein and the first serious reversal of the war for the Axis forces impended, Hoggart's regiment, its guns in tow, ground in low gear towards the docks on the Clyde at the edge of Glasgow, ready for embarkation to North Africa.

In a characteristic flash of recollection, Hoggart half a century later recalled passing, in a deserted street, a pair of coarse and cheerful Glasgow girls who hospitably lifted their skirts and flashed their knickerless loins at the startled soldiers who went, laughing helplessly and gratefully, on their way, Hoggart with the recollection of Mary's excellent legs keenly present in his mind.

At the docks they boarded a big old cruising liner, the *Otranto*, its dingy vacationing comforts from the 1930s barely visible in the tangle of hammocks strung in every corner below deck, the piles of kitbags dumped anywhere, the great guns being lowered by crane into the hold. When the liner sailed, the natural excitement of the departing troops, without any handkerchiefs fluttering below on the quay, quickly reverted to the usual tedium of warfare. The *Otranto* was due to hide herself away in some deserted loch while a huge convoy assembled until all was ready for the five-week voyage to Algeria.

They were seen off by Admiral, not yet Earl Mountbatten, and Hoggart snarled a little to himself at 'the divisive peacockery of monarchy', while the convoy turned sluggishly west and then south in a wide sweep, losing one troopship to an Italian submarine, disembarking by boat a little way out of Algiers before going by jeep, one ton truck and, for Hoggart and the junior officers, motorbike, into the city and down to the docks for their guns, there to be greeted by the news that the French army in Algiers, then commanded from Vichy, had surrendered. The 58th Regiment set up its 3.7s in the grounds of

81

a grandish hotel outside the city, fired off at the occasional air raid, and waited for the Germans.

They turned up all right, and destroyed a large 25-pounder field gun emplacement near Souk Ahras, three days' drive over cratered roads towards Tunis. Hoggart was assigned to take fresh guns and their vehicles with which to restock the ruined battery. There was no protection available either from infantry or the air. The roads were covered thickly with mud, steering the big trucks with the guns on trailers on greasy, broken surfaces damnably difficult, the occasional random attack from a single Stuka, the ripped air screaming through the louvres in its tail causing the men, at the officer's order, to dive into the ditch, made for an intent journey, the hours fleeting by, the beautiful desert nights a pleasurable interval, your friends sleeping lightly around you.

It sounds a bit rum perhaps, but usual for men of his lucky temper, to be able to find and be warmed by a little glow of happiness in a bracket left by times of routine watchfulness, even of mortal danger. The glow shone on these miniature camp sites, given off by tiny meals of canned meat-and-vedge warmed in messtins over a cube of methylated wax, followed by sweet tea. Around them, at dawn and dusk, the sands shone pinkly, a quiet, friendly routine framed the day, until Hoggart gave the word to start up the big Bedford trucks, each vehicle with its 25-pounder guns in tow lurched heavily onto the battered road and they were on their way, the driver leaning forward, peering at the broken, greasy surface under his wheels, his companion scanning the sky for the distant specks which would rush up from space and become in a trice enemy aircraft strafing their arbitrary targets at three hundred miles per hour.

Each time the troop piled into the ditch, and piled out again unhurt. Once, a coarse, gobbling sort of REME captain tried, in an angry panic, to stop Hoggart and his men sheltering in the ruined farmhouse he had appropriated for his own unit. He didn't have the authority to refuse cover, the young lieutenant knew it, and faced him down.

So Hoggart handed over his guns and vehicle to the hard-hit Field Regiment, whose CO he found making steady provision to write at once to the families of the dead. His adjutant commandeered all Hoggart's drivers to replace his lost men and sent Hoggart back to Algiers – no time to train him in 25-pounder drill – with one truck, one driver, and a recommendation that he be 'mentioned in dispatches', a minor military recognition of doing a job well and bravely. As you'd expect, there were other such relief exercises, on one of

82

which the truck skidded and crashed off the oily road, and Hoggart and his driver got back to base covered with blood.

The vast and living body of the army was gathering itself together for the mammoth engagement which would turn into the defeat of the Germans in North Africa, not exactly the turning point of the war – the struggle for Italy would be too terrible for that early victory to count for so much – but momentous nonetheless. Hoggart kept always by him, to reach for and use as reassurance and as a magic summons of Mary's voice, an anthology of poems which she had compiled and written out by hand.[3]

It was pocketbook-sized, nearly all of the entries poems shared during their studies of English literature at Leeds, some of them poignant and immediate as a touch: Rilke, '. . . again and again, we go out, two together / Under the old trees make our touch once more.' 'Since there's no help, come, let us kiss and part'; Auden's 'Look, stranger, on this island now'; Owen's *Futility*, 'Move him into the sun . . . / If anything might rouse him now / The kind old sun will know . . .' – lines made the keener by a tank battle one night next to Hoggart's position. At first light, the battle over, he went cautiously across to find burned-out tanks, the local Arab stripping the corpses, the young faces unmarked, beautiful, the flies loathsome, worst of all the smell of human decomposition, sharp, sweetish, chemical.

At almost that very moment, at Homs near Tripoli, a young poet in a tank was describing a German corpse, and was 'filled', as he wrote, 'with useless pity'. Keith Douglas notices a keepsake photo of the German's girlfriend, 'Steffi, Vergissmeinnicht':

> But she would weep to see today
> how on his skin the swart flies move,
> the dust upon the paper eye,
> and the burst stomach like a cave.

Hoggart memorized these lines long after Douglas's own death outside Zem Zem in 1943.

His solace had to be one of Mary's own poems, included in the anthology: 'Beloved – streets I discovered – / You had just walked down them . . .' as well as Eliot's greatest poem, *Little Gidding*, a copy of which was posted to him in Algiers as soon as it was published in 1942, and which gave its grand historical understanding to the atrocities, the waste, the awful boredom. Eliot's lovely pastoral, its timelessness notwithstanding, was addressed directly and with heroic

---

[3] Hoggart papers, 2/3/27.

radiance to the terrible crisis which the poet's chosen country faced. It could say, with no patriotic afflatus, 'History is now and England', and teach its eager, puzzled readers how to look for a political as well as a religious direction as the artillery thundered and shook, and the gunners, stripped to their shorts and shining with sweat, slid the shells into the breech with blistered hands.

III

The final, terrific barrage in Africa led to a slow victory. The air raids recurred and ack-ack regiments were kept in practice, but the dangers eased. The rhythms of modern warfare had however taught the gunners that, if for now they could drive easily into Tunis city and go bathing on the beach at Sousse, then something big and unignorable was waiting.

It is a fine and touching discovery that in among the frightfulness of that campaign there were men still making poetry out of its hideous strength. On the same beach at Sousse where Hoggart went paddling with thoughts of Bridlington in his mind, another young officer saw the likeness of his soldiers to those in a Michelangelo cartoon, a Pollaiulo painting.

> The sea at evening moves across the sand.
> Under a reddening sky I watch the freedom of a band
> Of soldiers who belong to me. Stripped bare
> For bathing in the sea, they shout and run in the warm air;
> Their flesh worn by the trade of war, revives
> And my mind towards the meaning of it strives. . . .[4]

Hoggart had, however, a prior appointment to keep during the Italian campaign, before returning to poetry. The Germans withdrew from Africa, the Italians surrendered in tens of thousands, and the invasion of Sicily began. The 58th was ordered to join an expedition to capture a tiny volcanic island halfway between Tunisia and Sicily with an inconvenient airstrip, called Pantelleria.

It possessed, like everywhere in the ancient sea, a bit of history: the Neolithic settlement of Mursia; it circumscribed a bottomless volcanic sea-lake like Santorini's; it was more recently, as his friend and fellow-soldier Alan Beatty told him, an anti-Mafia headquarters. As a military destination, it was grimly inhospitable and such moorings as there were damned hard to find and tie up to.

[4] F. T. Prince, 'Soldiers Bathing', *The Doors of Stone*, London: Hart-Davis, 1963, p. 57.

The small force set off from the docks at Bizerta, bucketing across the Mediterranean in ten flat-bottomed tank landing craft. The Stukas came screaming down, and one of their bombs so narrowly missed Hoggart's tinpot boat, swamping it in a huge wave, that his colonel, following a little way behind, said to his adjutant, with the flat meiosis the British army taught its men so thoroughly, 'Well, there goes Hoggart's lot.'

But they hadn't. They came ashore to find a blasted island, corpses everywhere, and a few huddled and dazed peasants, ignorant of the war, still clinging to existence in their prehistoric and window-less *trulli*, the peasants' beehive hovels. One of these nearly killed Hoggart.

The troops, divebombed punctually by Stukas every day, did what little they could in the intervals to clear rubble and bury bodies in the stony earth. Hoggart learned that one of the hovels contained the corpse of an old man dead on his high crude bed beneath which his goats slept. The beehive was roaring with thick torrents of swart flies, the body crawling with maggots. Hoggart and his sergeant took with them a five-gallon jerrycan of petrol, put on gasmasks to hold off the stench, then Hoggart soused the body in gasoline, led a trail of juice a few yards from the door intending to skip out the way after ignition. It was June 1943 and the Mediterranean sun ablaze. The gasoline in the oven which was the *trullo* vaporized instantly. Flames flashed and roared through the door, Hoggart was set on fire from head to foot.

His sergeant beat the flames out, God knows what with. They called up the doctor on the 88 set and carried Hoggart back to the camp on an old door found among the rubbish which lay everywhere. It was a mile over broken ground. The wounded man was in agony and desperately ill. The medical men had to perform the gingerly task of detaching the gasmask, the frame and rubber of which was melted onto his head.

The mask had, however, saved his sight, his very life. His hands and knees were badly burned but the flames had been put out before they could burn his body. Heaven knows – Hoggart didn't – how the (American) doctors prised away the melted mask without recourse to plastic surgery; it must have been an operation of exceptional artistry.

But slow; so was recovery. He lay in a hospital tent in the fearful heat, unventilated and immobile, with a drip up one nostril and the dreadful flies busy up the other and on his bandaged face. He had the misfortune to be tended from time to time by a weirdly Anglophobe and sadistic Italian-American doctor who took pleasure in ripping off the bandages as painfully as he could, snarling the while, 'stop whining, Limey'. Alan Beatty visited often, and so did his CO and the adjutant, and his troop sergeant, for the young officer was well liked and respected, easy to like come to that, open and cordial, but with a kind of authoritative reserve as well.

He also had stout physical reserves to call on. By October he had rejoined his regiment, Allied forces had landed at Salerno and then Anzio, cutting off the gigantic harbour at Naples. The seething capital of southern Italy was taken, and ack-ack regiments were duly installed along the seafront where so many wealthy English moved in 1770 or so, and around the bay as far as Posillipo, looking across from the bluff towards Vesuvius.

Writing, two years later, a valedictory article for the Forces' *Journal* Hoggart edited, he referred to the 'rubbish-tip desolation'[5] of Italy, and it was, it still is, so. All the same, he loved Naples – 'Leeds with knobs on'[6] – its colour, noise, crudeness, tumult, splendour, murder, crime (Hoggart saw a man stabbed to death in a knife fight on the Via Roma, bang in the middle of the morning crowd). The regiment was billeted underneath the football stadium; it turned out for the air-raids, nightly to begin with but thinning out as the Eighth and Fifth Armies made their grim and slow advance north.

The regiment and its parent army began, as armies do, to settle in for the duration. It learned the street ways of Naples; American Italians taught the British the nature and customs of local, necessary corruption; they also taught the magnificent hospitality of the Italians, the horror and the glory of Italian culture. The glory Hoggart found in the black stone palaces, the Capodimonte museum, some of its treasures looted by Göring, many of them – Titian, a Botticelli, Peruginos – remaining tranquilly on show behind sand-bagged windows and the barbed-wired entrance.

The horror, too much perhaps. One horrifying anecdote will do. Also in Naples at the same time was a conscientious but far too open-minded and cosmopolitan officer in the Intelligence Corps called Norman Lewis. His duties took him deep into the dangers of the underground, into the Camorra, into the lives of starving aristocrats and well-fed black marketeers. He noted nonetheless in his diary, 'A year among the Italians has converted me to such an admiration for their humanity and culture that were I to be given the chance

---

[5] Hoggart papers, 'Good-bye to England', 2/3/5.
[6] Hoggart (1991), p. 48.

to be born again, Italy would be the country of my choice.'[7] Lewis, like Hoggart, was an involuntary tourist, learning the ways of local life randomly. He too saw the horror of what his fellow transients do to the people who live in the foreign land becoming to him a home which time will force him to leave. He is helpless to help, like all tourists. In one horrifying epiphany, dining in a grubby restaurant off sticky, undressed pasta, he and a Neapolitan friend are interrupted by the arrival of 'five or six little girls between the ages of nine and twelve'.

> They wore hideous straight black uniforms buttoned under their chins, and black boots and stockings, and their hair had been shorn short, prison-style. They were all weeping, and as they clung to each other and groped their way towards us, bumping into chairs and tables, I realized they were all blind. Tragedy and despair had been thrust upon us, and would not be shut out. I expected the indifferent diners to push back their plates, to get up and hold out their arms, but nobody moved. Forkfuls of food were thrust into open mouths, the rattle of conversation continued, nobody saw the tears . . .
>
> The experience changed my outlook. Until now I had clung to the comforting belief that human beings eventually come to terms with pain and sorrow. Now I understood I was wrong, and like Paul I suffered a conversion – but to pessimism. These little girls, any one of whom could be my daughter, came into the restaurant weeping, and they were weeping when they were led away. I knew that, condemned to everlasting darkness, hunger and loss, they would weep on incessantly. They would never recover from their pain, and I would never recover from the memory of it.[8]

The Armies – American and British – turned into a mass of long-staying tourists, not Neapolitans but knowledgeable about the city, indifferent to its horrors, casually appreciative of its amazing spectacles – the glorious ruins at Paestum, the blue grotto at Capri once the island was accessible and the U-boats gone, and the amazing display put on by Vesuvius when she erupted in grand pyrotechnics on 19 March 1944, illuminating the whole bay, lending the regular little outings to Pompeii a more than archaeological keenness.

Hoggart was reading his way through Shakespeare. It's a funny but familiar thing even with the greatest writers and even for their most likely admirers that for some time, maybe for ever, one is immune to

---

[7] Norman Lewis, *Naples '44: An Intelligence Officer in the Italian Labyrinth*, London: Eland Books, 1983, p. 203.

[8] Lewis (1983), p. 53.

their power. The unlikeliest people cannot hear the enchantment of Mozart or see the grandeur of Cézanne. Then one day and for no discernible reason, the real thing happens. The original force makes itself felt, just as it is supposed to, the words (in the case of Shakespeare) become alive in one's being, not just heard, heard even admiringly, but present to one's body and mind, as if the words and sounds and rhythms have for those moments become oneself. It is a fulfilment and a discovery. Shakespeare or Mozart or Cézanne summon a person, and that person discovers his or her own self exactly as they give themselves to this great epiphany, allow themselves to be carried outward far beyond the control of the will, subject to an action rather than a passion, an energy compounded of mind and flesh.

It is love, of course. Hoggart had loved the poetry he had read at Leeds, loved the poems in Mary's handwritten anthology. But one day somewhere in North Africa after he found a tattered copy of *Macbeth*, Shakespeare spoke and it happened. As he said ruefully himself when he told friends of his revelation, 'they must at least have wondered why it had taken until then and that unlikely place for me to discover the power of a work by one of the few great literary names they knew'.[9]

A couple of years later, in Naples, he had swallowed the complete works whole. He had also made close, immediate friends with the son of Jewish émigrés to London on whom his wealthy parents had bestowed an English ruling class education at Westminster and Balliol, an education which had given their son the best of itself – a love of learning, a keen taste for politics, high spirits, boisterous zest for argument, a love of literature – and none of its awful side, its class arrogance, its narrow bigotry and coarseness.

This was Andrew Shonfield, gifted on his own account with irresistible charms as well as with the qualities and talents of the European intellectual who never overawed Hoggart but the cast of mind of whom was so unlike his own. Shonfield was reckless and playful in ways which were not Hoggart's but which he relished, and in any case laughter and happiness came easily to 'Sunny Jim'. So he and Shonfield fell into burlesque Shakespearean parodies, gritty arguments about the future of socialism (Shonfield's classic *Modern Capitalism* two decades away), mimicry of idiotic fellow officers, and they went together to the opera company's performances gamely surviving in Naples, to hear chamber concerts in the gaunt, half-abandoned palaces, to the Forces' own movie house to see *Gone with*

[9] Hoggart (1988), p. 196.

the Wind and, released in 1944 in anticipation of victory, Olivier's *Henry V*.

For those tens of thousands of soldiers stranded in Naples as the terrible siege of Cassino played itself out, life was a long, often boring preparation for the peace. Hoggart, naturally recoiling from NAAFI culture and the Neapolitan way of things embodied in the blind little girls, was determined to do his bit for the brighter side of Army culture, given its untapped vitality by its 'ingenious civilians' still reading and writing prose and poetry, still painting, still playing as best they could untuned pianos in always musical Naples. So Hoggart became the moving spirit behind the Three Arts Club, discovered a quiet and generous Education Corps major who provided premises, and a similar US Education Officer who provided rather good quality paper for the Club's poetry anthologies, run off on a Gestetner copying machine.

They opened in June 1944 at 68 Via Santa Brigida, just off the Via Roma and close to Naples' huge Victorian shopping arcade, presager of so many malls a century or more later. Once through the door, there were no differences of rank, there was only a common longing to regain touch with the three arts: literature, painting, music. Neapolitans were welcome, they brought their chamber quartet. The now-much-admired painter, Peter Lanyon, then in the RAF's Air-Sea Rescue unit and already seized with the passion for gliding which was to kill him in civilian life, painted a huge mural of landscape-seen-from-a-swooping-and-curving glider across the large rear wall. There were exhibitions of paintings, some by Italians; there were poetry readings and drama productions, of Shakespeare naturally, of Shaw, and one of Pirandello's *Six Characters in Search of an Author*, which went down well among civilian soldiers playing parts they hadn't written for themselves.

There was a four-hour lecture-and-performance from an American pianist accomplished at playing swing, taking place during a heavy air raid. One French infantryman came to listen to Beethoven the day before departing as a member of a desperate action. A Neapolitan lectured on D'Annunzio; *Desert Highway*, an anthology of poems and essays, was published on the expensive American paper; there were six hundred submissions. *Verses from Italy* came out in September, and in January 1945 *Comment from Italy*, much longer and with a commemorative introduction written by the ancient grandee and anti-Fascist philosopher, Benedetto Croce, just released from house arrest by the Americans (although the house in question was a splendid villa on the cliff above Sorrento). Croce's idealist aesthetics had been kept alive in Britain by the work of the metaphysician R. G. Collingwood, but in Italy his was an august name, honoured for his oeuvre, his saintly life, his principled refusals to countenance Fascism or to give Mussolini audience.

The Three Arts Club, thanks to Hoggart's good offices,[10] managed to get a bit of money from the *New Statesman*, from the Women's Voluntary Service, and from Penguin, where he first made acquaintance with Penguin's visionary founder, Allen Lane, then in uniform, a contact which was to count for a great deal later in his career.

There were several more collections published – *The Four in Hand*, *Voices from Italy* (with a contribution from Shonfield) – but as the year turned Hoggart, by now a captain, was offered promotion and special training in Intelligence work in the Middle East. It would have meant, at least for a while, becoming not a conscript but a regular soldier. There could be no question of it, even though it was a good job, and the prospects for sympathetic work at home, where Mary had been waiting for fifty-four months, entirely uncertain.

It was early 1945. The military campaigns in France and Germany, and in Northern Italy, were still fiercely fought. But away from the fighting, the hundreds of thousands of men and women in uniform were looking forward to going home, to the joyfully anticipated, painfully to be lived reunions, to the safe, reassuring, humdrum routines of home and work.

IV

A great many of those same men and women were also determined that the routines would be changed, that although they might go back to the same clothes they had put off when changing into khaki or blue, they would not return to the same orders, the same squalor, to paying threepence a week to the Prudential and whatever-you-can-afford to the doctor's 'panel'. Much has been written of the British armed forces and their joint resolution to change when they returned to the unequal, unjust, snobbish and incompetent old country they left in 1940. It had proved surprisingly durable and intransigent during the war – after all, it could count on its Empire for markets as well as men – but now! Well, now, things would be different.

Remembering that moment in 1945, shortly after he was a tank commander of twenty-one leading his squadron on the edge of

---

[10] Hoggart papers, 2/2/00 and 2/2/7.

Perugia, the great historian E. P. Thompson (later a friend and ally of Hoggart's) wrote:

> I recall a resolute and ingenious civilian army, increasingly hostile to the conventional military virtues, which became – far more than any of my younger friends will begin to credit – an anti-fascist and consciously anti-imperialist army. Its members voted Labour in 1945: knowing why, as did the civilian workers at home. Many were infused with socialist ideas and expectations wildly in advance of the tepid rhetoric of today's Labour leaders.[11]

There is some dispute these days as to the degree of egalitarianism abroad in the air of 1945, and even the excellent Peter Hennessy, stout defender of Hoggart's and Thompson's kind of herbivorous socialism, has his doubts about 1945 as being much of a new world.[12]

All such historical conclusions come out as saying 'It was, and it wasn't.' What was certainly the case is that many of those in uniform or in overalls thought, like Hoggart, that the grimness of 1930s Hunslet from which he had (so far) made an escape, must be tidied instantly away along with the bombed-out houses and smashed-up factories. He imagined, in one article written in August 1945, 'Goodbye to England', making a loudspeaker address to his people, after the manner of a candidate in the just-completed election which swept the Labour Party to power with an unprecedented Parliamentary majority of 145.

> We have just finished six years of killing, six years of such strain for us all that the number of neurotics alone is now an awesome thing – holocaust, atom bomb, on Europe's mainland murder, rape and pillage are common, mass prostitution, incidental violence are everyday affairs.

It was Wellington who, perhaps apocryphally, said at Waterloo, 'After a defeat, the saddest thing in war is victory.' The history of the aftermath of 1945 is largely a matter of either first-hand reminiscence or of the reordering of nations according to new alignments and constitution, in Europe, the history of the declaration of Cold War. But they weren't ordinary neurotics coming back to Britain; they were, in large numbers, mad as hatters, and they returned especially in London and the south-east to a society in which normal rhythms and customary sanctions were suspended, replaced by a crazy market of

---

[11] E. P. Thompson, *Writing by Candlelight*, London: Merlin, 1980, p. 131.
[12] See Peter Hennessy's *Having it so Good: Britain in the Fifties*, London: Allen Lane, 2006, especially the chapter 'The British New Deal and the Essentials of Life'.

bartering and piracy, of hectic drinking and desperate sex, of a gleeful anomie and a blasted economy.

One can contrast Hoggart's quiet and unfailing reasonableness with the account of the first postwar year given by René Cutforth, later a BBC reporter of foreign news, mostly wars, whom Hoggart met and liked while working with the Pilkington Committee in the early 1960s. Cutforth had been a prisoner of the Germans for three years. By the time he made it home, after underfed peregrinations around occupied Germany, he was quite barmy, pleasant and courteous in manner, invaded by black and appalling rages on the inside which leaped unpredictably out of him such that, when casually barged into by an unlikable young man in a bus queue, he smashed the offender in the face and laid him out on his back. The psychiatrist who had allowed Cutforth, with some misgivings ('very depressive type, educated, high IQ, possibly disturbed. Marked aggression' said the interview notes)[13] to go home to his wife, was very put out.

One quite general version of England at that date was being lived in London SE20. It was set in the crumbling wastes of Forest Hill in a jungle of unkempt rhododendrons and towering gloomy yews all sprinkled with bombed-out suburban mansions. In this dark chaos there thrived a culture, as people now say: a culture of boisterous drunkenness, habitual black marketeering, extraordinary gaiety and generosity, hand-to-mouth living and sudden ecstasies of plenty. The class system hadn't collapsed, but its sometime system of forbidding signs – No Entry, Trespassers Will Be Prosecuted, Keep Out – was simply ignored. Cutforth and his chum, an even madder squadron-leader of proven heroism and many medals, went round to the house of the Fiddler, who could fiddle any amount of illicit drink. The garden of the house can stand as a metaphor for some large part of British culture at the date. Hoggart found its other half in a small seaside town on the Yorkshire coast called Marske.

> ... the wrecks of various cars lay about on what had been the front lawn of a large Victorian house called 'The Hawthorns'. From the window of the basement where he led us we could see a vast expanse of dripping lawn, bald nearly all over and patterned with double V's from the feet of ducks, geese and chickens which were pottering about in wire-netting enclosures. Two goats were tethered to posts. A couple of turkeys strutted under the long wispy trees. And the basement itself had cages full of rabbits in one half and all the mess of a motor mechanic's workshop in the other. There was also a churn, a cheese-press, a box

---

[13] René Cutforth, *Order to View*, London: Faber and Faber, 1969, p. 119.

containing about a thousand packets of American cigarettes, some very fine pieces of antique furniture and rows and rows of good motor tyres. The Fiddler sat us down on one of these, a huge specimen which must have belonged at one time to an American army ten-tonner.[14]

Cutforth's truthful account of a mad, high-spirited communality holds its own against the sober practicalities of Captain Hoggart turning all his energy to the education of a new model army determined to make of bartering Britain a society in which work was steady, pay was fair, and doctors were required to tend the sick whether or not they had any money. In one of the most uplifting moments of national history, the wartime government had set the Liberal peer, Lord Beveridge, to draw up a programme for what was to be called the Welfare State. It was 1942, it was far from certain that there would still be a British state left to provide any welfare when the fighting was done. But the report was firmly written, national insurance payments from all citizens would be so organized that the unemployed would have rights to benefits, the elderly would retire on a pension, all children would be schooled until fifteen and the brightest 20 per cent or so (the proportions, as we heard, varied by region) would be sent to Grammar Schools,[15] and all medical treatment would be free.

It was a magnificent declaration of faith: of faith in freedom and equality, as well as faith that right would triumph. Of course, this being Britain, there were opponents of such handsome generosity who struck a mindless attitude of resistance to all such overdue emancipation, for all that it was ratified by Left and Right in Parliament. Richard Hoggart's later comrade in what was known as adult education, E. P. Thompson, then a tank commander, recalled with a kind of bitter amusement being asked by a senior officer to 'discuss the Beveridge report with the chaps'; he couldn't do it himself because 'it would be so difficult to speak against something when you know nothing about it'.[16]

Hoggart noted in his little article of 1945 that 'now a surprisingly high proportion of the troops do feel themselves involved in mankind'. The old social class rigidities of the army had necessarily been shifted by the huge invasion of civilians come to the necessary task of defeating the enemy, and then, the job done, to count the days to their demobilization. Within the military at least, there was also a discernible shift in common sentiment. Indeed, one might guess that it was then, in 1945, as world war ended but with an unforeseeable

14 Cutforth (1969), p. 123.
15 This decision not confirmed until the Education Act of 1944.
16 Thompson (1980), p. 132.

time remaining in uniform and away from home, that Hoggart found himself seized by the theme of his intellectual life's work. That infinitely difficult subject, solid, heavy and invisible as the atmosphere, was to be the task of taking the weight of culture, and judging the quality of the emotions it shaped into a civilization.

There was in this discovery, as for such a man there had to be, a moral imperative to teach. The political moment confirmed this order. Hoggart's strong feeling that there were many men around him convinced that the dangers they had passed warranted as recognition and as achievement a new version of old Britain received unexpected institutional embodiment.

There truly was a new current of social feeling-and-thinking flowing past the old, blind fixities. During hostilities, there had been set up, in the same spasm of enlightenment which had commissioned Beveridge, the ABCA – the Army Bureau of Current Affairs. A strikingly intelligent and capacious civil servant called Philip Morris had been tucked into a grand uniform with red tabs as Director-General of Army Education. His deputy, a skinny little radical from the Welsh valleys called William Emrys Williams, later a great force as Allen Lane's lieutenant at Penguin commissioning (and writing) in the Pelican series, had been directing the production of a series of pamphlets describing how the postwar world would be, and how it ought to be as well.

The pamphlets, with worthy titles such as *Education and the Citizen*, and *The Responsible Citizen*, were taken for discussion by the soldiers with an officer in the Chair and to hand a guide to such sessions written by A. D. Lindsay, lifelong Labour member, Master of Balliol, and Quintin Hogg's defeated opponent in the famous 'appeasement bye-election' in Oxford in 1938. Lindsay wrote, 'ABCA is laying the foundations of an enlightened society which will one day enjoy the peace.'[17] Lurking in Lindsay's text is a conscious view of education as class struggle, of the best of Balliol informing the resurrected spirit of the Putney Debates conducted during the English Civil War in the 1640s. The pamphlets taught their readers straight; they were not socialist propaganda (for all Bill Williams's vehement Welsh socialism), still less the view from the ruling class. They taught straightly about trade unions, economic planning, social welfare policy, the 1944 Education Act and the new experiment in London's LCC with so-called comprehensive schools.

---

[17] See Martin Lawn's excellent article, 'The British Way and Purpose: the spirit of the age in Curriculum history', *Journal of Curriculum Studies*, 1989, 21, 2, pp. 113–28.

Hoggart came to know them well as he assumed without presumption – the man was a born teacher, after all – the role of regimental education officer. This was very much a matter of advising the dozens of men on their way back to civilian life after five years away on what to do about applying for jobs, how to be parents to little children they had scarcely seen, whether they should seek special training or qualifications, how to reclaim wives who might have found their wartime independence a liberation and had quite new domestic terms to offer a husband, not at all like the settlement of the 1930s.

He had been sent home from Italy to attend a 'resettlement' course by way of preparation for all this, only a week or two after the war ended in Europe. Nobody could then know when they would be released from military service, but it was only natural to feel at once wound up tightly with anticipation, to look out all the time for the papers announcing release, to know that the dangers of sudden death or mortal wounding had abruptly dissolved and that the promise of going home – that piercing phrase – would finally be kept.

In the event, it was another ten months before Hoggart went to claim his demobilization suit from a drill hall in Ashton-under-Lyne. When he flew back in a battered old Lancaster in the summer of 1945 it was only to learn the sufficiently decent provisions of 'resettlement' and to take them back for the long preparations of his regiment towards disbanding.

He had a week in London. Mary was waiting for him, had been waiting for four days with no certainty he would make it. After the course finished, Hoggart had a week's leave which the couple spent first with Mary's parents, hospitable as always, and then alone in Cornwall, inured as they were to long train journeys. They were, according to their then expectations, well off; Mary's schoolteaching salary and a captain's pay left them with ready cash.

Hoggart thought back to T. S. Eliot's lovely poem, *Marina*, which he had first read at university.

> This form, this face, this life
> Living to live in a world of time beyond me, let me
> Resign my life for this life, my speech for that unspoken,
> The awakened, lips parted, the hope, the new ships.

He had hopes for the new Labour government. He looked out for people to recognize the horror of all that had happened, the holocaust of six million charred Jewish, communist and gypsy bodies, the dust-heap of Hiroshima; all he heard was people grumbling about rationing and the petrol shortage. Nonetheless, 'the hope, the new ships' were sailing landwards. By the time he flew back to the army, Mary was pregnant.

Simon was born on 26 May 1946 and his father learned the news by telegram in Italy. Hoggart had filled in the unconscionable wait with the heavy duties of resettlement and education officer for his regiment and then the brigade. He had also, and typically, been writing academic essays, one on Sydney Keyes, one on W. H. Auden, the latter later to turn into his first book and acquaintance with Auden himself. He was as generous then as always subsequently with his own time, lecturing to his former enemies about Shakespeare at the *Istituto Orientale* in Naples.

At last his papers arrived, at the very end of his service speeded up a little by his being called to an interview for a job as an extramural teacher at the University of Hull. The journey home took another lifetime: by train from Naples to Milan via Rome, Milan to Genoa and trickling along the French coast to Marseilles, then north to Lyon, to Clermont-Ferrand in the heart of Vichy country, bypassing Paris and trundling laboriously through Picardy to Amiens and, at last, Calais, the final couple of hundred miles – Bethune, Arras – redolent of troop trains and warfare to two generations of British conscripts.

The rails were in bad condition. The journey took several days, broken by solid army fare in temporary cookhouses alongside the railway, and nights spent in hurriedly assembled dormitories in warehouses. The army was good at all that, the men, as ever, dogged and cheerful and on their way home. Hoggart made instant friends on the way with Bill Connor, a memorable war correspondent, later the immortal columnist 'Cassandra' of the left-wing *Daily Mirror*, caustic and affectionate voice of the industrial working class. Connor's noble little book, *The English at War*, written when things were worst in 1941, ends:

> Fighting for democracy loses some of its point if it is going to lead us back to where we were on September 3, 1939. The English can and will endure anything, provided they are able to believe in their cause. That cause would be immeasurably fortified if the people knew that they were fighting to hold the better things that belong to the past and the far finer things that can be wrested from the future. VICTORY WITHOUT A NAME is a laurel wreath laid in desolation and sorrow. To struggle for life alone may be to lose everything that makes life worth while. But to fight for a way of living that is more kindly and that is more merciful and more tender is the only reason why this war can be justified.[18]

---

[18] 'Cassandra': *The English at War*, London: Secker and Warburg, 1941, p. 128.

— 5 —

THE EDUCATION OF THE PEOPLE

I

When the British novelist, J. G. Ballard, came home to England after spending his thrilling teenage years as a boy prisoner in a civilian Japanese POW camp outside Shanghai,[1] all he later recollected was the unremitting grimness and dreariness of everyday life in the home country which had never been his home. In his 2008 memoirs,[2] he wrote, with offhand contempt, of the general misery of British life in 1946, the wretched acceptance of awful public services, tasteless and indifferent food, daily hopelessness at work, at home. . . it's a long-familiar dirge, the responsibility often laid simply at the door of the Labour Party's then government.

That Labour Party had a lot on its plate. Almost bankrupt after the unbelievable extravagance of war, its transport systems running on empty and in any case long left without capital or investment by its quondam owners, shipbuilding living on old technology and a pre-war reputation, medical services inaccessible to many, overpriced to most, inadequate for everybody. . . the list[3] of shortage and of poverty is endless. And yet. . .

And yet the new postwar government, with arresting confidence, took all these faltering, capital-starved institutions – ships, railways, steel, coal, electricity and gas – into public ownership by 1948. In the same year a National Health Service was inaugurated which promised medical attention to the whole society 'free at the point of use' and

---

[1] J. G. Ballard, *Empire of the Sun*, London: Victor Gollancz, 1984.
[2] J. G. Ballard, *Miracles of Life: Shanghai to Shepperton*, London: Fourth Estate, 2008.
[3] Given its detailed history by Peter Hennessy in *Never Again: Britain 1945–1951*, London: Allen Lane, 2002.

paid for by universal contributions to a national insurance scheme. Perhaps most importantly, the new government, with its unexpectedly huge majority, set in train an enormous programme of rebuilding cities and their homes, going far beyond the bomb-damaged zones of the industrial north and midlands, let alone London. The results were often aesthetically horrible, but – in Leeds, Sheffield, Liverpool, Glasgow, Birmingham, Bristol, Swansea and the East End – they were light, airy, electrified, sanitary, and roomier than anything Hoggart's people knew in the 1930s.

The vast and vastly productive economic machine of Britain cranked itself up for peacetime production still much favoured by imperial preference and tariffs across one fifth of the globe. Rationing of food and petrol was however maintained over some goods until 1954, three ounces per person per week of cheese, one pound of meat, half a pound of sugar, three ounces of chocolate.[4] The international habits of wartime thought kept up the Cold War and therefore the mammoth distortions of military production and development. The consequences were inevitably veering even as the mighty postwar boom began so suddenly to take off, and dreary old Britain, unequal as ever, began to delight in new colours, clothes, cars and recreations.

For Ballard is far too partial in his recollection of the first ten postwar years, and Hoggart gives him the lie even as he too remembers the dreadful hotels he had to use in his first job, the grim, dour landladies, the bitter cold of the winter of 1947 when the coal ran out, the perpetuity of class snobberies which neither war nor socialism eradicated, the unthinking stupidity of so much class resistance to social improvements and individual emancipation.

The most important kind of history is social history, and social history is the consequence of the ideas men and women have about how to live. A Labour government might have – did have – plenty of plans for making and providing. It had none for changing human passions. How could it? So what indeed remained dreary and stale about British life in 1946 when Hoggart came home to baby Simon and Mary now perforce without a salary was much of what they found in Marske-on-Sea.

---

[4] Figures in Christopher Driver, *The British at Table, 1940–1980*, London: Chatto and Windus, 1983, p. 26.

Mary in 1945.

II

During the interminable wait after the German surrender in May 1945 while the Allies tried to restore some kind of normal productive life to the ruined cities of Italy, Mary Hoggart had sent Richard's applications for nine or ten jobs as university lecturer (the British title). Hoggart had first-class honours, an MA and a distinguished backer but he wasn't from Oxford or Cambridge and those who were took the first places in any academic queue. Thus and thus the throttling grip those two institutions held and hold on English intellectual life became an intrinsic part of Hoggart's life-inquiry, indeed gradually posed themselves as the momentous question: how is it that one's deepest values and allegiances are given form and content by the chance distributions of history and geography, and their composition shaped by privilege, the brutality of money, by genuine talent burnished or exaggerated by advantage, by mere presumption unchallenged by timidity or ignorance?

Hoggart had already found these grand themes modestly carried by the questions and pursuits of innumerable soldiers behind the lines of the Eighth Army as they puzzled over the Army Bureau of Current Affairs pamphlets or tried their hands as poets, short story writers or journalists at the Three Arts Club. From then on there had been little doubt about his vocation, indeed there had never been any doubt in Dobrée's mind – the interview at the *Yorkshire Post* notwithstanding – since politics and literature had so coincided in his life as a student, let alone in the giant crisis of European civilization. In agitated necessity, he had applied for a traineeship at John Lewis's then incipient chain of department stores, but the call to interview finally came from University College Hull and then in what was called until recently its extra-mural department, where lecturers were designated tutors, and the subject specialists (English literature, local history, politics and industrial relations, modern languages, music, general science), although teaching separately, had administration, social life, intellectual argument and, on the whole, political commitment in common. The beaten boundaries of departmental dispute were much less pronounced in the teaching done outside the walls. What was at stake was the common pursuit of personal inquiry and, it may be, of class endeavour. At the heart of such work was far less any kind of social advancement or the making of vocational qualifications; what counted for teachers and students was the search for understanding the world better; for a richer sense of life's fulfilments and possibilities; for breadth of mind and liveliness of imagining; for largeness of education. No one thought of the students as either customers or consumers, and their numbers were not checked against targets nor the tutors assessed for performance. When, thirty-five years later, Hoggart chaired a committee at Goldsmiths' College where he was by then Warden, conducting some research into what it was that urged mature people into part-time study, the students told him they wanted to become more 'whole' by learning more; they ratified every one of the old values. 'You wanted to throw your hat in the air',[5] the Warden said.

It is easy to idealize such departments back in 1946. Less easy when you recall the ancient ceremony of the interviewing panel which appointed our man in Hull.

Such panels were made up of some eight or so members of the university's staff drawn partly from the department in which the appointment was to be made, partly from the intra-mural staff, the full-time

---

[5] Richard Hoggart, *An Imagined Life: Life and Times 1959–91*, London: Chatto and Windus, 1992, p. 214.

specialists from which required the deference of the extra-mural less-than-specialists who only taught evening classes and summer schools fifty miles away and (by and large) published no books. In Hoggart's case, the committee was chaired by the Professor of Philosophy, one Tom Jessop, another of those portly, bonhomous, pin-striped academic grandees of the day with a terrific manner, high standing in the Methodist church then dominant in south-east Yorkshire, and a decent social conscience to match.

The committee's members each quizzed the candidates one by one, asking what and how they might teach a mixed bunch of about fifteen voluntary students seeking no qualification but wisdom and a larger slice of life, turning up for two or more hours in a church hall or a local primary school one winter evening every week. Some questions were asinine, some searching, some questioners elaborate and judicious, some kindly and helpful, the head of department, Billy Mayfield, five feet two, soft-voiced, dedicated, percipient, the person whose judgement would end the day.

Mayfield was the ideal head of extra-mural studies as they were then conceived. He felt and shared the force of the feeling for education sweeping through the immediate postwar society, civilian and military alike. The Army Bureau of Current Affairs connected straight with extra-mural studies (and with Penguin books) in a determination to break into those rooms in the culture kept locked against the wrong classes and opened only to those who spoke in the correct way. Mayfield wasn't a Yorkshireman, but he was devoted to an ideal of radical education well beyond the puffed-out breathlessness of Professor Jessop, devoted also to the ideals implicit in the teaching of drama as an activity breaking open the one-way imparting of knowledge by a single tutor to a group of students, dispersing classroom authority, demanding that people pretend that things are other than how they are, and thereby help to make them so.

So Mayfield saw plainly how the short, stocky Yorkshireman, still in his captain's service dress, talking easily and fluently to the committee, matched and contrasted with his own vision of what his department was about. Hoggart was appointed three notches up the salary scale at £400 a year. Mayfield assigned him to the far north of his departmental empire, which ran south from Teesside and Darlington, then County Durham, down East Yorkshire by way of Scarborough, Bridlington, and Hull itself, across the wide Humber (then crossed by only one bridge near the beginning of the estuary) into Lincolnshire and Grimsby. Seaside resorts, fish and, along the Tees, the vast and sprawling dominion of black and smoky industry – coal, steel, shipbuilding, and the colossal estate of ICI's chemical works at Billingham, provided the mixed and earnest students of extra-mural evenings. Middlesbrough, on the Tees, was the grimmest of the industrial towns of the north, surrounded by the steelworks of Dorman Long and Head Wrightson's, whose mighty furnaces lit the night sky above the beaches at Marske where the Hoggart trio first settled. Saltburn, where he took a class for three years, was on the other hand a stout little resort a mile up the road, with three or four high, white and handsome hotels, built for the Victorian middle classes trying to get out from underneath the thick black smoke belching out along the estuary, and to take a brief sojourn beside the North Sea, visiting in summer the Pierrots on the long cast-iron pier, bending into the stiffish breeze along the hard yellow sands glittering with coal dust.

The location of Hoggart's classes took in the most beautiful and the most darkly satanic of north-east Yorkshire, from stately Scarborough perched high on the cliffs above its two bays, to the railway marshalling yards and boiler repair factories at Darlington; from the solidly unchanging market towns of Thirsk and Malton (so lovingly restored to the national imagination by James Herriot) to the dismal fairground tat and cheap neon-and-plastic of Redcar, the working class's daytrip destination a dozen miles from the works.

Wherever the tutor was teaching, however, the class inevitably foregathered in one of those uniform meeting places provided by schools, churches, the working men's institute, village halls, occasionally a room above a pub (not always tactful in the days when the temperance league was stronger than it is now). In these bare, sometimes chilly surroundings, on wooden chairs and wooden floors and the limited technical aid provided by a blackboard, a record-player (the tutor's own) and a piano, some twenty students worked their way, between September and May, through courses on 'The English Novel', 'Roman Britain', 'Tudor Yorkshire', 'The History and Politics of Trade Unions', 'Parliamentary Democracy', 'From Newton to Einstein', 'Beginners' French', 'Choral Music from Handel to Vaughan Williams', 'Shakespeare and Elizabethan Drama'.

Students were asked to write essays, tutors usually opened the evening with an introductory talk, sometimes a full lecture delivered from a typescript. Once, in his earliest days, giving a course on modern poetry in Middlesbrough's Constantine College, a mechanics institute from the nineteenth century, Hoggart read aloud from the book he had discovered himself to be writing on W. H. Auden. A seasoned woman student (who deserves to be named, Violet Trimbull) stood up – often an ominous sign in such audiences – and complained that it was no doubt an interesting essay, but that it gave students no way in to discussion, gave them no purchase on the poems with which to attach poem to person, no way to question themselves on the significance, the very meaning of the poet's words.

These are fearsome questions, and only a teacher whose soul is dead has failed to face such criticism on one occasion or another, whether made by a student or by him- or herself. Either way, Violet Trimbull stands for something important in the tradition of Adult or Extra-Mural Education. She was one of those invisible leaders who, undaunted by shyness or by respect for the better-informed teacher, was able not only to make her objections and her feelings plain, but to redirect the line of the seminar towards common understanding, to show it the way towards shared endeavour, mutual comprehension, towards that supreme educative discovery, that culture is communal, that human life reflects itself in all its variety to itself, that civil society is its best work of art.

Hoggart's seniors, like Bill Williams in the ABCA, and Billy Mayfield at Hull, were fired by this visionary ardour. So too were Hoggart's contemporaries, soon to become authors and soon-to-be-celebrated teachers of the people in the same vein of feeling as his own, Edward Palmer Thompson, already mentioned, Alasdair MacIntyre, and Roy Shaw, all three next door in the Leeds extra-mural department, Raymond Williams at Oxford, Douglas Brown and Leo Salinger at Cambridge.

These men counted themselves part of 'a movement'. They called it that. It was a movement, they believed, of popular energy. The term had its origins in the new forms of mass politics which emerged after the First World War and were, for better and worse, a measure of new feelings of strong participation in politics, a new requirement by a people that their leaders be popular, visible, unflinching.

The 'movement' for increased participation in the education of a people, and especially those many hundreds of thousands who didn't even know they lacked an education, was hardly an instrument of the masses. The history of adult education, of which Hoggart's classes in Middlesbrough and Bridlington were distant tributaries, is a vast, contradictory and protean chronicle in the making of a fissiparous United Kingdom. In the nineteenth century, the making of 'really useful knowledge'[6] into a curriculum was competitively pursued by chapel schools (for all ages), Mechanics' Institutes and the miners'

---

[6] See Richard Johnson's three essays in *Working Class Culture*, John Clarke, Chas Chritcher and Richard Johnson, eds, London: Hutchinson, 1979.

libraries which supplied the 'underground university' – Jonathan Rose's stirring slogan[7] – until it came to some kind of formal realization with the founding of the Workers' Education Association in 1903 and the revolutionary infiltration of Ruskin College within the ancient walls of the University of Oxford.

All historians of working-class education are beset by the blood-stained dispute as to whether the WEA and the extra-mural movement was politically radicalizing or socially anaesthetic. In his authoritative contribution to the debate, Stuart MacIntyre[8] saw the whole thing as an instrument of official policy to incorporate free radicals into the body politic at a time when the spectre of revolution, as Marx foretold, was stalking Europe, and even the British police had gone on strike.

The early heroes of 'the movement', A. D. Lindsay and R. H. Tawney, radicals certainly in the seats of the ancient universities, would heatedly deny such an interpretation. Hoggart, as we saw, stood in their tradition and held firmly to the judgement that the pamphlets of the ABCA were incomparable instruments of popular enlightenment, and gladly recalled that even the sometime enemy of the people, Winston Churchill, had given them his blessing. It was to take, as Hoggart later discovered, another thirty-odd years for a Tory Education Minister, the preposterous Keith Joseph, to revive old nightmares of Reds under beds[9] taught revolutionary politics in evening classes held in primary school classrooms.

The Dave Spart chestnut about adult education as social soporific got no hearing from Hoggart. Egalitarian to his bone marrow, he was also and all his life alert and sensitive to the vivid quiddity of other people, whether he liked them or not. What he and his now famous colleagues in adult education – Shaw, Thompson and company – brought to their classes and powerfully deepened and extended as they taught them, was the certainty that intellectual discovery was a joint activity, that if knowledge was a product, it was more like a communal work of art than a facticity, that it was the precious end of joint study.

Some such belief seemed to surface in common agreement in educational theory a generation ago, and then vanished from sight under the deluge of vocational training and the coarse, bullying insistence

[7] Jonathan Rose, *The Intellectual Life of the British Working Classes*, New Haven: Yale, 2001, especially chapters 7 and 8.
[8] Stuart MacIntyre, *A Proletarian Science: Marxism in Britain 1917–1933*, London: Lawrence and Wishart, 1986, pp. 89–90.
[9] Hoggart (1991), p. 126.

on the instrumentality of learning, the deadly conversion of education into cash. These lethal tendencies have worked to cut off knowledge from inwardness, to separate knower from known. The market principle creates a new dislocation. We have two distinct markets: one of knowledge and one of potential creators and users of knowledge.[10] This is the contemporary crisis of education. The originary contexts of adult education and its working out in the relationships of war and postwar settlement is one of the most magnificent of British cultural achievements, the Open University its pinnacle. It was Hoggart's discovery of this work of culture, in Italy and in north-east England between 1944 and 1956 or so, which was his own signal creation, which found its expression in his books as in his life, and the two as inseparable.

III

The road to the seaside village of Marske hardly lent itself to such high diction. When Mr Mayfield, his boss, assigned Hoggart to the north-east, he was still living necessarily with his in-laws in Stalybridge. He had to make the long journey up the country by way of trains to Leeds and Darlington, take a hired car paid for by the university until he and Mary could afford their own, and set off four nights a week from some dire commercial hotel to classes spaced at anything up to fifty-mile intervals, Middlesbrough, Filey, Helmsley, Seaton Carew.

One Teesside hotel so far encouraged the class struggle that one day, after standing up to a five-strong cadre of natty little suede-shoed salesmen on behalf of the Labour government, they saw him off to work the next morning by bawling 'Fucking Commie' after him, out of the high lounge windows. Things were quieter and more respectable, as well as with much better breakfasts, beside the seaside in Whitby or Bridlington.

It was a good job, nonetheless, if also a good job that he was only twenty-eight. After a year sharing half a terrace house with cheap old furniture and filthy carpets provided by a genteel snob of a landlady, the Hoggarts moved, in the wonderful hot summer of 1947, to Marske, a single street of a place halfway between Redcar and

---

[10] I am paraphrasing another great teacher of evening classes, Basil Bernstein, in his *Pedagogy, Symbolic Control and Identity*, New York: Rowman and Littlewood, 2000, p. 86.

Saltburn. It had a pub, a handful of shops with thin stock, and a few little stone cottages and bungalows for summer lets.

A far-off Hoggart relative, in those days of stronger family ties, had taken a considerate interest in the family. The local GP turned out to be the medical major who rushed to Richard's help after his dreadful accident on the island of Pantelleria three years earlier. A student from an evening class in tiny Marske told her tutor of a bungalow for rent at number 164A up a 'ginnel' just off the High Street. The idea of community still had plenty going for it. They found a battered little place, but homely, with a shabby garden and a sizeable wooden hut behind the single storey house; the hut served as a very rough study, bitter cold in winter but not bad after writing in desert tents, the backs of Bedford three-tonners, in Aunt Clara's cramped little bedroom, or at the edge of the kitchen at Newport Street.

So preparation for evening classes as well as his own writing went on a few paces from the back door of number 164A, where Simon, only fifteen months old when they moved in, couldn't penetrate. Hoggart had kept up his own writing in the spaces the war permitted, plenty of it in Naples, what with the publications of the Three Arts Club and his expository writing for his soldier-students as Brigade education officer.

There was plenty more for those so inclined in adult education, and two or three journals – Adult Education, the Tutors' Bulletin – in which to place strenuous contributions to the earnest, admirable debates of the movement about its best purposes. The best-known of these was The Highway, house magazine of the WEA and host to Hoggart as well as those others of his coevals in adult education much-mentioned in these pages, Thompson, Williams, Shaw and Holbrook. Indeed, although Hoggart often referred to himself as a 'slow writer'[11] and as hardly ever capable of 'knocking something out' in 'a spirit of only casual interest', he wrote a very great deal; consistently so across almost fifty years.

In Marske he wrote in his den. When it was coldest he rigged up a crazy Bedouin tent made out of awful old carpets found in the shed and pinned over cords with those monstrous safety pins long ago used to make triple or quadruple blanket covers for freezing bedrooms. The only source of heat was a short, four-bar electric fire placed close to his desk and scorching his shins. His books lived in the house. The little family's small savings went on a car: a hundred quid for their relative's ten-year-old Hillman, and of course Hoggart

---

[11] E.g. for one in *Speaking to Each Other*, vol. I, London: Chatto and Windus, 1970, p. 9.

used that for his often lengthy drives across the wolds, sometimes in snow, always in the dark, once or twice with failed headlights or windscreen wipers, creeping along moorland roads much populated by sheep, peering through a drenched windscreen and out of an open side window.

For some years he wrote and published an article every two months or so, many on adult education pedagogy, many more in the genre he was to make his own but already a century and a half old in English literature. It was the genre of Cobbett and Carlyle, of William Morris and John Ruskin, then of D. H. Lawrence's *Phoenix* and R. H. Tawney's *The Acquisitive Society*. Its contemporary master as Hoggart began to write was George Orwell, and the subjects which so delighted or repelled Orwell such as seaside comic postcards, boys' weekly comics, sex-and-violence thrillers, seized Hoggart also and pinned his attention and his genius to those of life's edges at which ordinary detail and routine suddenly flash with value: plates of food always, not-so-casual gestures and turns of phrase, lines of life on people's faces, movements of affection or rejection, above all the plunge of the imagination into cross-current narratives wherever found, on the page, on the screen, in conversation.

To begin with, he wrote about literature. That was his professional tradition and it was always to the great names of English and European literature that he reached out to steady himself when seeking a discursive lead. When in the army he had been struck by 'the simple but awful thought' that his men had 'virtually never in their lives listened to a writer trying to talk objectively, honestly, about life and its problems';[12] that simple thought pointed him to his magnetic north, whether in his teaching or his writing, and steered it for good.

Since Naples, or since his time at Leeds, he had been puzzling over the work of the contemporary poet who, alongside T. S. Eliot, meant most to him: W. H. Auden. Plenty of people were writing about Eliot, but not about Auden. He was only recently turned forty, he had a lot of writing in him. Hoggart began a lengthy essay on Auden after the successful publication of an essay on Sydney Keyes, a war poet killed in North Africa at the age of twenty-one, in *Poetry Review*.

He worked on the Auden essay in Marske while also writing shortish pieces of, so to say, ethnographic observation – on railway bookstalls visited as he waited for the little local trains on his way to evening classes, on trade unionism (for the local Labour Party), on the working of the magistrates' bench in his in-laws' home town,

---

[12] Hoggart (1991), p. 61.

on the public library in Saltburn, on the Sunday church parades of the Scouts, the Guides and the Boys' Brigade. Tosco Fyvel, a Jewish polyglot of shrewd cordiality, had taken over from Orwell as features editor of *Tribune*, the left-wing weekly in a newspaper format, and he gave Hoggart space and a small fee.

But the Auden essay went well beyond the limits of a periodical. After a year and a half of progress inside the stale carpets it had swelled to 35,000 words, Dobrée had an approving look, and Hoggart posted it off to Cecil Day Lewis, poet and friend of Auden's, then an editor at Chatto and Windus and unfailingly kind and generous to young new writers.

Just as well he was; the draft was critical of his own work. Day Lewis asked for greater length and, over the summer of 1949, Hoggart doubled it; Chatto, leisurely as all publishers were in those days, brought out *W. H. Auden: An Introductory Essay* two years later.

By then Hoggart was a bit borne down by something much weightier. The book on Auden, with its caricature of a frontispiece showing the poet in his twenties urgently lighting a fag, was the first full-length study of the poet, for English departments were smaller then and less rapaciously in search of monograph material to paint over. Hoggart takes his readers carefully in step with his subject, much as he would in a three-year tutorial class. He is wholly undaunted by Auden's by then international stature. He warns admirers, with striking assurance, not to mistake

> . . . an almost insolently smart incantation or a rhetorical flourish for the assured movement of a major poet. All this is most in evidence in the very early work; it is what tempted so many knowledgeable young men to imitate Auden without having his fundamental seriousness.[13]

Then, with a stringency *and* the kind of welcome he would extend to those of his students who could manage it, he tells us that 'the reader must be capable of feeling with a sensibility equal to that of a writer'.[14] This is the large egalitarianism of literary study. Auden himself came up to scratch when he met Hoggart in the 1960s; he said he thought his critic was 'all in all, over-generous'.

'Over-generous'? I don't know. Lucky for sure, for what Auden's amazing garrulity led him to say after 1951, in his *Dichtung und Wahrheit*, could not really lend itself to straight exposition. Yet

---

[13] Richard Hoggart, *W. H. Auden: An Introductory Essay*, London: Chatto and Windus, 1951, p. 17.
[14] Hoggart (1951), p. 18.

Hoggart tackles that long and very strange poem-with-prose, *The Sea and the Mirror*, with great blitheness, lines up the characters Auden takes from *The Tempest*, gives each his or her say (Miranda's helplessness left a bit coldly to fend for itself), and paraphrases Caliban, who sounds like a loving parody of Henry James, until Auden sounds more than a little trite.

Hoggart is far and away at his best with Auden's youthful best, though one wishes he could have told us what he would make of Auden's two masterpieces, 'In Praise of Limestone' and 'The Shield of Achilles'. That early best work – 'Let History Be My Judge', 'Venus Will Now Say a Few Words', 'Musée des Beaux Arts', 'In Memory of W. B. Yeats', stretches of 'Letter to Lord Byron', every poetry-lover has their own list – enclosed, shaped, expressed the sensibility, even the world-outlook, of a generation of serious-minded, politically alive, afraid and courageous soldier-housewives and citizen-antiFascists. Hoggart's book is their acknowledgement of this great achievement.

What impended in 1951 was indeed, as Auden diagnosed in his poem-drama, *The Age of Anxiety*. By then, Auden had been in America for five years where perhaps the anxiety was greater. The quest of Auden's characters for 'The Good Place' (*Eutopia*, as More had it) mostly leads these insufferably talkative people back to somebody's apartment for a drink, after which they disperse down mean streets.

At the end, Hoggart turns away from what the great poet, only eleven years his senior, has become. The streets of Marske, if not mean, were plain and dowdy, the tent of carpets stale and smelly, England herself run down, scruffy, still bomb-damaged, still class-bound, still looking along foreshortened political perspectives. But at the end of the little road on the right just along the High Street was the hard yellow beach and the shallow waves of the North Sea. In 1948 sister Nicola arrived to join two-year-old Simon. Her father, in the meantime, had begun to grasp that the portly and dog-eared file of papers, essays, articles and scrappy notes (for Hoggart kept everything he wrote, including his memoranda, in careful order) which carried his mingled impressions of his life and times, were taking on the mass and energy of a single, irresistible demand.

IV

It had a long way to go. When *Auden: An Introductory Essay* came out it was variously and quite well reviewed. Like any author with his first book, he felt very exposed to the possible slights and incomprehension of reviewers working quickly, and regardless of the sweat shed in the making of it. In particular, he looked out for a review in *Scrutiny*, the journal edited by F. R. Leavis, who had early spotted Auden's enormous talent and then written in strong and bitter terms of his tendency to lapse into flip allusions, unearned magniloquence, cheap flourishing, shallow epigrams, all of them charges duly considered by Hoggart.

The review appeared; it praised the author's powers of 'sensible' discrimination but rebuked him for seeming 'not to realize what all these particular criticisms add up to', for 'a summing up both cautious and unspecific', for, in short, not naming what *Scrutiny* took to be Auden's acute deficiencies.[15] In ensuing correspondence Leavis was also drawn in and, while making his by then habitual criticisms of Auden's poetry, betrayed the fact that he hadn't read Hoggart's book. Quite rightly, Hoggart wrote to point this out. Leavis, with a sincere contrition he rarely showed, wrote a personal letter of apology.

Hoggart had however a much bigger, longer-running dispute with the Leavis household and its intellectual methods. For as his own great subject began to come clear to him by way of his writing in the years after the war, he understood, dimly, as is the way of wholly new ideas looming up out of the fog of history, that this subject was no less than the making of its subjectivity by a whole social class. As commercial culture emerged from world war, and as the systems of a new kind of capitalism led by the USA seized hold of its opportunities, swift, shallow, powerful surges of creative reproduction offered to fill, to satisfy, to overcome the imaginative life of whole societies. The cinema, a torrent of cheap and shiny illustrated magazines, another torrent of cheap, gripping fictions, plus the rapid spread of radio reception, all offered entrancing nourishment to class imaginations cut off by the killing forms of mass labour from a traditional culture no longer able to answer the demands of life and death.

Leavis's *Scrutiny*, in its diminutive scale, represented a collective effort to think through this crisis of culture. Formative in its inception had been the pioneer work of Queenie Roth, soon to be Queenie Leavis. She had begun a PhD at women-only Girton College, Cambridge, at a time when doctorates for women were rare indeed. The dissertation turned into *Fiction and the Reading Public*, published in 1932 and the first ever close and serious study of what now would

15 Review by R. G. Cox, *Scrutiny*, vol. XVIII, 1951–2, Cambridge: Cambridge University Press, reissued in 20 vols., 1963, pp. 160–1.

be called, I suppose, 'reception theory', which is to say the study of how people receive and digest cultural narratives. Her husband, in a famous pamphlet called *Mass Civilisation and Minority Culture*, had sketched a history of the collapse of old rural culture, its replacement by mass commercial culture the moral sustenance offered by which had a strict cash value, and ended by calling for 'an armed and conscious minority' to fight on behalf of traditional (literary) culture and 'the storehouse of recorded value'.[16]

This was the formidable apparatus framing *Scrutiny*. It was embattled but pessimistic. Queenie Leavis, fiercely self-protective, pitiless in opposition, hard and harsh in intellectual and personal combat, argued with every justification that the popular press inaugurated by Lord Northcliffe had 'put literature out of reach of the average man',[17] that there were no longer shared standards of judgement for a reading public, that common reading capacity was unprecedentedly low, and that a new kind of fiction, the 'best-seller', incarnated by such as Edgar Rice Burrough's Tarzan novels and Warwick Deeping's bluff gentlefolk, worked 'to solidify herd prejudice and to debase emotional currency by touching grossly on fine issues'.[18]

It was an irresistible case. It energized the periodical and fired its minority readership. As part of *Scrutiny*'s historiography, its contributor guerrilla took for granted the permanent rupture with traditional culture. The poetic language still spoken by country people in 1900, the sanctions and transmitted craft and artistry of old working principles (in a key example, the wheelwright) still surviving in August 1914, were gone, destroyed by the ruthless routines of mass production and the shallow, saccharine products of the new industries of leisure.

It became a very general malediction in the academic class. In a much-admired book,[19] the Professor of Metaphysical Philosophy at Oxford, R. G. Collingwood, repeated it in resonant accents. Dobrée at Leeds had spoken it but to a less hectic tune. Opposing the inevitable tide of commercialization in imaginative life was one version of their work which the tutors of the movement would offer their classes, asking them implicitly to join the armed and conscious minority.

---

[16] Q. D. Leavis, *Fiction and the Reading Public*, London: Chatto and Windus, 1932, reissued 1965. F. R. Leavis, *Mass Civilisation and Minority Culture*, Cambridge: Gordon Fraser Minority Press, 1930.
[17] Q. D. Leavis (1965), p. 224.
[18] Q. D. Leavis (1965), p. 67.
[19] R. G. Collingwood, *The Principles of Art*, Oxford: Clarendon Press, 1938.

Hoggart was armed and conscious all right. But the years at war, the early years on the road and the rails to evening classes had shaped in him the strong conviction not simply that all was not lost, but that the charges of 'escapism', of 'living at the novelist's expense', of the destruction of a moral language and the ruination of a former grace and courtesy were wrong and wronged the people at whom (other people, of course) they were pointed, not without sanctimony.

So, as he puzzled over his nameless and intractable subject-matter, and tried to discern what strange shapes there were moving through his life experience and troubling his dreams, he came to see that even his not very conventional inquiry into popular reading for the not-very-often-reading public would be insufficient to his purposes. He had intended to call his peculiar and, in 1952 or so, shapeless book *The Abuses of Literacy*. But the more he pondered his material and the more odd and unexpected articles he published in *Tribune* or in an excellent journal combining the practical concerns of teachers with larger cultural matters, called *The Use of English*, the more he realized that he was trying to judge without sentencing the idiom of his people.

That is to say, his subject-matter turned out to be the changing sensibility of a whole social class, and the way that sensibility found speech to say what it felt, but also found itself being sold a language which was not its own, which did not say what it meant, but which it spoke in any case. So Hoggart was in a tight fix. He was writing in the language of the academy, but found that language too distant from his allegiances. However, to make his book tell (in every sense) it had to ring right its intellectual coin while at the same time it had to be faithful to its origins in another language, spoken as it were in another land.

There again, the signs of the times were happily portentous. Hoggart had at his elbow Eliot's lifelong meditation on the use of English; never more so than in *Little Gidding*, sent to him in 1942 while in North Africa, an amazing work of affirmation written at just about the grimmest moment of the war.

> Since our concern was speech, and speech impelled us
> To purify the dialect of the tribe . . .

These lines come after the reader's being advised,

> And what the dead had no speech for, when living,
> They can tell you, being dead: the communication
> Of the dead is tongued with fire beyond the language of the living.[20]

---

[20] T. S. Eliot, *Complete Poems and Plays*, London: Faber and Faber, 1969, pp. 194 and 192.

Hoggart was listening to the speech of his dead mother and grand-mother, but also to the still-living aunts, the neighbours of Newport Street and, beyond them, the Working Men's Institutes (there was, there is, one in Marske High Street), the little tea-rooms, the Woolworths (all folded up in 2010), the charabanc outings, the sing-songs at the club, the fairgrounds, the corner shops. These signs of the times, these little glowing lights were what he sought to give speech to, before turning to the newer, coarse and brutal language which, as Hoggart heard before anybody else, threatened with extinction the old warmth.

That he was offered hospitality by *The Use of English* is no surprise and is worth the detour. The journal was edited for twenty-seven years by Denys Thompson, a pupil of Leavis's and for ten years an editor of *Scrutiny*. He was a lifelong schoolteacher and leader of schoolteachers of English, and took as his vocation the transforma-tion of the school subject 'English' into a force redemptive of culture. Not that he ever wore the redeemer's mantle, being a man rather of quiet and persistent courage as well as high intelligence; but he spotted in Hoggart, who was reading from the work in preparation at a *Use of English* conference, a likeminded dedication to purifying the language of the tribe and heeding the communication of the dead, less than ten years after peace broke out with a few new hopes.

V

The manuscript became progressively stouter as the 1950s advanced. Towards the end of 1949, Director Mayfield ordered Hoggart south to Hull, to give his extra-mural classes rather closer to the ramparts of the university itself.

The Hoggarts were glad enough to leave the bungalow and the Bedouin tent, and to bring their two little children to the big city, little enough in all conscience. In Hull, you are always aware of the river, what Philip Larkin, whose name and whose poetry is so closely asso-ciated with the city, called its 'level, drifting breadth' . . . 'Where sky and Lincolnshire and water meet'. With the water came, in those days before the industry collapsed, the everywhere smell of fish. Beyond the city, Yorkshire and Lincolnshire are as flat as the Netherlands and, like them, portioned out into long rectangles by ditches, 'rheins' they are in the Somerset wetlands, another bit of Holland, and the ditches hold the floodwater, mostly, and irrigate the sodden land where the rapeseed grows in bright yellow profusion.

The city itself, miles away from the tourist routes, is widely built beneath the big sky, like enough to the other northern Victorian cities and their universities, except for the traces of its older significance, when the port was a trading host to the magnificence of the mighty Dutch empire in the seventeenth century, and Andrew Marvell was its MP. A century and a half later, the Member was one William Wilberforce and his heroic efforts to stop the slave trade were conducted in line with Hull's traditions of puritan dissent; Thomas Fairfax had held the city when the Royalists briefly besieged it.

The docks dominated Hull, each named after members of a royal family long reconciled to one of the capitals of the regicides. Albert, Victoria, Alexandra and King George docks[21] received mighty cargoes while below them, like a busy little sea rat, ran the ferry which plied the Humber from Yorkshire to Lincolnshire and back, and sometimes carried the tutor to evening classes in Grimsby.

From 1951 the Hoggarts lived at 26 Park Avenue, just across the Park from St Augustine's church, in 'The Avenues', a handsome suburb of sizeable Edwardian provenance – big, high rooms, a hallway with stained glass windows to the entrance porch, wide stairs with shapely banisters, a spacious bathroom and separate lavatory, no cellar (the water table brimful beneath the roads) but a large loft. After a year or more in a first floor apartment rented from the university, the family could afford the hefty mortgage needed to buy number 26 and make a new nursery room ready to take the third child, Paul, born in 1952. There wasn't a lot of money to spare, but there was a lot more than in 1946 as well as the living space, the garden, the domestic plenty which began to flow from the postwar boom. The British economy may still have been in a parlous state, and rationing still in force, but a different spirit was abroad, and after all with Mr Churchill back in Downing Street, the age of austerity was slowly closing.

The rhythms of the Hoggarts' family life – and this biography must be as much an everyday story of domestic folk as it is a tale told of a solitary intellectual – were naturally more spacious and much better upholstered in Hull than in Marske. The University College had high hopes of becoming a university in its own right and freed from the seigneurial rule of London. It was increasing staff and student numbers as the government began to grasp the new importance of higher education in the postwar polity, the enhanced expectations,

---

[21] I am grateful to Roy Hattersley for his reminiscences, one afternoon in Rowsley, of his time as student in Hull, beginning in 1951. See also his *Goodbye to Yorkshire*, Harmondsworth: Penguin, 1978.

Richard Hoggart and family playing at home in Hull.

the force of a novel political concept, 'equality of opportunity'. These changes and the self-confidence they brought to the small academic class meant that social life in 'the Avenues' was thriving. There were dinner parties of a kind hitherto unknown to the quotidian middle classes; there were regular concerts at the university (as it became in 1954) not, as now, numerous and contrastive in style and cultural allegiance (and the attire to go with it), but magnetic, authoritative, formal, all this as well as musically pretty good. Hard to realize now, but it was only in the late 1950s that British universities became such busy markets of cultural production, with rival film societies, little student theatres, cyclostyled newsletters and even their own typeset newspapers, a medley of political parties (at Hull, the Lab soc and the Soc soc; Hoggart addressed both), new jazz and old Bach, art exhibitions, carnivals with student floats, and everywhere the signs and weaponry of strange new pastimes and games, canoes, skis, lacrosse sticks, squash racquets, climbing ropes, archery targets.

At the same time the tough schedules of extra-mural teaching remained inflexible. Four evenings a week from October to the end of March, with more than a sprinkling of weekend courses and conferences, kept Hoggart out of the house most nights until the happy release of Maytime, and the knowledge that there were no formal examinations to mark. There was, however, no question of his relaxing the self-imposed discipline of writing. What had started out, in part as a riposte to Mrs Leavis's 1932 classic, as an effort to find what it was in poorish writing which nonetheless pleased and gripped such an enormous readership, had now become a long and faithful history of the moral imagination of a social class. Moreover, that social history – one for which there was no recognized method of inquiry, no approved conceptual vocabulary nor recognized *style* – was in the throes of drastic change, and consequently all the harder to write about.

More than by Mrs Leavis's wholehearted malediction, however, Hoggart had been much affected by a polemical paragraph in Ezra Pound's marvellous little pamphlet, *How to Read*. Famously, Pound wrote in 1931,

> ... the governor and legislator cannot act effectively or frame his laws without words, and the solidity and validity of these words is in the care of the damned and despised *literati*. When their work goes rotten ... when their very medium, the very essence of their work, the application of word to thing goes rotten, i.e. becomes slushy and inexact, or excessive and bloated, the whole machinery of social and individual thought and order goes to pot.[22]

Hoggart had begun from a strong feeling that things in the home country *were* going to pot; that the literary and imaginative life not so much of 'casual' reading as of the *only* reading done by the working class, was such as, in the title of an essay he wrote in 1952, to 'unbend the springs of action'. The only nourishment in the cheap magazines, the cheesecake photography and titillating short paragraphs, was 'candy floss' – frothy, sugary, pink and evanescent.

Reading these judgements today, one is bound to think – as Hoggart himself acknowledged in his revaluation of 1995, *The Way We Live Now* (which waits its turn in chapter 10) – how much worse things are now. Forty years of the *Sun*, of the degradations of a reckless and irresponsible tabloid press, of public mendacity and late night pornography on half-a-dozen television channels, only serve to bring out how accurate and prescient Hoggart was with very much less to go on.

In discovering, as he did, that nonetheless he had a quite different book on his hands than a communication spoken over 'mass art' and slack-jawed 'indifferentism' (Hoggart's coinage), he found his very own sensibility telling him other, better, more reassuring things as

---

[22] Ezra Pound, *Literary Essays*, T. S. Eliot ed., London: Faber and Faber, 1954, p. 45.

well. Hence his turning his book back to front. The front half now became a revaluation of what was enduring, strong and companionable in a culture built out of two hundred years of life in the industrial city. W. H. Auden wrote, in a poem just too late to be mentioned in the book about him,

All sane affirmative speech,
Had been soiled, profaned, debased
To a horrid mechanical screech.[23]

Hoggart now placed as the first half of his book his careful retrieval of sane, affirmative speech insofar as it was still spoken.

That older order, as he came to call the first part of his great study, comprised the language of home, the definitions of motherhood as these were carried by language and transformed into carriage and conduct, the forcefield of geography as that marked out a neighbourhood, the solid, trustworthy rituals and customs of such off-duty practices as gossip, tea-sharing, jokes, gambling, drinking at the club, allotment-tending. In the final typescript, Hoggart could still write, 'Even today, I should guess, you would find fifty people who could take up "the Hallelujah Chorus" with you from any moderate-sized working-class crowd in Hunslet.'[24]

That this would now, well over fifty years later, be more unlikely is not merely a matter of the deturpation of culture, the end of civilization as we know it. The *Messiah* is still very widely performed, the class membership of choral societies much more fluid; what is called in the book, without irony, 'the full, rich life' is now lived in shopping malls, on package holidays, on sight-seeing trips to stately homes as much as to football grounds (the numbers visiting the former comfortably exceeding the latter).[25] But there can be no question in these pages of our trying to match Hoggart's appraisal of class and country with a parallel set of judgements grounded half a century later on a new ethnography. (My impressionistic first chapter is no more than an effort at contextualization.)

What is here at stake is how he did it. When we know that, someone else can try to do the same thing, differently, for a different epoch. (This is once more to paraphrase T. S. Eliot.) What he did was threefold. He started out from the discipline of the criticism of literature which he had learned as a student. This provided him with

---

[23] Auden, *Nones* (1951), omitted from the *Collected Poems*.
[24] Hoggart (1958), p. 150.
[25] *Social Trends* 2009, London: HMSO, tables 34–5.

a reach-me-down theory of how a literature expresses and qualifies the spirit of an age, together with a more precise instrumentation with which to test the accuracy of writing, its realization of a lived experience in words, the exact quality of the emotion the writer was seeking to express.

His second method – to call it that, it was more like the assumption of a style of thought-and-feeling together – was to write autobiography but to tell it at a distance. Thus in 'Scholarship boy', the section of the book which brought him most correspondence, all of it *in recognition* of a common historical experience, he searched out what it was for a boy of his class, from a very poor, all-womanly household, to make his way out of his class along the roads of scholarly education.

Thirdly, he filled out the history with what one might first think of as the material of the novelist, the observer 'trying to be one on whom,' in Henry James's words, 'nothing is lost'. In practice, however, this third style is more like that of Baudelaire's 'painter of modern life'. This much-hailed, elusive figure is in part the *flâneur* or idle stroller, in part a detective (Baudelaire, like Dickens, was much impressed by the arrival in storytelling of the urban plain-clothes policeman), in part 'a spectator who is a *prince*, everywhere rejoicing in his incognito'. Baudelaire goes on,

> The lover of universal life enters into the crowd as though it were an immense reservoir of electric energy. We might also liken him to a mirror as vast as the crowd itself, or to a kaleidoscope endowed with consciousness which, with each one of its movements, represents the multiplicity of life and the flickering grace of all its elements.[26]

This is a bit too high-flown for Hoggart and he might have looked doubtfully at Baudelaire's city dandy. But Hoggart's calm, self-assured, sympathetic pedestrian is like enough to the dark-suited *Symboliste*, missing nothing, belonging everywhere, and invariably liking it here.

This was a new kind of figure in academic life, and plenty of people didn't know what to make of it. A rare old tumult broke out when *The Uses of Literacy* was finally published in 1957, but even friends and colleagues who looked at the manuscript handled it gingerly. Thus the old Left looked in vain for the embattled heroes of trade union struggle – the sort of figures who would indeed appear in

---

[26] Charles Baudelaire, *'The Painter of Modern Life' and Other Essays*, trans. Jonathan Mayne, New York: Da Capo, 1964, p. 9.

Edward Thompson's *The Making of the English Working Class* six years later – and less politically minded people fretted anxiously, as academics will, about its flouting of disciplinary boundaries: was it social history? was it sociology? what on earth was it?

There was in those days only one British publishing house hospitable to intellectual novelty and academic category-shattering, and that was Chatto and Windus, with their inevitably discreet offices just off Trafalgar Square. Hoggart duly sent off his peculiar, insistent, bounding and irrepressible kangaroo of a book, and awaited the verdict of Cecil Day Lewis (who saw immediately how good it was), of the shrewd and kindly Ian Parsons (who said, on publication, that he thought it would prove a sound backseller), of Leonard Woolf, Virginia's widower and doyen of the Hogarth Press and intellectual pillar of the Labour Party, who wanted to reject it. But in the end, which, as always in those leisurely days for publishing houses, was a long time coming, a contract was issued.

Two or three months later, a bombshell arrived in the post. Rattled rather, in their genteel offices, by a book addressing quite so bluntly the venality of the daily press and the exploitative brutality of so much popular fiction, the company had consulted a libel lawyer. He was of the view that the book, at that stage to be titled *The Abuses of Literacy*, perpetrated deadly libels the particularity of which were made worse in law by the general forcefulness of the argument. He advised against publication and was, a short time later, supported in this and line by line by a barrister in Inns of Court.

This grandee went through the manuscript with Hoggart and Parsons who now, in the nature of things, had their blood up and were determined to win the day for some version of the book. So Hoggart suggested taking off 'Ab' from 'Abuses' which seemed more emollient, and he proved ingenious in inventing on the spot snatches of journalism which caught the inanity or phoniness of the original example without direct, and therefore actionable, quotation. But the barrister dug in deep against the section of the book dealing with sex-and-violence novels, most of the passages in which were taken from a revolting classic in the genre shortly before enjoying a huge *succès de canaille*, being read on the train, in a spirit of anthropological curiosity you understand, by respectable businessmen.

This new kind of bestseller burst open the decorous limits of Mrs Leavis's research. James Hadley Chase's *No Orchids for Miss Blandish*, the work in question, could hardly keep company with Edgar Rice Burrough's manly, courteous Tarzan or Ethel M. Dell's fluttering courtesans. The change in tone and style went deep. It was central to Hoggart's evaluation of the moral imagination of his day. His adroit and instantaneous emendations of earlier passages, made at the meeting with the lawyer, were all very well. Miss Blandish was another matter.

Hoggart went back to Hull resolved, as well he might be, to defend his masterpiece and get it into print. Astonishingly, he replaced all the direct quotations with his own imitations. The tricky part was then to keep faith with the artistic impulse, horrible but nonetheless truthful as it was, and not to write a parody in the manner so often called for in those days by the *New Statesman*'s weekly competition for victorious pastiche. Perhaps the difficult aesthetic point is made by noting that once, when the *New Statesman* competition set as the subject for parody the writing of Graham Greene, Greene himself entered under a *nom-de-plume*, but was only placed third.

So Hoggart's mimesis had to be, well, perfect. As he says himself, the aim of these writers 'is to make their readers feel the flesh and bone of violence'.[27] So to speak, they run their thumbnail along the line of an open nerve so that readers sense the thrill and vivid pain as immediately as an odour. The power of such writing is physical first; thereafter it is the power of subjugation.

> Suddenly Fatsy brought his knee hard up into Herb's groin. Herb's face came down sharp and Fatsy met it with his ham-like fist. The knuckles splintered the bone and made blood and flesh squelch like a burst pomegranate. Herb fell back to the tiled floor, retching teeth. He was bubbling gently as he lay there, so Fatsy gave him one in the belly with his steel-shod shoe. Then – just for luck – Fatsy ground his foot straight on to the squelchy mess that useter be Herb's face.

Identification of the self with another person by way of the word is intrinsic to the experience of literature. Thus the right reader is made into a poet by reading a great poem. Dr Johnson once wrote of Gray's *Elegy in a Country Churchyard* that

> I have never seen the notions in any other place; yet he that reads them here, persuades himself that he has always felt them.[28]

Hoggart makes himself into the kind of debased artist who dramatizes the horrible fight. It's a risky game, and he found it easy. But then he has to wriggle out of his disguise, and name it for the dreadful thing it is.

---

[27] Hoggart (1958), p. 265.
[28] Samuel Johnson, 'Gray', *Lives of the Poets*, vol. II, Oxford: Oxford University Press, 1956, p. 453.

He wrote his imitations in a few days. The lawyers were mollified, Chatto began the machinery of publication. Hoggart knew how original and audacious his book was – friendly colleagues had told him so, sometimes reproachfully, but he could not of course anticipate its reception, maybe, if things went badly, its disappearance.

In any case, there were still four evening classes and the journeys to-and-fro to make every week of autumn and winter, and he and Mary were beginning to turn their thoughts to working inside the university's walls, where timetables permitted a lecturer to go home, stay for supper, see his or her children and, in those days, have no weekend conference duties; by mid-June he would have polished off the exam papers and be able to turn to the fulfilments of personal research or, for many, of gardening and happy indolence.

Certainly, in the 1950s there was little of the transatlantic academic traffic which was to crowd the airways by 1975, still less was there the grotesque insistence on mere productivity on the part of all lecturers, including those whose products withered at the light of day. But the curses to be spoken over the deformations of university life as those came to twist erudition and pedagogy into such horrible new shapes awaited the revolutions of the Right in the 1980s. For a literature tutor aged thirty-seven in an extra-mural department, the change, if it could be brought off, and the high ramparts of intellectual snobbery stood in the way for sure, to a senior post in an English department looked a good idea.

So it was a bit of a surprise and a bit of a rush when Billy Mayfield suggested putting his brightest spark up for a visiting professorship in Rochester, New York. The wonderful Senator Fulbright had, in 1946, put up a sizeable portion of his family's fortune to pay for such passages nationwide, but they hadn't touched very many. Mayfield, lively always in the care of his department's standing, saw the chance. The professoriat was out of the competition, closeted in defence of its five-yearly national grant allocation and in any case wasn't, beside the Humber, alert to the significance of the boats going west from the Solent. Hoggart was a star on the rise; Mayfield knew his man; Hull and Rochester agreed the deal. On 7 September 1956 the Hoggart family embarked for New York.

121

— 6 —

BEST OF FRIENDS: THE BOOK, THE CENTRE AND THE MORAL COMMUNITY

I

They sailed on the *Queen Elizabeth*, still at that date the latest thing in ocean-going liners, still at that date rigorously British, the barriers between the classes impassable except to those with a great deal of social nerve, three separate cinemas carefully graded as to comfort, the third class no more than a miniature church hall, with high-backed dining chairs to sit on, and *Brigadoon* to watch.

It was thrilling, all the same. The three children ranged their allocated portion of the ship – with Fulbright's help they were travelling second class – delighting in the very idea of a little swimming pool sloshing gently with the rhythms of the Atlantic, excited by the expansive dining room and the unfamiliar pleasures of hotel life, braving the companion ways as if aboard a naval vessel and at war, the boys' imaginations very properly filled with images from *In Which We Serve* and *The Cruel Sea*, hanging onto the rails under parental watch and gazing seawards for a glimpse of a distant smokestack.

The terrific imagery of the Atlantic passage sunk deep in the cultural memory of all British people is of course consummated by the sight of the Statue of Liberty, and beyond it the amazing skyline of Manhattan. All liners headed for West Side past Ellis Island and up the Hudson River to passenger terminals 90–99, where the huge ships docked and the hordes of passengers, up and dressed for departure since dawn, tumbled slowly down the gangways into the vast, overcrowded, slow and painstaking customs halls. The officers were tough and exacting; they opened most suitcases and trunks; taxi-drivers jostled for fares and favours – 'you look after me and I'll

122

see you right' – the whole ordeal took two or three hours, the children hot, tired, hungry, and the Hoggarts still with the length of New York State to travel up to Rochester.

Rochester is a nice city, neat and nice and solidly built and the house the family were given for the year, on Anthony Street, pleasant, solid, roomy. Simon fared well at Harley School, Nicola at a local high school known only by its number, Paul still too little for school. They were bright, articulate, eager, accustomed to plenty of visitors, Simon even then formidable with words, quick and sharp, Nicola tiny but self-sufficient, Paul a gentle family junior, all five of them open, likeable, wholly free of any of that insufferable English muf-fledness, let alone any taint of snobbery towards the Americans. They were held within the perfect freedom of their loving family; Mary, good-looking, well-built, her husband's height, perhaps its ultimate authority, wise and quietly witty anyway.

British academics hadn't quite begun, in 1956, the compulsory pilgrimage to the States and Hoggart was a rare bird. As always he made swift friendships, with the Kaufmans, the Schillings, particu-larly with Charles Frankel, good scholar, lavish host, brave man too, many years later murdered – shot – in his bed as he tried to talk a drug-crazed interloper down to earth.

The practices of adult education at home were a help; they pre-vented the too-easy judgement of the British academic fifty-odd years ago that half the American students shouldn't be at university at all, were unlettered, unable to write, had no stamina for reading . . . Hoggart was accustomed to discerning intelligence and commitment in the most uncertain stammerings of students as they groped their way through *The Waste Land* and *Sons and Lovers*. He was teaching a course in modern English literature, Hardy, Hopkins, Yeats, Eliot, Lawrence, Forster, Joyce, and his own particular choices on whom he had written at home, Graham Greene and W. H. Auden. Modernist aesthetics is *difficult*, that is part of its point, and was a lot harder then as being less familiar. Some of the students took it hard as well, even when trying their best. They came from comfortable homes, they may have known the war stories and had had parents in uniform, but these things had little immediacy. Eliot's canal and its rats, its broken pentameters and distracted neurasthenic took some facing up to; Lawrence's hot domestic quarrels and drunken miners were a long way from Rochester.

So he was kindly enough with his grades once he had the hang of the credit system, and found, as he had found on the Yorkshire coast, touching instances of students being radically disconcerted by their reading, opened up maybe, but also horrified, disjoined from what they knew and loved about their pretty little well-kept home towns: Auburn, Palmyra, Carthage.

Richard and Mary confided homesickness to one another from time to time. But they had behind them long practice at separation and at pacing themselves through such passages. Besides, the place was so congenial, the people so hospitable, Mary made so welcome, his children so cheerful, so attractively touched with Americanism – turns of accent and speech, suntan, clear skin, T-shirts. Only the pay proved a point of strain: the exchange deal left each beneficiary with a home-salary equivalent, and British pounds fell well below dollar expenditure, so that Hoggart had to make up the difference with summer school overtime.

So a year away was nothing, except to qualify and extend Hoggart's gifts of judgement and analysis in all aspects of life. He accommodated America as he later would the polyglot environs, the endless travelling at UNESCO. He saw, he envied even, what an American friend, no chauvinist but a sharp-eyed, sometimes caustic observer of his country, meant when he said 'Ah, but you see, I love America.' The Englishman Hoggart, patriotic enough and his feet planted deep in his country's soil, wouldn't say, I guess, 'I love England.' Who would? There again, he would say, 'I love great stretches of the English landscape' and would do honour to its greatest democratic achievements – the National Health Service, naturally, and Allen Lane's Penguin books – but English patriotism has to be tough to thrive, as well as to be caustic about, in Hoggart's own phrase, 'a snobby little island'.

There was a kind of relish for the family in their brief exile. They were insulated by the ocean and by the Americans' happy indifference to Britain and all her works; so much so that when, in November 1956, Anthony Eden launched his crass and doomed attempt to recapture the Suez Canal from the upstart General Nasser, his American colleagues, themselves Anglophiles to a man and woman, jointly shook the Hoggarts into abrupt awareness of just what irreparable harm the country was doing to its moral standing. *The Daily Express* headline on 4 November was as shameful as any the Yellow Press has published in its long and disgraceful rule over the English mind: 'Red Devils Go In. It's Great Britain Again!'

Mostly the Hoggart family, always and still its members' own strongest and much loved moral geography, a redoubt when needed, a harbour always, and with plenty of traffic in and out, mostly the family took America as it came. Doing so, they were able to greet and to share the best of the country, and in a time and place which – in a phrase Hoggart himself always looked out for – brought out the best in both hosts and guests.

This creative capacity to live where they were also kept at a distance the most consequential event of Hoggart's academic life, which was the publication of *The Uses of Literacy*, subtitled with a nod to the conventions in such things, 'Aspects of working-class life with special reference to publications and entertainments', dedicated, with much more than nodding conventionality, to 'Mary, with love'.

II

It came out on 27 February 1957. It was everywhere reviewed. That was less a mark of distinction in 1957 than it would be nowadays; there were many more weeklies, and the broadsheets reviewed more books then than now, and scarcely touched broadcasting except for the BBC's own *The Listener* which had in any case its own ample book review section.

That said, it was an astonishing reception, one that reveals something much bigger-hearted and more benignant about the cultural climate of the day than one would find thirteen years into the new millennium. Perhaps the most handsome as well as the most emblematic welcome came from the Labourist *Daily Herald* which gave the book, as well it might, at the hands of its house correspondent Basil Davidson a whole page on two consecutive days, the second a questionnaire to readers appealing for recognition of the judgements made in the book. Davidson had been a legendary hero of Special Operations Executive, parachuted into the Balkans to work, on the run, with the partisans. He had also been much mixed up with adult education and in South Africa alongside the ANC. There couldn't have been a better voice to welcome a book about the cultural health of the mangy old British lion facing up to the new world with its old weaknesses. Davidson wrote:

> . . . this man Hoggart is not a patronizing do-gooder, and that is why his book is important. Is there so much to choose between the Russian 'Party line' and the Big Brother of mass entertainment?

and in his questionnaire he asked, in capitals, 'Do You Mind and Does It Matter . . . that many children who have passed the 11 plus and gone to Grammar School leave at 15?'

The Daily Telegraph, reviewing on publication day, found inevitably a mournful Tory moral in the book, but it saw its distinction: 'the cultural desert is accurately surveyed and mapped without anger or exaggeration'. Dwight MacDonald, doyen of American Leftists and propagandist for *Scrutiny* in the USA, writing in the June *Encounter*, praised the book's 'eye for detail and ear for the colloquial', said how 'thoughtful, literally full of thought Mr Hoggart's book is', and quoted Hoggart directly in the coda: 'Most mass entertainments are in the end what D. H. Lawrence described as "anti-life". They are full of a corrupt brightness.' Kingsley Amis, not yet a self-parodic right-winger, assimilated Hoggart to Peter Wilmot and Michael Young's classic ethnography, *Family and Kinship in East London*, and praised it accordingly; Tosco Fyvel gave it the Party's salute in the April number of *Socialist Commentary*; the *Manchester Guardian*, speaking from Cross Street on the other side of the Pennines, described the book as 'serious, disturbing and admirably written', as 'moving and thoughtful'; and the professional sociologists called, in the case of Charles Madge,[1] for more data about 'effects' and 'the capacity of the masses for fine living' (which was to ask a lot), and on the part of Mark Abrams, for a reckless curse to be spoken over the whole of the young working-class as being 'cynical, irresponsible, pleasure-loving, self-indulgent', all this, apparently the fault of 'Mum' who was, of course, so much revered in section C of chapter 2 in the book.

Hoggart's mailbox was pretty full as well, one letter coming from the novelist John Braine, whose novel *Room at the Top* had just met with huge sales and which described the desolate success and empty arrival at the top of a working-class Yorkshireman who had spent his years in a German POW camp not digging tunnels under the wire but doggedly passing his exams to qualify as an accountant. Braine wrote in recognition of Hoggart's struggle as being like his own 'not to be too damned literary', and spoke with envy of Saul Bellow's having 'the living speech' of Chicago Jewry to draw on.[2]

Two tributes, at this juncture over fifty-five years later, stand out of this copious sheaf of felicitations. The first is in a letter not written until 1971, when Hoggart was working for UNESCO in Paris and met Claude Lévi-Strauss, with Clifford Geertz the anthropologists' world champions who placed the subject at the pinnacle of the human sciences. Lévi-Strauss's own autobiographical reflection on his science and on himself in *Tristes Tropiques* has much in common

[1] *Glasgow Herald*, 28 February 1957; *Listener*, 18 July 1957.
[2] John Braine, letter dated 4 September 1957, Hoggart papers, 3/11/309.

with Hoggart's preoccupations, even though couched in a much self-stricken and dramatic set of attitudes. Lévi-Strauss wrote, with rare warmth and intimacy, of the book's

> ... vivacité, une pénétration, une sensibilité qui en fait non pas seulement une étude scientifique, mais aussi et en même temps une oeuvre littéraire. Et quelle leçon vous donnez aux ethnologues![3]

The second tribute comes from the then undergraduate magazine at Cambridge, *Granta*[4] (named after a tributary of the river Cam). In it, one Christopher Foster, during a graceful encomium, spotted that Hoggart's crucial value of community was embodied in, first, the family and, second, the neighbourhood, and used this insight as a lever to prise away what were at the time the intellectual student's sacred texts: 'Hoggart's book is worth more than all the social thought of Sartre and Camus and of a thousand Colin Wilsons.' When the book came out in Penguin for four shillings, there were Hoggarts in hand all over Cambridge, in the cafés as well as the libraries, on the river as well as for sale in Downing College, where the Doughty Society, cadre of Leavis's own, invited Hoggart to speak in November of that year.

Leavis had to miss the meeting and wrote with his usual punctiliousness to Hoggart to apologize, and to commend his deputy, Morris Shapira, to do the honours. Shapira, however, was a Leavisite for sure but of that repellent kind which used once to use Leavis's own unconventional judgements to test other people for suitability as allies and recruits, 'fighting the class war in negation' as Raymond Williams once put it. This Shapira was determined to display his feathers before the students and put an uncrossable gap between the Leavises and this person from the world of adult education with his Yorkshire accent and his criticism of Queenie. So, smirking more than a little, and oscillating his head with nervous self-satisfaction, he asked 'Mr Hoggart, might you be described as the intellectual man's J. B. Priestley?' He couldn't however faze Hoggart, who replied equably that he admired Priestley's *English Journey* but had the quite different purpose of revaluing the quality of life in a social class and a particular area. It was a courteous deflection; Shapira prowled away.

By the end of 1957 Hoggart's old friend from the days of Army Education, Bill (later Sir William Emrys) Williams, had made a deal with Chatto, strongly approved by Allen Lane, for publication in

---

[3] Lévi-Strauss to RH, 28 November 1971. Hoggart papers, 3/11/349.
[4] *Granta*, March 1957.

Penguin. The hardback cost twenty-five shillings, quite a stiff sum; the paperback four bob. The hardback sold a most respectable 8,000 in its first year; the Penguin sold 33,000 in its first six months, and 20,000 every year from 1960 to 1970, keeping up a steady six or seven thousand for several years thereafter, being sampled in innumerable anthologies and textbooks, and appearing in a dozen translations as well as an American edition.[5]

What the publishers expected to be a 'steady back seller' turned out to be, for the form in which it was written, a smash hit, and within a few months was granted canonical status, at once a *succès d'estime* and a scandal. The same questions insistently pose themselves once more. What sort of thing, after all, was it? Was it sociology? No, not enough numbers. Was it autobiography? No, too much generalization. If it was about working-class history where were the unions, the blackened faces and hobnailed boots; where was the General Strike? Was it literary criticism? Well, perhaps, but then who on earth would write criticism of sex-and-violence thrillers or agony columns?

Like all great works, *The Uses of Literacy* created for itself a quite new form. Hoggart had found the historical theory latent in the teaching of English literature he studied at university at once compellingly confident, and wrong. It taught that the self-explanatory decorum and sacred rhythms of an agrarian culture were gone, and that mass commercial and subhuman forms of popular art had replaced them.

It was and is a powerful story; single-handedly, Hoggart rebutted it. He brought F. R. Leavis's practical criticism to bear on the moralizing saws and dicta of his class ('landscape with figures'), on the great but living archetype of the working-class mother, on the goodness of 'a good table', its 'tasty' black puddings and tinned salmon, on the great swell of feeling accompanying the songs at the club, on 'the close-ribbed streets' (in Larkin's irresistible words already intoned) 'like a great sigh out of the last century'. There he found not a lost proletariat but a mighty continuity, a strong, living and active culture, carried as I said before by the old big words, for sure – solidarity, neighbourliness, community – but also by its jokes, its tiny gestures, its biking excursions and seaside outings, its downright bloodymindedness before the facts of social life.

But things are going wrong. 'Unbending the springs of action' tells us of the softening of old resilience and uncovers on the page a new

---

[5] There have been several since, one published with a postscript by John Corner, by Transaction Publishers (2000) and a new Penguin edition in 2009 with a very good introduction by Lynsey Hanley.

literacy of reflex cynicism. Hoggart, as I have already said but it bears saying again, took a grim but minutely careful rollcall of an imaginative class life nourished by a corrupt and phoney matiness in its daily and weekly papers, and distracted from boredom by the deathly fictions of brutal punchups and panting, pointless sexual sadism.

Accused of indiscipline, the book created a new discipline of itself. Cultural studies would spring autochthonously alive at Birmingham. Worldwide it became over the decades a new sort of multicultural and industrial anthropology. The subject is nowadays liable to local doses of moral hypochondria, sanctimony and dreadful prose at times, but it keeps alive Hoggart's originary vision of the evaluation of ordinary life, the cherishing and the sharp criticism of, in the master's later title, 'the way we live now'. When this now almost sixty years old and international confederation falters, it needs only to go back to its founding father. Hoggart teaches by example how to shape and hold the defining practice of the human sciences and, when it is rightly done, its high and wide epiphany. In his great book, we see and feel how judicious objectivity and loving kindness become synonyms, and feel directly how keen moral sympathy dissolves into historical understanding.

This is the expansion of the mind and spirit sought by all practitioners of the human sciences: the melting of compassionate inquiry into true judgement, the discovery in human endeavour of the best that is in it and the accurate naming of things ill done and done to others' harm.

Hoggart's name, now made, was always to be attached to that single work. There is a justice in this, for in all the later books, and in the public life which was the ground of their existence and is inextricable in its meaning from his everyday conduct *and* what he wrote, the unity of vision in *The Uses of Literacy* gathers together a divided people. Hoggart's sure grasp of autobiography as not merely belonging to the individual concerned, the way one family's life opens out into a moral community, and how a little local neighbourhood stands for and against a nation, connect book and author to comparable great achievements in such monuments of art as Wordsworth's *Prelude*, George Eliot's *Middlemarch*, Ruskin's *Unto This Last*, Vera Brittain's *Testament of Youth*.

It is worth adding, in the name of building moral communities capable of giving the shape of lives and human effort a public meaning, that in the years which saw *The Uses of Literacy* come to fruition, there were a number of other writers working within the same structures of feeling and of 'practical rationality'.

129

The phrase belongs to Alisdair MacIntyre. He is the moral philoso-pher whose ambition was and is to oppose the thinness and myopia of liberal ethics with something somehow combining the solidarities of socialism and the practicalities of the rural life of smallholding Scotland in which he was raised by his devoutly Christian parents, both local doctors. MacIntyre, twelve years younger than Hoggart, wrote to him in 1987 to say, *a propos* of his own classic *After Virtue*, 'This moral sense of community was awakened in me by you in your *Uses of Literacy*, three decades ago in a steel works.'[6]

At the time to which he refers MacIntyre was working under Tom Hollins at the University of Leeds Extra-Mural Department. In the same department were Roy Shaw, later one of Hoggart's closest friends, and Edward Thompson, then only thirty-three and deliberating his mighty study, *The Making of the English Working Class*, which came out in 1963 to acclaim and contention as noisy as greeted *The Uses of Literacy*, and which represented a quite new kind of political history – the coming-to-consciousness of itself, by way of chapel homilies, strikes and street resistance, dreadful oppres-sion, secret trade unions, daring and illicit publications, of the new industrial working class. The lessons for the students of adult educa-tion were plain: it was *their own* social history which Thompson had collected from them, and recounted on their behalf.

At the same time, in the extra-mural department in Oxford but based in Hastings, another ex-captain of tanks, Raymond Williams, was turning *his* teaching of evening classes into another revision-ist work, in which the great critical tradition of English social and literary commentary was arraigned for its unacknowledged class bias and historical distortions, and then, by way of William Morris, D. H. Lawrence and R. H. Tawney, given a new and radical edge with which to cut open the tough old conservatism of Britain in 1958. Williams's *Culture and Society*, and his optimistic *Long Revolution* which followed three years later, marched to the same music as Thompson and Hoggart.

In the summer of 1959, Hoggart and Williams were recorded discussing their work together, and Williams said, 'Though we were often writing about the same things, we hadn't each other's books to refer to.' Hoggart replied,

> I had begun in 1952 too, by writing one chapter which doesn't appear. I was thinking then of something quite simple in scope and size – a

---

[6] Alisdair MacIntyre, *After Virtue: A Study in Moral Theory*, London: Duckworth, 1981. He was referring in particular to pp. 220ff.

series of critical essays on popular literature. Soon I began to feel that I wanted to relate this material to the day-to-day experience of people. After this, a strange thing happened ... things I'd been writing since 1946 (bits of a novel and some unconnected descriptive pieces) began to fall into place in the new book.

RW: It's interesting, the way the books were built. I can remember my own first impulse, back at the end of the 'forties. I felt very isolated, except for my family and my immediate work. The Labour Government had gone deeply wrong, and the other tradition that mattered, the cultural criticism of our kind of society, had moved, with Eliot, right away from anything I could feel. It seemed to me I had to try to go back over the tradition, to look at it again and get it into relation with my own experience, to see the way the intellectual tradition stood in the pattern of my own growing-up.[7]

The two men were at one in matching a formal curriculum for their students to their own feeling for their history. It is the way T. S. Eliot tells us that 'tradition and the individual talent' meet and tussle,

... and the poet cannot reach this impersonality without surrendering himself wholly to the work to be done. And he is not likely to know what is to be done unless he lives in what is not merely the present, but the present moment of the past.[8]

The same truths stood for Hoggart and Williams, maybe stand as truths about life for any serious person, certainly as true about the life of Richard Hoggart, but about the lives also of a number of men and women at that time who had been stirred by a common purpose, touched by a common genius, shaped by world war, resolved to make a better country than they came back to, and by and large finding the rhetoric of a herbivorous socialism useful for the task. There are many names I haven't mentioned in this tradition[9] – Thomas Hodgkin, Secretary to the Oxford Delegacy, Asa Briggs, another social historian and later first Vice-Chancellor of the University of Sussex, Roy Shaw eventually and rightly ending his career as head of the Arts Council, that most handsome embodiment of wartime optimism about a nation's self-education, and David Holbrook at the Cambridge department, third ex-tank troop commander, who boldly

[7] Conversation published in *New Left Review*, 7 January 1960, reprinted in *Border Country: Raymond Williams in Adult Education*, ed. John McIlroy and Sallie Westwood, Leicester: National Institute of Adult Education, 1993, pp. 111–20.
[8] T. S. Eliot, *The Sacred Wood* (1920), London: Methuen, reissued 1960, p. 59.
[9] I am drawing here on a similar brief history I wrote in *Raymond Williams: The Life*, London: Routledge, 1995.

turned these new ways of seeing to inspiring use with forgotten poor children in secondary modern schools.

It was more than coincidence which led these figures to their positions as leaders and writers for a new generation of teachers and students. It is always an elusive thing to be trying to catch, this 'common genius', but the most thrilling thing in the world to find in historical action.

III

The first explosion of interest in *The Uses of Literacy* and the excitements that went with it were, as I said, muffled by distance, and in any case hard to feel without being able to read the reviews as they came out. Certainly the pleasure the family took in a telegram from brother Tom announcing the birth of his baby son was as great as the news winging its way across 3,000 miles about the success of the book, still confined to the hardback, and in any case hardly read in the States for a long time.

So they finished their year in a big old American banger, driving those vast American distances from New York State to Virginia and then back to the long quays of Manhattan, homeward bound on the SS *Empress of Britain*.

In his absence, Richard Hoggart had become a name to conjure with. Always detached and modest about his achievements, he was sure he could get the job he and Mary knew would now suit them best after ten years on long and dark roads four times a week to evening classes. Departments, whole universities, were much smaller and jobs in any case fewer in 1958; he applied for a vacancy at the University of Leicester, another of those middle-ranking Midland academies, built on the foundations of local industry rather later than Leeds, but in a gentle landscape unblackened by smoke and just emerging by the usual progression – from a college under tutelage from London to University College, to (in 1957) university in its own right.

The head of English at Leicester was one Arthur Humphreys, who became – in a long line of such friends – one of Hoggart's closest, one of those of whom Hoggart would often quote, as a kind of prayer of thanksgiving, Yeats's wonderful couplet,

> Think where man's glory most begins and ends,
> And say my glory was, I had such friends.

But Hoggart's first application to Leicester failed. It was hard at that time to climb the symbolic walls which separated intra- from extra-mural staff – it's sometimes hard to recollect just how hide-and-classbound British society was in 1958 – hard, that is, until one recalls with a shock the return to government of the Old Etonians in the general election of 2010.

Humphreys was, however, wholly uncontaminated by the filth of old snobbery. For the first appointment he had given the post to a poet, George Fraser, then three years older than Hoggart, wartime warrant officer and a veteran of British Council appointments in the Far East as well as of the boozy literary pubs in the aesthetes' village of London's Fitzrovia hard beside the LSE, where Fraser drank as heavily as the great William Empson, and wrote him a poem for his fiftieth birthday, what's more.[10]

Fraser wasn't an obviously safe bet for appointment as a literary scholar, but Humphreys was happy to settle for the author of these lines – a man, moreover, with a deadly accurate eye for academic windbags and for clever colleagues with underhand or scurrilous habits of debate:

Summer, at evening, on her basket chair,
A blowsy frump, her glass of beer before her.
Can change her frock, put scent upon her hair,
And in the cool night we again adore her . . .

Hoggart was already senior lecturer and obviously could only afford to apply for an equivalent post. Dramatically, a sudden death in Humphreys' department left a similar vacancy a year later. Hoggart was appointed. Fraser and Humphreys had strolled Victoria Park beside the university – they had become fast friends because, unalike as they were, they shared the same quick, accurate gift for spotting cant and insincerity, the same warmth and sensitivity to straightness and integrity even when concealed by diffidence, in others. The new appointment would have to act as Head of Department the following term when Humphreys was to be a Visiting Fellow at the Folger Library in Washington. Could somebody new to administrative life inside the walls do the job? Fraser agreed that Hoggart was the most interesting candidate. At the interview, somebody was ill-advised enough to raise doubts with Hoggart himself about the scholarly standing of his extra-mural syllabuses. Hoggart dispatched him; he got the job.

Fraser and Humphreys became his cherished friends though Fraser

[10] Published in the *New Statesman* and cited by John Haffenden in vol. II of his biography, *William Empson*, Oxford: Oxford University Press, 2006, pp. 397–8.

was watchful at first, wary in case Hoggart's sudden fame and recognition in public life disqualified him from admission to Fraser's gregarious heart. A public grandee, the Countess of Albemarle, had already invited Hoggart onto her Royal Commission inquiring into the Youth Service. She had read *The Uses of Literacy* and responded to its plain sympathy with and criticism of the lives of the young urban poor, their dismal leisure and their helpless availability to the sharks of commercial culture. Bill Haley had barely begun to rock around the clock and teenage pay packets left scarcely anything over for what, ten years later, would be to all appearances the very brave new world of pop.

Royal Commissions are almost forgotten nowadays, more's the pity. Their work is now done by public policy institutes and, as they say, thinktanks. But once upon a time governments took advice and appointed a committee of worthy, even distinguished and original souls, to advise it from weighty enough experience and soundish judgement what to do not for the sake of ideological zeal or partisan advantage, but for the common wealth and the prospects of a good society.

Hoggart's membership of the Albemarle Committee, which reported in 1960, was an unusual qualification in a forty-one-year-old, and Fraser narrowed his eyes at it. In an obituary address for him, Hoggart wrote:[11]

> If he detected you in even a marginal dishonesty of the imagination, he would give a wicked little laugh and produce some phrase which cut you right down.

But Fraser couldn't take coarse attack and Hoggart, tougher than his friend, had more than once to repair brutal damage done by some academic thug to that always shaky self-esteem of Fraser's, which was the unexpected verso of his boisterous drinking parties. In one typical act of toleration, he phoned Fraser about some student interviews which had been arranged. 'Yes', Fraser said, he was looking forward to them. 'They were yesterday, George', said Hoggart.

Arthur Humphreys was the moral centre of the department, and his calm authority stemmed from his unimpeachable probity. He is hard to overpraise were it not that such a description might make him sound of improbable saintliness. Well, he *was* saintly; he overworked on behalf of his department, ten hours a day all week, taking on a teaching load as heavy as any colleague's, taking on also

---

[11] January 1980. Hoggart papers, 4/2/38.

a heavier-than-usual administrative and committee burden and doing
so out of a conviction that the blessed republic of letters should be
self-governing, and that professional administrators left to themselves
will lead intellectual life into the dreadful quagmires of managerial
and corporate stagnation. He was prescient in this as in much else.
For that is what has happened, and for a season the managers have
occupied the university, and rotted its purposes.

Humphreys' most famous book, *The Augustan World*,[12] is of a precious kind not much written now. Once it would have been dubbed
'a background book', a sort of set of theatre flats against which the
great *littérateurs* – Johnson, Pope, Garrick, Hume – play out their
parts on stage. But it provides much more than background. It is
more like an example of what is now called 'Cambridge historicism'.
This is a term applied to a newish tradition in the history of ideas,
whereby the canonical texts are set deep in the contexts which gave
them life, and the thinkers' thoughts are explained in terms of their
deliberate responses to the urgent questions of political life around
them. According to this array of interpretative methods, writers mean
what they say; artistry is purposive and persuasive. Humphreys'
splendid book is like that, and it was a consequence of the simple and
self-dedication which he brought to being in charge of his department
that he didn't publish much more.

He died of cancer in August 1988, aged seventy-seven. When
Hoggart visited him for the last time he made his farewells and,
leaning forward to the weak and seated invalid, kissed his forehead.
When, in March 1992, he sent Humphreys' widow Jean a copy
of the third volume of his autobiography recounting the years in
Leicester – 'easily the happiest place I've ever worked in,' as Hoggart
said, typically and publicly, when given an honorary doctorate – Jean
Humphreys wrote back with this noble candour:

> Volume three arrived this morning and I have spent this morning crying
> like a child . . . he had such love and respect for you and you never let
> him down.

In his obituary for Humphreys, published in the *Guardian*,[13] Hoggart
wrote of his friend's 'equable, charitable, fair-minded and generous
spirit', of 'his moral authority with no sense of self-importance', of
'his splendid and shining company'. Is it now the case that universities
conduce far less to the display of such qualities? that scholarship has

---

[12] Arthur Humphreys, *The Augustan World*, London: Chatto and Windus, 1954.
[13] *Guardian*, 12 August 1988.

The Hoggarts on holiday in France 1959.

become instrumental, and the common pursuit of true judgement has been poisoned by the fatuities of competition?

Hoggart arrived in Leicester in autumn 1959 but fame was hunting him down. The sheer readability of his great book meant that his was suddenly a recognizable name in circles of the powerful not well known for their use of literacy. So it was that he was invited to join a new and much more prominent Royal Commission. He got good references from the Countess Albemarle, he had published a much-noted essay in the house journal of the intelligentsia, *Encounter*, entitled 'the uses of television', he was a novel figure in the schedules of public duties. So he seemed a natural for membership of the Committee on Broadcasting, to be assigned to the marginal sections of the report which would deal with such highminded irrelevance as public responsibilities, and television's nod towards standards of criticism and creation.

No sooner had Hoggart, with his amazing givingness of self, accepted this public duty than he joined the exacting labours of evidence-collation, witness-questioning, collective mind-making, which took, the Report tells us,[14] 78 whole-day meetings, 43 sub-

---

[14] *Report of the Committee on Broadcasting*, London: HMSO, 1962, pp. 3–4.

committee meetings, a couple of dozen excursions to visit various television company headquarters including, of course and several times, Broadcasting House, receiving testimony from a total of over 450 interested and garrulous parties.[15]

He had barely started when Allen Lane got in touch as, after the huge success of *The Uses of Literacy*, he not infrequently did. Hoggart, he could see, knew things about the temper of society, its quarrels with itself, its sudden forays of imagination and interest, which he himself didn't but which mattered to Penguin, not so much for its greater profit than for its services to the public mind. This time, however, though all these things were at stake, the meaning of his question was wide open. He asked Hoggart if he would be one of the 'literary experts' to be called in the legal dispute of Regina against Penguin Books, in the case of the publication of D. H. Lawrence's famous, infamous novel, *Lady Chatterley's Lover*.

It's now well over fifty years since the trial and it retains its strong hold on the collective social memory. It was only the day before yesterday, in 2006, that the BBC broadcast at peak time the excellent Andrew Davies's new dramatization of the trial, of which there had already been several, for radio, TV and live theatre, thereby buffing up the mythic occasion in national recollection. Sex being at the living heart of the matter and honest speaking about the importance of sex in everyone's life being rare in a court of law, it's no surprise just how glowing a force the whole story retains.[16] The glow is however all the brighter and the deeper for the explicit clash of class and culture which gave it such a dramatic simplicity.

The legal framework was this: Allen Lane had been publishing the full run of D. H. Lawrence's novels; he now braved the publication of *Lady Chatterley's Lover*, officially banned by law as an obscene publication. In the past, James Joyce's great classic, *Ulysses*, had only dodged its way into an unbowdlerized edition by various such tricky manoeuvres as Parisian publication. *Ulysses* was prosecuted by the New York Society for the Suppression of Vice and, after many delays in Britain as assorted public figures snorted with outrage, was finally brought out by Allen Lane himself, no less, then of Bodley Head, in 1936, for the stiff price of three guineas.[17] At the same time,

---

[15] *Report*, Appendix B, pp. 299–330.

[16] The account is taken largely from C. H. Rolph, ed., *The Trial of Lady Chatterley*, Harmondsworth: Penguin, 1961.

[17] Gordon Bowker, *James Joyce: A Biography*, London: Weidenfeld and Nicolson, 2011, pp. 243 and 274, and *passim*.

however, Radcliffe Hall's novel about a lesbian love affair, *The Well of Loneliness*, was banned by law.

There used to be an advertising slogan for *The Daily Telegraph* which ran, 'Times change, values don't.' But the end of an era is marked precisely by changes in values, which are in turn registered by changes in language. In 1959, Roy Jenkins, then Shadow Home Secretary for the Labour Party, saw through Parliament his Private Member's Bill, the Obscene Publications Act. This made it possible for literary and artistic merit to be evaluated in defence of a work of literature formerly arraigned strictly on grounds of obscenity, about which there could not, it seemed, be any doubt. After the new law was passed, a 'tendency to deprave and corrupt' might be mitigated by 'literary merit' and the legislation made it possible for expert witnesses to be called to testify in defence of the work in question.

Allen Lane, from much more than profit-making motives, set himself and Penguin Books to complete the D. H. Lawrence list. Lawrence's reputation, always publicly controversial during his lifetime, had by 1960 been much revalued and his achievement understood as matching the best that had been known and thought and written by George Eliot and Charles Dickens. Much of this change had been wrought by a series of highly influential essays by F. R. Leavis, from which this judgement about *Chatterley* was a key formulation:

> What may be called the hygienic undertaking to which it is devoted commands one's sympathy – the undertaking to cleanse the obscene words and to redeem from the smirch of obscenity the corresponding physical facts. But the willed insistence on the words and the facts must, it seems to me, whatever the intention, have something unacceptable, something offensive about it; it offends, surely, against Lawrence's own canons – against the spirit of his creativity and against the moral and emotional ethic he in essence stands for. He felt that here there was something so urgent to be done that it *must* be done, whatever the cost. But that there *is* a cost – that, I think, needs to be said.[18]

It was Leavis also, writing at about the same time as Hoggart was grappling with such intractable stuff, who found in the life of the characters in *The Rainbow* all that local tradition and the language which shaped it conduced towards by way of 'the finer contemporary human consciousness'. Leavis was more highly wrought in such expressions than ever Hoggart was; Hoggart, in *Uses of Literacy*, went straight to the living force felt in touch, taste, lovingness,

---

[18] F. R. Leavis, *D. H. Lawrence: Novelist*, London: Chatto and Windus, 1955, p. 70.

and the edge of misery. But Hoggart wrote to Leavis during their correspondence about the book on Auden,

> I'd like to take this opportunity of saying in complete sincerity that I have learned more from you and from *Scrutiny* – far more – than from anyone else.[19]

Leavis spoke at several points in his study of Lawrence's 'reverence for life' – his praise is shot through with religious vocabulary – and quotes his subject's wonderful remark made in a letter, 'I labour always at the same thing, to make the sex relation valid and precious instead of shameful.'[20] Leavis also, in redress of those capering about at Lawrence's licentiousness, concupiscence and so forth drew attention to something admirable, something indeed puritanical in Lawrence's ethics, by which he meant a severe sense of active responsibility in all one's moral choices. (For the Puritan there is no such thing as a non-moral choice.) The two words – 'reverence' and 'puritan' – would resound in the court room.

Everyone remembers the courtroom drama: the Crown's Attorney General, Mervyn Griffith-Jones, egregious, condescending, incredulous that his coarse commonsensible sexism did not carry the day *as* commonsense; Penguin's counsel, Gerald Gardiner, handsome, clever, upright, later Labour's Attorney General; Judge Byrne, dry, creaking, openly prejudiced against Penguin; and, amid the respectable medley of middle-aged, middle-class, autumnally dressed and palefaced literary experts, the greatest living novelist, Edward Morgan Foster, as well as an unknown lecturer in English in a tweed jacket from some provincial university.

No one can resist quoting the wretched Griffith-Jones's rhetorical question put to the jury early in the trial; certainly not me.

> Ask yourselves the question, would you approve your young sons, and young daughters – because girls can read as well as boys – reading this book? Is it a book you would want to have lying around the house? Is it a book you would want your wife or your servants to read?[21]

It's rare for one's own self-righteousness to be so handsomely vindicated by the ruling class.

The courtroom drama was dramatic indeed. Seriously commonsensible ladies from the Oxford and Cambridge English departments – Helen, later Dame Gardner, Joan Bennett, tough scholar of

[19] 4 May 1953, Hoggart papers.
[20] Letter to Miss Pearn, *Selected Letters*, New York: Anchor Books, p. 285.
[21] Rolph (1961).

seventeenth-century poetry – bore their careful witness to Lawrence's seriousness of purpose as well as to the lyrical exaltation with which he wrote about sex. The most famous such teacher was of course Leavis, and in his full-length study of Lawrence he had, as we heard, acknowledged the moral and artistic costs of Lawrence's willed explicitness.

Those scruples kept Leavis from the witness box as well as, surely, his instinctive rejection of *anything* which he took, wrongly in this case, to be a show of *bien-pensant* liberalism. Straightly and finely as he spoke in his book, in company he simply could not join the crowd. His personal intransigence, his recoil from anything he considered 'herd-feeling', mattered more than justice to his very own literary subject. (For what it's worth, I don't myself believe that Leavis thought out at all the legal issues at stake.)

It didn't matter. For one thing, the jury had all read the novel in a special retiring room and it was Hoggart's own conviction that the book's artistic power had done its work for most of them at once. Griffith-Jones made much of what he called 'the bouts' of love-making, but his locker-room coarseness and courtroom habits of bullying could not annul the lyrical tenderness, let alone the unrivalled splendour of passages such as these:

> And it seemed she was like the sea, nothing but dark waves rising and heaving, heaving with a great swell, so that slowly her whole darkness was in motion, and she was ocean rolling its dark, dumb mass. Oh, and far down inside her the deeps parted and rolled asunder, in long, far-travelling billows, and ever, at the quick of her, the depths parted and rolled asunder, from the centre of soft plunging, as the plunger went deeper and deeper, touching lower, and she was deeper and deeper and deeper disclosed, the heavier the billows of her rolled away to some shore, uncovering her, and closer and closer plunged the palpable unknown, and further and further rolled the waves of herself away from herself, leaving her, till suddenly, in a soft, shuddering convulsion, the quick of all her plasm was touched, she knew herself touched, the consummation was upon her, and she was gone.[22]

In Andrew Davies's admirable dramatization of the trial he very properly follows C. H. Rolph's account and gives a voice to those jurors who were indeed scandalized by the book, but he also brings out plainly that these were a minority, that the case was most probably won and lost before it was fought out, that in particular the

---

[22] D. H. Lawrence, *Lady Chatterley's Lover* (1928), Harmondsworth: Penguin, 1960, p. 181.

prosecution's oafish and arrogant presumption – let alone the Judge's own *parti pris* – did everything to clinch things.

But legal trials may not be foreshortened; all five acts must be played out. Happily for drama, Hoggart was called late on the second day. He was asked, with portentous irony, whether Lawrence could be said, as earlier witnesses had claimed, to be on the side of 'virtuous behaviour' (in this case, virtue and vice were simply counterposed by the prosecution as meaning inexplicit sex within marriage and explicit sex outside it). Hoggart replied that Lawrence's concerns were virtuous, even 'puritanical'. The Judge penned, with elaborately raised eyebrows, a note of this word, and the prosecuting counsel girded himself up for a fine legal frenzy the next morning.

When he did, he was met by Hoggart's unafraid and composed intelligence. Asked to justify 'puritanical', Hoggart set out plainly the historical tradition which culminated in Lawrence's view of sexual morality as truthful feeling, sexual desire as precious and tender, love itself as a sacred giving of oneself to another person. All this was spoken with Hoggart's characteristic directness and unassuming self-confidence. Griffith-Jones was so rattled he made the bad mistake of telling Hoggart off for 'lecturing the court. We are not in the lecture hall at – ha – *Leicester* University here.' A little later, E. M. Forster, now seventy-one, Lawrence's coeval and acquaintance, was called, and the defence asked him about the use of the word 'puritanical'. Forster said judiciously, 'I think the description is a correct one, though I understand people might think it paradoxical.' By then, Hoggart was the front page figure who said in court, 'The fact is this: one fucks', and who quietly replied to Griffith-Jones when asked incredulously by him whether a lover might show 'reverence to a man's balls', 'Yes indeed'. *Private Eye*, to its great discredit, dubbed Hoggart 'Hogballs', but other journals dealt better with the witness, best of all in the case of Bernard Levin, whose natural effusiveness led him to say:[23]

> Mr Hoggart, patient, clear, brilliantly analytical, transparently honest and honourable, devoted, passionate for truth and learning, he made me reflect that the students at Leicester are fortunate indeed.

Wayland Young, a *Manchester Guardian* columnist, also a peer of the realm who forswore his title, was probably the most accurate in saying that Griffith-Jones was 'obliterated by the fire of Lawrence's writing . . . and the single cautery of clean English prose'.[24]

[23] In the *Spectator*, 4 November 1960.
[24] *Manchester Guardian*, 4 November 1960.

The following month, E. M. Forster himself wrote to Hoggart, suggesting he consider applying for a three-year Fellowship at King's, and saying of the trial,[25]

> The victory gained ... seems to be due mainly to you, anyhow it was for you to bear the full insolence of the prosecuting counsel, whom it is difficult to believe not to be a cad, privily as well as publicly.

There was a curious little after-eddy to the case when John Sparrow, Warden of All Souls College, Oxford, no less, and a clever, self-preening Mephistopheles of literary London, wrote an article for *Encounter*, proud organ of Anglo-American political-cultural piety, that not only had 'the defence reeked of humbug', but that the novel was in any case 'extremely distasteful' and 'a failure as a work of art'.[26] Sparrow then, assuming his favourite role of candidly unshockable shocker of the rightminded (though plainly shocked himself), went on to prove to his great satisfaction that Oliver Mellors had perpetrated anal sex with Connie Chatterley but that no one dared say so. Finally, delighted with his *succès de scandale* and man enough to recognize Hoggart's independent manliness, he invited the hero of the hour to All Souls to give the Churchill Lecture in 1961.

The morning after the jury's verdict, the queue outside Bumpus' big bookstore stretched far down Baker Street. When the doors opened, customers were met by a great pile of copies of the novel in Penguin's orange-and-white uniform, Lawrence's phoenix in the centre of the cover. Few people spoke. There was no need to ask for a copy. They handed over their three shillings and sixpence and by the end of the week the first print run of 200,000 was sold out.

The whole event wasn't really a liberation of literature; rather, it released for publication a torrent of pornographic sewage unendangered by the law. What was achieved, however, was the public acknowledgement of the greatness of D. H. Lawrence's art, uncontaminated by any slur or snigger. Something nasty in the culture was flushed away, and a surge of sexual emancipation was, for better and worse, inaugurated.

There is an entertaining footnote to add to the long mythology of the trial. When Andrew Davies' TV dramatization was cast, the great Shakespearean actor, David Tennant, got the part of Hoggart. He came to talk to the family who were delighted by the selection but expostulated plaintively that their father would never have dreamed

---

25 Hoggart papers, 4/3/25.
26 *Encounter*, February 1961.

of wearing the sideburns sported by the actor. 'I am so sorry,' he said, 'but I am playing Dr Who the next day, so they'll have to stay.'

IV

Hoggart's was now a national name and, new at Leicester while at the same time taking over as Head of Department for a few months while Arthur Humphreys was at the Folger, he became invisibly a forceful presence on the Committee on Broadcasting whose membership was announced in September 1960. Hoggart's name had probably been proposed by Edward Boyle, a highly literate and egalitarian Tory then parliamentary secretary to the minister. The Chair of the committee was Sir Harry Pilkington, chairman of his family's huge glassmaking company in Lancashire, toweringly tall, formidably authoritative, honestly public-spirited.

Peter Hall, already a sovereign figure in theatre direction, only lasted four months' membership. But one member must be done honour, and that was Joyce Grenfell, a well-known, well-loved comedienne on TV and in music hall, always self-deprecating ('I never went to university') but determined to grasp complex arguments – about access, effects, about the uneven democracy of culture – and to envision what was best for a nation in the way it spoke to itself about itself. Her stage persona was not so very far from her own self: cut-glass English accent, deadly accurate about class pretension and arrogance, tender to the weak, tough with the bland buccaneers of the airwaves. As you'd expect, she and Hoggart, and Mary, became fast friends and allies.

In his article about television for *Encounter*[27] in that year, Hoggart had praised, as one always must, the wonderful scope and variety which television makes possible as well as noting the utter bafflingness of the puzzles set to broadcasters by the massive irregularities of audience response, to content, to tone, to intellectual demand, to what is known and trusted, to what is known and mistrusted. He sees early, and regrets, 'a decline . . . in the importance of local, face-to-face communities as educators in manners', he sees the non-moral innocence – 'a world prior to the knowledge of good and evil' – of the imaginative society of advertisements and, giving credit to his country for its 'leathery . . . caution, its patience, phlegm and good intentions',

---

[27] Vol. XIV, 1 January 1960, reprinted in Richard Hoggart, *Speaking to Each Other*, vol. I, London: Chatto and Windus, 1970, pp. 152–62.

nonetheless sounds a warning bell about 'some people with commercial reasons for wanting a very large and very quiet audience'.

Nowadays the audience is kept in thrall, among other devices, by having held out to it the promise of one day appearing on the screen itself – as applauding audience, as quiz show member, as unreal citizen of television's reality. In 1960, with only two channels and another impending, both hellhounds and seraphs lived in a much smaller box.

The Pilkington report owed plenty to its calm, commanding chairman, who held his members in a circle of argumentative consent. It owed much to the civil servant who wrote much of the final version. Dennis Lawrence, London working-class-and-grammar-school, was keenly awake to the public importance of the report and his duty towards it. For it is a classic in the genre, although published at a time when many fine, even noble reports emerged under such notable names as John Newsom, Lionel Robbins, Lady Plowden, each preparing the political ground for the true benefit of all, fifteen-year-olds, university students, six-year-olds. For it is safe to say, in the days before the abrupt politicization of absolutely everything which so changed the temper of the country after, say, 1983, that governments of either blue or red saw their responsibility as being to the nation as a whole, and their duties as defined by the common good of peaceability and safety in work and at home. Beyond the frontier the Cold War froze history in its tracks, the empire slowly peeled away, but at home what counted was domestic benefit and steady employment.

Pilkington was of a piece with this climate. Much was lent it by the chairman's authority, much more by the civil servant's intelligent seriousness, by Joyce Grenfell's stamina and natural goodness, by Robert Smith-Rose's command of technological matters, bang up-to-date, and by Hoggart's unshakable resolution that democracy be served at the same time as its moral standards, without which democracy is mob rule, be given strength and youthfulness.

Naming these qualities well into the twenty-first century tolls a solemn bell. For much has been lost in sane public debate, much more from the manners, the content, the very respectability of television. 'Respectability', that is to say, as denoting worthiness of respect, respect for the enormous force of the medium and for the multitudinous variety of its audiences. There is still respectable work presented on the dozens of channels, and the BBC no doubt still merits the respect as well as the affection accorded to it, in spite of the shameful abuse so long poured over it by the now shamed empire of News International. But to turn away from the unspeakable Babestation or

144

the fatuities of QI and the adolescent dreariness of the Dave channel, and to go back to Pilkington's discussion of 'triviality' in chapter V of the report is like leaving a smelly, raucous playground for a fresh spring morning.

Dennis Lawrence, with Hoggart's counsel, wrote the exemplary chapter III, 'the purposes of broadcasting', and broadcasting must include radio as well as television. The report set out the essential certainties of a broadcaster's world: that

> ... the presumption must be that television is and will be a main factor in influencing the values and moral standards of our society ... by its nature broadcasting must be in constant and sensitive relationship with the moral conditions of society.

The report met squarely the slack-jawed justification much voiced then by the beknighted barons of commercial television and still the cliché reached for by their sons and daughters that 'they were giving the public what it wants'.

'No one can say', the report went on, 'he is giving the public what it wants, unless the public knows the whole range of possibilities which television can offer and, from this range, chooses what it wants to see.'[28] The vital point was made that an unexpected surge in the popularity of symphony concerts, of competitive swimming, of programmes about classical literature all betokened lively interest and response where none might have been predicted. The resonant, relevant judgement had been made to the committee by the testimony of no less than T. S. Eliot, author it should be remembered of *Notes Towards the Definition of Culture*, who bore his witness as President of the Third Programme Defence Society in a pale grey summer suit and carrying a Panama. Eliot said – the dictum should be added to the façade of Broadcasting House – 'Those who say they give the public what it wants begin by underestimating public taste; they end by debauching it.'[29]

Hoggart himself wrote chapter V. Paragraphs 97 to 102 are headed 'triviality'. It was preceded by this ringing declaration:

> Broadcasters ... must accept as part of their responsibility a constant and living relationship with the moral condition of society. Emphatically, this is not to say that where there is virtue, there can be no cakes and ale; that gloom is good and gaiety godless; that there

[28] *Committee on Broadcasting* (1962), pp. 15, 17.
[29] Ibid., p. 17. The reporter weakened the remark by replacing the semi-colon with a comma.

can be no pleasure on Sundays. Nor is it to say that the sordid and harsh truth must not be shown. For television's picture of the world must be realistic, and people can come to suffer as much harm from being led to believe that there is no evil in the world, as from seeing it over-emphasized.[30]

Time and manner are unmistakable. No contemporary report – one might think here of the 2010 Browne report on universities – would dare speak like this. Low populism would do it down. What would it make of this?

> The criticism of triviality as we have described it was that trivial programming was a waste of the medium, and represented a failure to realize its potentialities. But the sin was not merely one of omission; too often, because it had positive results, it was also a sin of commission. Thus subjects billed as controversial sometimes avoided the controversy, and so served rather to reinforce than to disturb prejudice and complacency. Programmes which exemplified emotional tawdriness and mental timidity helped to cheapen both emotional and intellectual values. Plays or serials might not deal with real human problems, but present a candy-floss world.[31]

Hoggart closed the section with a favourite quotation of his from R. H. Tawney, another public moralist of great force and humility: 'Triviality is more dangerous to the soul than wickedness.'[32]

The committee recommended that selling advertising should be done by a separate arm of the Independent Television Authority, who would then commission programme companies to make their own programmes. It recommended against pay-TV because, in the days before fibre optics, the distribution of access would be confined to the conurbations. The committee judged – good gracious, yes – that commercial television, as then broadcast, was working badly, that it went headlong for the biggest audiences and thereby limited its scope and its quality. It could sell low-intensity, cheap programmes to millions; it could indeed debauch their taste; it should be reined back.

Without mentioning that their own profits were often invested in commercial television, the feckless popular press let rip. The distribution of invective wasn't predictable. The report, in its formal, judicious way, addressed something close to those centres of meaning and value over which the press had assumed jurisdiction. It touched, in its

---

[30] Ibid., p. 31.
[31] *Committee on Broadcasting* (1962), p. 34.
[32] Denied, mistakenly I think, by Mary Midgley in her book *Wickedness: A Philosophical Essay*, London: Routledge and Kegan Paul, 1984.

The Pilkington Committee, with Joyce Grenfell fourth on the right.

polite formality, those exposed, naked but disregarded tendernesses of public conversation which the press at large and the discussion programmes on commercial TV took to be, precisely, untouchable. To accuse, in whatever restrained language, the manners of daily newspapers of the gross insincerity, phoney cordiality, worked-up hysteria, revolting sentimentality which mark their every utterance is a declaration of civil war. In its discussion of triviality the *Report* was doing no more than its duty when it summarized testimony as follows:

> On the general quality of television programmes, viewers expressed both disquiet and dissatisfaction. Indeed, one of the main impressions left with us by written submissions and spoken opinion is that much that is seen on television is regarded as of very little value. There was, we were told, a preoccupation in many programmes with the super-ficial, the cheaply sensational. Many mass appeal programmes were vapid and puerile, their content often derivative, repetitious and lacking in real substance. There was a vast amount of unworthy material, and to transmit it was to misuse intricate machinery and equipment, skill, ingenuity and time.[33]

The *Daily Sketch*, a now-forgotten tabloid then with a circulation of two million, covered its front page in high headlines, 'Pilkington

[33] *Committee on Broadcasting* (1962), pp. 33–4.

147

tells the public to go to hell'; the *Mirror*, with large investments in commercial broadcasting, reached for tired old horror stories of totalitarianism – 'Given the chance, Pilkington would recommend the suppression of your favourite newspapers'; and in a juicy giveaway in the *Sunday Pictorial* (also now defunct) a Labour MP of irretrievable sanctimony, substantial wealth and interests in commercial radio told his readers that the *Report* depicted them as 'trivial people' who 'will have to brush up their culture'. 'Big Brother TV' was on its way (Orwell's great novel was early appropriated by exactly those currents in the society he most detested). The usual mindless abuse was scattered all over the dailies, and *The Times*, still at the time the respectable voice of the ruling class and its settled conservatism, picked up the careful use of the adjective 'moral' in the *Report* – 'the moral condition of society' – and took it to mean flatfooted moralizing; its junior sibling, *The Times Educational Supplement*, followed suit.

The terms of abuse were strong and, you might say, heartfelt. That is, they filled to the brim the convention that, in a fairly reticent society, the language of its daily newspaper conversation be madly highpitched, bawling, excessive, then to be switched off or just switched over to the next overheated topic the following morning. The Committee was called 'authoritarian', 'socialistic' (naturally, a bad thing), 'puritanical' (Hoggart himself just as naturally named 'a provincial puritan', after his turn in court), paternalist, arrogant ('a haughty conviction that whatever is popular must be bad'), pompous, prim, priggish . . . One thing that became clear above the worked-up cacophony was the accuracy of Hoggart's analysis of the Press in *The Uses of Literacy*.

What counted above all in this lowering failure to *listen* was the very meaning of old democracy itself. The rabble-racket response to Pilkington as raised by the newspapers was that democracy is merely a matter of thoughtlessly thinking whatever one likes. On the other hand . . . – but it is far more than something that can be placed on the other hand. Pilkington – like those exemplary reports published, nearly enough, at the same cultural moment under the names of Albemarle, Newsom, Robbins and Plowden – aimed to say something definite about the conversation of a democratic culture. It met head-on the slackjawed idea that 'all demands are satisfied if there are symphony concerts for the highbrows and quiz-shows for the masses', as Hoggart put it later.[34]

---

[34] In a lecture given at the Teachers' College, Columbia University, in the spring of 1963. Reprinted in Hoggart (1970), as 'The Difficulties of Democratic Debate', pp. 185–200.

As to what it achieved, Pilkington remains a landmark, certainly; but it marks a lost bearing nowadays. In 1962 it brought commercial broadcasting up sharp; it prepared the way for the best days of Channel 4 and the excellence and severity of the *Annan Report* in 1977. Then the tide of mass broadcasting and two hundred channels swept past and isolated them both. The BBC has been left fighting for breath and struggling to swim athwart the effluent vilifications of the imperial Murdoch. Democratic debate shrinks to the chop-chop of political parties in *Question Time* and the bogus forensics of *The Week in Politics* and *Newsnight*, the amicable emptiness of Party leaders' debates before general elections.

Things could be worse, and in any case no one seems to mind very much. One thing is sure, and that is, democracy would be feebler if the Pilkington Committee had never met.

V

It was hard to hold the balance between doing the job at Leicester and the exigent demands of the Committee. The family house at 21 Central Avenue, just beside Victoria Park near the university, thrived under the unflappable authority of its ruling presence, Mary Hoggart. Both boys took places by way of the eleven-plus examination at the well-known grammar school, Wyggeston School (boys only), Nicola further away at the girls' grammar. Dad's trips away were mostly brief visits to London, the new friends – the Humphreys, the Frasers – close and gregarious, often found with coffee in the kitchen, the Frasers much given to parties, and the new social breed of graduate research students turning up at the house, scarcely ever turned away.

It was neighbourhood life, enviably solid and affectionate. Its rhythms and its geography conduced to the discipline of writing, but the heavy rush of public office as well as the long aftermath of his world-changing book meant that Hoggart's writing, though so very crowded, had now to be more short-winded. He had no big work on the go.

For he was man of the moment. He and his family settled quickly in Leicester, the house was bigger than their home in Hull, it had a garden, the department was companionable and, typically, Hoggart took on post-Albemarle duties on a committee at a new college in the city for the training of Youth Service leaders. He was asked to write semi-official pieces arising from the still-heated argument over

Richard Hoggart at Leicester. Reproduced with the kind permission of the University of Leicester.

Pilkington and saw them also as called for by acceptance of the public office. So he appeared in newspaper reviews and articles in the normal places – the *Guardian* (as it became after moving to London) then under the watchful literary editorship of Bill Webb recruiting as always the best new voices, *New Society, The Listener*, the *Observer* as well as such less predictable pages as those of *Esso Magazine* (on educational change) and the *Advertisers' Weekly*, for advertisers in those days were touchy about attacks on their business, Pilkington had put their trade at the radical centre of its recommendations. Naturally, these didn't happen, but the implications upset the admen.

Life at Leicester ('the happiest place I've ever worked') was flowing along easily, Hoggart was teaching the modern literature he knew and loved best – Auden and Eliot, Thomas Hardy, D. H. Lawrence and

Graham Greene – his Shakespeare course, and third-year lectures on Blake, Jane Austen and Keats. He felt immediately at home. He was well liked by students and made his criticisms of their work speedily apocryphal. When David Howe, then in his second year, came for his essay to be discussed, Hoggart said, 'You've flattened the village, Mr Howe. You were only told to bomb the petrol pump, but you've flattened the village.' But the times were on the move in 1961 and he had helped to start them off.

He received a letter early in the year from Terence Spencer, the handsome, beautifully suited and well-known Professor of English at Birmingham. Spencer ran the Shakespeare Institute as well as his department, he was much revered in the United States, he was a kingmaker with powerful friends; he had a roving eye. He wrote, with a slightly teasing as well as self-aware speculativeness, of his twelve-strong department as looking for a second professor, as not having had any success, as himself seeking advice in the matter. They needed, he wrote,

> ... someone different from me ... someone who takes a more radical view of English. Even if you weren't interested in Birmingham yourself (having other openings for the future) I should value your opinion.[35]

It wasn't an offer; it was a probe. Hoggart replied guardedly, in the English way, he was invited to lunch by the Vice-Chancellor, Sir Robert Aitken, a New Zealander, 'to talk about the Chair without commitment', for 'you seem to be much sought after', and to meet interested parties. Hoggart, usually quick in such perceptions, didn't realize he was to be given a once-over by the chaps, but he was, and was duly approved. So on 3 June 1961,[36] Spencer wrote in generous phrases that he had said to the Vice-Chancellor 'that I knew nobody who would, in my opinion, make a more lively and valuable and humane contribution to English studies'.

So the thing was done, but in an elasticated kind of way. No one in the Hoggart family wanted to move from Leicester just yet. Simon had A-levels approaching in two years, Nicola's O-levels were due the year after, they had all of them only been in the house since 1959. So the new professor temporized. He was taking over the care of the Leicester department again in the spring term of 1962 when Humphreys was revisiting the Folger Library. He asked for and got permission from Aitken to be a commuting professor – Leicester is

---

[35] Hoggart papers, 4/2/52.
[36] Hoggart papers, 4/2/55.

only thirty or so miles from Birmingham, the university two or three stops up a local line from New Street station.

His foremost condition, however, was that once arrived in his new department, he establish a graduate and research centre for what he dubbed 'contemporary cultural studies'. The coinage was his own; it is no slight thing to found a new intellectual discipline, still less at a time just before Britain's great university expansion began after the Robbins report was presented in 1963. English departments at that time didn't have 'centres' for specialized research, but the Vice-Chancellor waved a courteously airy hand by way of permission and only required that somebody else, not the university, would have to pay for it. Then, in the discreet way of such manoeuvres, the Registrar wrote to say that his salary would be £2,800 per annum, the appointment appeared in the *Birmingham Post*, and Dobrée sent a congratulatory telegram just to say 'hooray'.

Birmingham is probably the grandest-looking of the old civic universities, each placed near the heart of the regional capitals. Its most dominant buildings were largely the gift of the local Victorian caliphs, the Chamberlain family, who also provided the country first with a foreign secretary, then a prime minister. Doing things in style, their architect placed a lifesize copy in red brick of the slender ninety-metre *Torre del Mangia* which dominates Siena, setting it off with large and stately Italianate buildings to match. By the time Hoggart arrived, the university spread expansively across Edgbaston, with playing fields, a running track, a well-stocked art gallery called the Barber Institute and the huge Queen Elizabeth hospital just down the road.

Within such an empire, it was surprising that the initials of the CCCS cut such a dash. Hoggart couldn't raise much money – there was no Arts and Humanities Research Council then – but he didn't need much: enough to hire a deputy, to help out with a bursary or two, to buy a secretary and stock a small library. So he turned instinctively to Allen Lane who turned instinctively to Bill Williams, his lieutenant and chief editor at Penguin since he put off his uniform. Hoggart asked for £2,400 a year for seven years, the minimum he needed to start up. Because income tax for semi-millionaires in the good old days stood at 97 per cent, tax-deductible donations cost the donor sixpence in the pound. Hoggart recalled Williams saying, with the brutality permitted by long friendship,[37] 'Oh give him what he asks, Allen. You've made a fortune by riding cultural change without understanding it.' Chatto and Windus together with the *Observer*

---

[37] Hoggart (1992), p. 90.

chipped in a little, premises were assigned and the post of Senior Research Fellow advertised.

Contemporary cultural studies, as Hoggart conceived them, would take from the canonical study of English literature its most developed intellectual strengths. That subject had only been going strong since it was founded at Cambridge in 1917 and then given its lead by the stalwart labours of I. A. Richards and the genius of F. R. Leavis. Oxford preceded Cambridge by two decades, but in order to try and make the subject as respectable as classics ('Greats'), burdened it with Anglo-Saxon origins and heavy-engineering historiography. What cultural studies wanted from English was fourfold. First, its minutely close reading of a text for what it said, for sure, and even more for what it implied, for its *tone*, its assumptions about its audience, the tremors of meaning above and around its explicit statements. Second, the student of culture-in-the-present learned from English a theory of reception, learning from a different kind of social inquiry what individuals and social classes make of the imaginative confections in front of them. Third, Hoggart hoped that the student who would come to the Centre would go beyond the written texts within which English *tout court* must be confined to the vast agora of cultural life expressed in language certainly, but extending far beyond words to gesture, ritual, ceremony, manners, all the untheorizable density of living by which the human world is created and recreated. For fourth and last, the goal of inquiry in cultural studies was to be the understanding, and then the evaluation of 'forms of life' (the phrase is Wittgenstein's). Such evaluation would not be that of a judicial sentence (though there would be tussles with the Marxists over judgement and severity). To evaluate a work of literature is to discover the human relevance, for present and future, of its way of saying what it says. To evaluate contemporary culture is to find and name in everyday expressive life what brings out the best and the worst in people.

One doubts very much that Hoggart would endorse, though he certainly knew, T. S. Eliot's famously eked-out, grimly resigned epigraph, 'these fragments I have shored against my ruins'. Hoggart had been, he still was 'sunny Jim'. He wanted the new discipline (to call it that) to test culture and society for liveliness and deathliness. The modestly titled Centre would shape itself into a moral community whose members, one of another, would leave it looking for, in Matthew Arnold's famous slogan, 'the best that has been known and thought', hoping to find it in the commons of everyday life.

153

HOGGART-WATCHING:
ARGUMENTS WITH MARXISM,
ASPECTS OF WORLD GOVERNMENT

I

His rather syncopated move to Birmingham – first doing his duty as Head of Department at Leicester, thereafter commuting daily to Birmingham while the children passed their exams – was for Hoggart nonetheless crowded with new work and heavy duties. His was, after all, a nationally known name, his colleagues were bound to look at him a bit sideways. There were, in the strictly bounded landscape of the disciplines, more than a few neighbours – in philosophy, sociology, history, foreign languages – leaning over the fence to see what on earth these new people were doing, digging in muddy, unmarked ground quite off the proper map of knowledge. What was more, the new chap was supposed to be a professor of English, and English itself remained something of a cuckoo in the nest of the humanities, shouldering its way past historians and philologists, laying claim to supplies and room for eggs in social science's nest next door.

So when, early in 1963, Hoggart gave his inaugural address to the university in its central hall, there was a big turnout, the *Birmingham Post* carried a report, and well-wishers alongside the envious and the malicious crowded in to find out what to expect. The word was already out that Penguins were to pay for the strange new Centre, and the news created high enough excitement of both an anticipatory and a vengeful kind.

Inaugurals express something placid and courteous in the life of British universities. On this particular occasion, Sir Robert Aitken did the honours after leading a little procession, flanked by the beadles (the Chamberlains' is a very traditional university and does things in a style compatible with its Renaissance redbrick architecture) up to the platform, the new professor in academic gown following modestly behind. Then he had his say, was politely applauded, and everyone went away to dispute what it would all mean for the changed life of the university itself.

Hoggart's title was typically ecumenical, but large in its embrace. 'Schools of English and contemporary society'[1] committed him to welcome pieties about the care and health of language, and the damage done to it in public by propaganda and advertising. He quoted, as well he might, Ezra Pound's famous dictum we have already read about the importance of 'the damned and despised literati', still such a rousing as well as accurate warning about their duty and the dangers to their labours; no apology for repeating it:

> When their work goes rotten ... when their very medium, the very essence of their work, the application of word to thing goes rotten, i.e. becomes slushy and inexact, or excessive or bloated, the whole machinery of social and of individual thought and order goes to pot.[2]

Pound's remark remains as blunt and as sharp as when he made it in 1931. Hoggart stuck to it in every book he wrote. As he said of himself, he was always talking, he didn't know when to shut up; he might allow himself deliberately clumsy informalities which belonged more to speech than writing; he was always aiming towards agreement and reconciliation, always working *for*, and only turning against when he had to.

These deep habits of disposition and formation called out hostility in more partisan listeners. When David Holbrook, ex-communist and ardent Romantic, read the inaugural he wrote with open anger[3] (as he often did to his correspondents) to Hoggart, reproaching him fiercely for a lack of fight, a failure to name and fire at the contemporary enemies of 'life' – 'life' which Leavis called 'the necessary word'. But Hoggart had quoted his standby quotation from Auden,

> All sane affirmative speech
> Had been soiled, profaned, debased
> To a horrid mechanical screech:
> No civil style survived

---

[1] Reprinted in Hoggart (1970), vol. II, pp. 246–59.
[2] Ezra Pound, *Literary Essays*, T. S. Eliot ed., London: Faber and Faber, 1954, p. 35.
[3] Hoggart papers, 4/5/9, letter dated 21 May 1963.

That pandemonium
But the wry, the *sotto voce*,
Ironic and monochrome.

He placed 'schools of English' at the centre of a contemporary and
hurtling, headlong rush of communication, and assigned to them the
huge task of steady, patient inquiry into the making of writers of
all kinds, into the shaping of society's innumerable audiences, into
the creation by society of its élites and their reputations (daring to
include his own in this programme), into (one eye on Pilkington) the
organizations which produce and circulate the official conversation
of the culture.

These unexceptionable purposes added up, no doubt, to a pretty
ambitious programme. They certainly corroborated much of the
future labours of the Centre in its ramshackle hutments which his
professorial address implicitly announced, although these latter
labours went ahead, in the later event, under rather different colours.
But the programme steered into a gathering current of criticism and
creation. It wrote a coda to the Pilkington report and did so by restoring the force of the adjective 'moral' to the study of a nation's efforts
to give voices to its seething variety, and not only to those loud organs
with all the money.

If it wasn't exactly a research schedule, it was a sign to hang over the
shop. Now there needed to be someone else to help Hoggart keep it.
In the summer of 1964 another small, stout-hearted sign of the times
was published, a book called *The Popular Arts*. Its authors, Stuart
Hall and Paddy Whannel, had been English teachers of the poor in
London secondary modern schools, carried there by the high idealism
of the self-styled New Left. Thereafter Whannel went as Education
Officer at the British Film Institute (another tributary of adult education) and Hall, for £500 pa (a good deal less than schoolteaching paid
then, supplemented a little by evening classes) became full-time editor
of an insurgent new journal, *New Left Review*, founded to capture
and develop a fresh and bubbling spring of feeling in the culture,
filled with generous-hearted and egalitarian ideals, thrilled also by the
advent of easier money, softening the harsh old prohibitions of social
class in bloody-minded Britain.

Hall wrote the brisk, fluent editorials, the journal sold teens of
thousands, he became *de facto* national organizer of the New Left
clubs, he and his comrades (Raymond Williams among them) raised
the money to buy, great heavens, a house in Fitzrovia at 7 Carlisle
Street, editorial offices upstairs, the *Partisan* (!) coffee house in the

basement, with lectures, guerrilla seminars, protest music (Woody Guthrie, Ewan MacColl). It all lasted for most of the 1960s, energized by the great rush of dissent which formed and held in an exhilarating political vanguard the Campaign for Nuclear Disarmament, while the journal subsequently became, under Perry Anderson's generalship, a permanent monument of the intellectual Left until the present day. Vivid and exhilarating as it was, the terrific overwork and squeezed-out salary wouldn't pay Stuart Hall's rent. He was invited by Hoggart to Birmingham to discuss the Senior Research Fellowship. He got the job.

Hoggart's career was, not accidentally, punctuated by a series of very strong-minded, larger-than-life, acutely social-conscientious intellectuals: Dobrée, Billy Mayfield, Bill Williams, Arthur Humphreys, Stuart Hall. He met them as equals, but without collision. Hoggart's way, easy, friendly, determined but concessive, was to talk past any obstacles until they dissolved once again into possibilities. From the start, Stuart Hall saw, with his habitual detachment as well as his high intelligence, what sort of man his new boss was, and how, as both of them wanted, professional collaboration should be transformed into – the key destination – moral community.

Hall was, is, or should have been a leading figure in British intellectual life these past forty-odd years, a figure, say, as unignorable as Richard Titmuss or Ralf Dahrendorf. Maybe he drew back, less at the immensity of the task, more at the horrible obduracy of Old Corruption (as Cobbett called it), the cast-concrete fixity of the English Leviathan? Maybe his political stamina was reduced by the ill health he suffered in his later years? However that may be, in 1964 he seemed man of the moment for the Centre, a mixed race West Indian of great good looks and good humour, of compelling presence, a former Rhodes scholar who arrived in Oxford in 1953 and joined the august company of Charles Taylor, Raphael Samuel, Alan Hall, Graham Martin, Gabriel Pearson (most of whom did time in adult education), collectively – in Hall's words[4] – 'appointing themselves keepers of the Left conscience'. Hall was a man of wonderful fluency, a spellbinder, overpowering on his day, high-principled, a touch aloof but congenial, and like Hoggart a rare talker. *The Popular Arts*,[5] what's more, could have provided a curriculum for the Centre. It tackled head-on the opposition between Folk and Popular Art, the

---

[4] In an interview with this author, reported in *Raymond Williams: The Life*, London: Routledge, 1995, p. 154.
[5] Stuart Hall and Paddy Whannel, *The Popular Arts*, London: Hutchinson Educational, 1964.

advent of mass consumer culture, the themes and narratives which had become so dominant in movies, on television, and supremely in the new and glittering world of pop music. The book did its bit towards comprehending the giant phenomenon of Elvis Presley, and it made frequent references to *The Uses of Literacy* as drawing the essential map of the ambivalences at the heart of the moral (which is to say the universal) imagination and the emotions it puts in order.

Hoggart and Hall made a powerful duo. The division of labour was such that Hoggart had his duties as the English department's second professor – duties to committees, to Senate, as well as to his prominence as new star in the university's firmament – but he also manned the defences of the Centre against rivals and assailants in the academy. Hall tended the intellectual life of the Centre, its seminar patterns, its students' progress. To begin with, the two men agreed they would only accept research students for an MA. They were resolved, a bit brutally, to prove to any malicious sceptics (there were several) that the intellectual standards of the new discipline would match anybody else's, and they picked the toughest examiners they could find.

For six years, their joint methods of social inquiry joined hands easily enough with the political allegiances and intellectual principles of the two men, and provided thereby a wide space for their students to work in. Hoggart's wringing out of the value and meaning of commonplace texts and domestic practice by way of the closest of 'close reading' taught the lessons of true and humane judgement as found out so very gradually by patient attention. Early in the collective life of the Centre, students spent a whole term in the practical criticism of women's magazines, learning to weigh up accurately their lovingness and their silliness, their seriousness and their triviality.

Hall, much further to the Left than Hoggart, a heterodox but hermeneutic Marxist, framed these delicate probings with a stout theoretic framework as well as bold revisions of category. Hoggart relaxedly confessed himself weak on theoretical issues – although Jean-Claude Passeron, his Parisian admirer, rebutted this in the French edition of *La Culture du Pauvre* – but in any case Hall seized the necessity of theory with his characteristic energy and clarity. These were the very beginnings of the 'theoretical turn' in British and American intellectual life, especially in the human sciences, and Hall was exceptional in his grasp of these, as well as in his own powers of theoretic invention, and in his great gifts of clear explanation.

'Theory' is always considered to sort badly with old English empiricism, these latter and native habits of mind recoiling from high Parisian abstraction, seeking always to ground themselves in ordinary language and to speak, as Wordsworth had said, in 'the real language of men'. Theory arrived with a loud, unseemly bang in the British university when it first heard of structuralism from Claude Lévi-Strauss,[6] and was much complicated in the very middle of the stormy unseemliness which accompanied the irruption of students into the centre of French politics in 1968 by Jacques Derrida's slippery proofs of the complete unreliability of language itself.[7] Built into every grand theory of the day, however, was the patriarchal presence of old Marx, insisting on the omnipotence of the economy and the ideologies which subtend it regardless of human reason or intention.

Hall was master of these matters. Much later in the day, well after Hoggart had left Birmingham for the world stage of UNESCO, Saturn's children turned on their mentor, seeking to devour all his ideas. It is a postscript to the history of the Centre we shall briefly return to. What counted in 1964 was the happiness of the conjuncture between the two men, the friendship which sealed it, the consequences for social thought.

For Hoggart, theory-without-a-capital-letter upholds his method by making experience and text synonymous. At the same time, Hoggart had avoided the mere individualism of autobiography by dissolving the personal into class consciousness. Class was the dominant structure in his analysis, but it was transformed from utter determinant into a critical and creative instrument of thought, and of the feelings which must shape it. The strong congruence of his work and his life meant that, treating everyday domestic life – conversation, manners, food, gesture, the stories the culture tells itself about itself (culture being just such an amalgam of narratives) – as his text, he offered to revalue that life on its own behalf and for the moral benefit of its society. Thus he was able, by the winning for his purposes of a plain, sober, tolerant style, to take the felt measure of all that was good and strong in the life of a much-belittled and massive class, and also to feel and register what was going wrong with it, what menaced its best parts, what it would carry forward from past to future. The Centre, in its communal endeavours, would aspire to make a language capable of correctly judging the moral advances and retreat of a people, and of its means of self-civilization.

---

[6] Whose *Structural Anthropology* was first published in translation by Basic Books NY in 1963.
[7] Jacques Derrida, *de la Grammatologie*, Paris: Editions de Minuit, 1967.

159

II

The task which the Centre gave itself – no doubt in a much more modest formulation – was therefore no less than so to shape the prose of the times that it would carry the best of those times – the finest life it could imagine – and thereby match up to the best wisdom of the day it could discover. Hoggart had shown that he could write English capable of the task. Hall's gifts and his biography as black Caribbean émigré and irresistible rhetorician of the abstract together summoned him to contrive a novel theory to fit both the facts and the values.

It is the purpose of theory to explain. Theory turns experience into patterns and configurations which have a meaning. To be master of a mystery is to hold the power of new knowledge. It is to gather together the many bits and pieces of experience and events in such a way that their pattern becomes visible and thereby to bring life a little nearer our comprehension. Theory is therefore the modern name for magic. The danger, as the hordes of the philistines are always quick to say, is that the magi speak their magic words without controlling or understanding anything, and for the sheer delight of incantation. All these stormy forces were jumbled up together in the little meeting place of the Centre.

It wasn't their phrase, but Hoggart and Hall were hoping to create that unplannable entity, a moral community of like-minded scientists of the human. In such a purpose, they presaged in their approach in 1964, their calm assumption of equality of dedication as well as of being-in-the-world, more than a little of the thwarted detonation of political feeling which exploded among students across Europe and in North America in 1968. The two men, with their high reputations and their quiet accessibility, enacted in all they did the ideals and principles of their intellectual politics. The weekly seminar was held for all students at the Centre, and was open to a good many outsiders also. By that date, the radical edge of Leavisian English had been turned, his fierce contentiousness absorbed by old English sedatives into the portly frame of daily study and its genteel administration. 'Hoggart's little outfit,' as they said at Birmingham, disturbed the schedules and spilt the tea.

After all, its members didn't so much deny the canon, the settled orders of cultural tradition, as ignore it. Their concern was less with the best that was known and thought, as with *anything* that had been known and thought. When they spoke of power, it was not the power of the Miltonic pentameter or D. H. Lawrence's prose that they meant, it was the power of press barons and their newspapers.[8] When they explored imaginative vitality, it was by way not of Dickens or John Keats but (another of the termly themes) in the company of police serials on television. Among the best writers of the day, after all, were Jack Rosenthal from *Coronation Street* (from 1961),[9] Alan Plater and Alan Bleasdale at *Z Cars* and, a little later, Andrew Davies with *A Very Peculiar Practice*. These were not assigned to any canon, but they fairly filled the imaginative life of millions in the nation.

So it wasn't just the syllabus of the little outfit, it was its whole style of life which was an affront to the contemporary idea of a university. The separation of staff and students was barely observed, the materials of study were demotic and unsanctified by time, and there was a disturbing smell of gunpowder about the premises, a political pungency which, as the contents and methods of contemporary cultural studies became known and whispered about, presaged the riotous echoes of the Parisian events of 1968 and, in the previous year, the march upon the Pentagon of American students protesting against the Vietnamese war.[10]

The ingredients of the Centre's communal life were such as were bound to boil over when international politics kicked open the door of the Senate House. But in the everyday life of the academy, Hoggart and Hall made an ideal intellectual partnership. For a start they were firm friends, Hall's natural authority of manner and his tranquil geniality absorbed into the easy atmosphere and the openness of welcome Hoggart created about him. There was always Hall's fluent and formidable powers of theoretic exposition to reckon with, as well as the grace with which he carried off his black independence, the years in front of dead-end schoolchildren, and the equable bitterness with which he addressed the imperial heritage. Beside him, the professor held at poise his natural vehemence, the authority of office, the weightiness of public success, and his own even greater seriousness of experience – Newport Street, Pantelleria, Naples, the labouring life of adult education. Both men were, as I have said, on the Left politically, Hall further along than the boss, but just as important was the openness and readiness of both when faced with these quite new landscapes of intellectual exploration and cartography.

For the 1960s saw a remarkable flowering of novel horticulture. Alongside the new university campuses being built at York,

---

[8] An early topic at the Centre, issuing in the publication *Paper Voices*.
[9] See his *By Jack Rosenthal*, London: Robson Books, 2005.
[10] Turned into literature by Norman Mailer's *The Armies of the Night*, London, 1968.

Brighton, Warwick, Colchester, Lancaster, new syllabuses were also under construction, old boundary fences and signposts taken down, acrimonious quarrels over proprietorship fiercely contested.

In its small way, the Centre shone a beacon over this genteel struggle. For a start, Hoggart dispatched his students to read the sociological classics, especially Max Weber, when to do so (in 1967) was to bemuse or affront the respectable scholar of the humanities. R. H. Tawney had told historians[11] to read *The Protestant Ethic and the Spirit of Capitalism* back in 1926 but there, there, Tawney could read German of all things, and was in any case an architect of the Workers' Educational Association and, though much honoured for his years, a bit of an odd fish, don't you think?

So when Hoggart wrote a little pamphlet setting out a reading list for his kind of student, it relaunched the tale of a tub and the battle between ancients and moderns.[12] It was published as first in an elegant little series from the Centre, with a shiny white and grey cover, and cost three shillings. To the author's surprise, it sold out at once, postal orders pouring into the office. By the time it was published, a new model army of heretics had been recruited nationwide, and students of Elizabethan literature turned to the new historiography of Christopher Hill and Rodney Hilton, set Marx at Weber's throat in order to determine the exact political colour of *Coriolanus* and *The Tempest*.

Such a battle of the books was simultaneously a skirmish in a national and an international confrontation between old and new orders. For it must be remembered that the second half of the 1960s saw the entry of the babyboomers upon the political stage. It was a moment of perhaps temporary but undoubtedly glowing hope and idealism. One measure of its ardour was the large number of English graduates who carried off their degrees not to an advertising agency, still less an investment bank, but to secondary schools in order to bring the tremendous and emancipatory force of a national literature to schoolchildren disinherited by mass entertainment and monopoly capitalism.

Slogans are not necessarily vacuous. That rush of vocation was a fine thing. The contrast of those ardent figures from 1968 with today's English teacher, much better paid, much less convinced, is merely painful. No doubt the period in which any given historical

---

[11] In R. H. Tawney, *Religion and the Rise of Capitalism*, London: John Murray, rev. edn, 1950.

[12] Richard Hoggart, *Contemporary Cultural Studies*, University of Birmingham, 1969.

narrative will hold up for its believers is always limited, and the message of salvation brought and taught by the great wave of enthusiasm which launched, under the leadership of Denys Thompson, the National Association of Teachers of English broke up on the rocky difficulties of multiculturalism, moral relativism and all the other -isms of reach-me-down social theory, not least the philistine obduracy of Thatcherism.

Hard to credit now that Hoggart's pamphlet was widely circulated among English teachers and reviewed a bit later in that subversive organ, *Teaching London Kids*. In conception, it was preparatory to the Centre's first big conference, held in July 1969. This was indeed an exuberant occasion, a party thrown under sunny skies against the dramatic backdrop of the Americans' first landing on the moon. It had all the things Hoggart's pamphlet said should mark contemporary cultural studies. It was international – Steven Marcus was there, whose new classic, *The Other Victorians*, a study of the unofficial literature of sex in Victorian England, was recently out; Leslie Fiedler, Hemingway's self-appointed successor, stout, hairy, boisterous author of 'Come up on the raft, Huck honey',[13] gathered what has to be called a bevy of admirers round him; Edgar Morin, small, contained, precise, membership of the Resistance on his CV, author of *Plodémet*,[14] a loving essay in ethnography as applied to a modern Breton village, marked the advent of the Parisians into British academic life; Edward Thompson, long a friend of Hoggart's, dashing and handsome in military shirtsleeves, spoke a malediction over statistical history as issuing from Cambridge's new Centre for such a thing and was, as everybody knew, at daggers drawn with 'Warwick University Ltd', the title of his 1970 polemic.

It was no doubt a celebrity conference, and its membership prefigured the new and necessary bibliography now being seized by the young *arrivistes* who thronged the gardens of the hall of residence; emerging starlets from the Centre like Alan Shuttleworth, lanky, self-deprecating Marxist-Weberian of formidable learning, new polymaths from new universities like Krishan Kumar from Canterbury, gorgeous in a seersucker blazer and canary yellow shirt, sociologist of a novel stripe, as much at home with Leavis as with Mannheim. Feminism only picked up speed at the Centre in the 1970s, but the conference attracted preachers of radical psychoanalysis like

---

[13] Leslie Fiedler, *Return of the Vanishing American*, London: Jonathan Cape, 1968.
[14] Edgar Morin, *Plodémet: Report from a French Village*, Allen Lane Penguin Press, 1971, just published by Arthème Fayard: Paris, 1967.

Margaret Rustin, sociologists of trade unions and social policy like Dorothy Wedderburn, cabbalistic historians of the ideas of Jewry like the late Gillian Rose, fierce proto-feminists and critics of Hoggart like Carolyn Steedman, then incubating her classic *Landscape for a Good Woman*. All these people, as Nick Carraway says of Gatsby's party, came to the conference that summer.

Two of the crowd were new colleagues of Hoggart and new stars in the galaxy of contemporary intellectual constellations. Both were novelists, Malcolm Bradbury in a well-cut pale flannel suit, whose breezy and mordant novel *Eating People is Wrong* presaged his future bestseller and hatefilled satire of libertine academics, *The History Man*, and David Lodge, hunched in a dire zip-up jersey which belied how funny he was, the recent success of his National Service novel, *Ginger, You're Barmy* anticipating his kindly picturing of apostate Catholics in *How Far Can I Go?*

These two latter figures became close friends and allies of Hoggart in the way he had of making friendship itself as much the centre of his life as his family and his writing. If Stuart Hall was not quite so close, that was a mere consequence of his slightly distant stance towards life, his magnetic charm notwithstanding. Michael Green, a very recent appointment in the English department, fresh from student life, rather shy, likeable, was made immediately welcome to the Hoggart home and noted there just how strong a presence Mary was, 'an acute questioner, at times mildly sardonic . . . not someone standing in her husband's shadow but a force – kindly, shrewd, sharp – in her own right'.[15]

These four men spoke for the Moderns in a department of substantial reputation and of sharp competitiveness within itself as between ancient and modern for sure, but also as between the calm monumentality of the Shakespeare Institute and the rest, and towards representatives of the new, tough, hard-edged discipline of linguistics. In his inaugural, Hoggart was at pains to stress the reconciling necessity of talking across the boundaries of the disciplines. In the pamphlet written for the 1969 conference he offered the kind of reading towards the common pursuit of true judgement about culture which he saw as necessary. At the Centre, the building itself so much resembling the old Army huts in which Hoggart had often held his adult education classes, an extraordinary succession of speakers had included, by the end of 1967, E. P. Thompson, naturally, Raymond

---

[15] Michael Green, 'Richard in a Working Context', in *Richard Hoggart: Culture and Critique*, Michael Bailey and Mary Eagleton, eds, Nottingham: CCCP, 2011.

Williams and Roy Shaw, ditto, Wilfred Mellers, author of *Music and Society*, a wonderful, canon-revising study of the power and greatness of Elizabethan music, but by 1965 revolving in his mind his just-as-handsome and then-astonishing study of the Beatles, Jonathan Miller, no less, the Australian novelist and cultural critic (*England, Half-English*) Colin McInnes, George Melly, who needs no footnote, Norbert Elias, doyen of Frankfurt social theory, A. H. Halsey, best-known British sociologist then and since, sexologist Alex Comfort, Troy Kennedy Martin, then a writer for *Z Cars* (in 1985 author of the greatest BBC drama ever made, *Edge of Darkness*).

It's hard to turn a list into a living history. Universities were thriving then as well as big news; new British architecture of a bold, civic kind was on show in York, Brighton, Colchester, Norwich; students were in fashion as well as showing it off. And they were in politics by way of occupation of vice-chancellor's and college principal's offices at LSE, at Hornsey College of Art, in Essex and Warwick and even Birmingham, where Hoggart, as always, tried in the huge, packed hall to coax straight answers to straight criticisms out of the Vice-Chancellor, to talk past bitter hostility and affronts to status until there was a chance of conciliation, rational agreement, mutual understanding.

It was his life's work and its meaning. He pursued it in the heated, angry, boring and self-righteous forum of the mass student sit-in, and he pursued it in the Centre's hut, where it enjoyed some of its happiest hours. The excitement of those meetings, their vivid sense that being in attendance would make new thought thinkable, that intellectual endeavour could indeed be linked to social improvement, that, most thrilling of all, a moral community was in the making in the room, was, for the season of the 1960s and at Hoggart's Centre, made real for its members and for its many occasional visitors also. Both feeling and achievements by way of ordinary academic communications – books, bibliographies, broadcasts – kept the promise of happiness implicit in all inquiry, quickened also the old excitement which is like terror at the prospect of imaginative discovery, of invention, of the shock of the new to one's very life.

III

Hoggart had been writing hard since he arrived at Birmingham; the weeklies, the review pages, the assorted platforms on which he had given invited lectures, let alone his hand behind so many pages of

Pilkington, all bore witness to that. But he hadn't had a book to work on, there was no grand successor to *The Uses of Literacy* on the way.

So when Ian Parsons, at Chatto and Windus, wrote suggesting he publish all Hoggart's recent and uncollected writings, it was a relief. The professor would be seen to be carrying on the work of public scholarship, Hoggart himself was surprised and pleased to find that there was more than enough in the files to fill well over 500 pages, he did a bit of editing and as the wheels of his life turned tremendously in a new and completely unexpected direction, *Speaking to Each Other* was published in 1970 in two volumes, as *About Literature* and *About Society*.

A biographer of a thinker and writer must be at pains to greet all the subject's writings as worthy of attention, and there is plenty in the two books to hold it, plenty also we have met already. Yet there is something bland about them, something repetitious also, as of 'a smiling, public man' telling his many audiences more or less the same things, talking plainly for sure, but – the occasions being what they were – urging such necessary, quotidian banalities upon people as may coax them to speak up a little more on their own push; these worthy pages were hardly likely to give them new ways of gripping and – well – theorizing their experience.

> Before making larger gestures and assertions, we have to learn to talk to each other and that includes listening to each other, more simply and directly.[16]

As an exasperated (and much younger) admirer wrote in a review at the time,

> The cast of mind leaves him also without any language to carry his inquiries not only into the souls of ordinary men and women (including his own) but also into the souls of men who would enslave other men. Only when he is angry, as in the sound essay which describes the planned misrepresentation of the Pilkington report, does he show any signs of seeing where the seats of power in our culture lie. I'm not telling him off for not being a Marxist, but if anybody is to discuss the mass media any more than externally then he must discern the difference between manipulation and expression. Hoggart knows these are the terms of reference (as we've all learned from *The Uses of Literacy*) but he brings them no precision of application, nor does he create a structure within which the terms would find meaning and traction.[17]

---

[16] Vol. 1, p. 49.
[17] In *Delta: A Literary Review*, Winter 1971, pp. 20–1.

Breezily said, perhaps; who after all *has* brought off such a thing, has contrived a theoretic framework whose key concepts will unlock aspects of the human heart, and do so in sane, affirmative speech (poems and novels can't count)? A few years after he published his two plain, straightforward, kindly volumes, his very own centre for humanly scientific study lost itself, as we shall hear, on the hot and stony sierra of high theory. His by now thousands of admirers fell back a little disappointed from books they had anticipated eagerly for thirteen years. It is a token of the personal affection friends and colleagues felt for him that, for instance, talkative man-of-letters P. N. Furbank could write in *The Listener* that 'it is part of his literary effectiveness to present himself so consistently on whatever topic, as a man of good will', and in the *Guardian*, his cheerful friend and colleague at Birmingham, Malcolm Bradbury, wrote of 'his bodying forth of a serious, responsible and above all considerate critical decency'.

'Decency' is a moral quality of which George Orwell, always a touchstone for Hoggart, made much, and Hoggart did so as well. What is it? Mostly, it rings as though coming in the middle range of moral actions and attributes, somewhere below heroism or gentleness, which so easily crosses into cowardice. Decency, however, is a tougher quality than most, more like a defining characteristic than an attribute; it is a shaping spirit of a person's life rather than something that flashes out from time to time. Decency in Hoggart's life showed in the immense kindliness he brought to his huge acquaintance, especially his juniors; it showed in the directness and truthtelling in all his conduct (he was afraid of nobody, not even his fearsome boss at UNESCO, René Maheu, whom we meet in a moment). Decency is uncontaminable, it is always trustworthy; it does its daily, domestic work. When, in 1971, Hoggart gave the BBC Reith Lectures, one could say that they represented a meditation on decency.

Their delivery took place after the most drastic and unlooked-for change in the life of the Hoggart family. By the late 1960s of course Simon had left Wyggeston to brother Paul and his passion for drama, had first taught for a year in Uganda and then cut quite a dash as an undergraduate journalist on *Varsity* at Cambridge, and meanwhile Nicola was beginning training as a primary schoolteacher at Goldsmiths' College in South London, anticipating by several years her father's later arrival there as Warden.

Hoggart was very fully established at Birmingham. Their house, to which they moved in 1964, 40 Richmond Hill Road in Edgbaston,

167

the very incarnation of a leafy suburb, was as solid as its predecessors in Leicester and Hull, but decidedly rambling, with outhouses and an appleloft as well as being as welcoming a home as Hoggart homes always were. The vertiginous inflation of house prices after 1990 or so has put such properties out of reach for most university lecturers, but in the 1960s they were taken, if not for granted, then, for the £10,000 (very cheap at the price because of a 35-year leasehold) which the Hoggarts paid, at least as a fine rounding off of the cultivated and scholarly life.

It was immense by comparison with its forebears, incoherently extended over the years since it was built in the nineteenth century, three cellars, echoing attics, three toilets (very rare then) in varied conditions of sanitary readiness and separated from the parent bathrooms in narrow coffins, half-a-dozen bedrooms, half-a-dozen living rooms, a big kitchen innocent of *Home-and-Garden* designer cupboarding but the family HQ anyway. The half-acre garden shaped itself round a magnificent cedar; the family, when it was together, sat out there often and, as Simon once reminded his father, 'laughed a lot'.

Hoggart was much talked about at Birmingham, nationwide come to that, at least in the lower-middle echelons of the power élite. Before he went to Birmingham, his name had been canvassed for a Chair in English at Manchester, his membership of the Albemarle Committee and, of course, of Pilkington, had made that name widely known even to Cabinet ministers, and his anti-commercial, pro-democracy stance on the committee caused a few wrinkled noses among senior Tories. Indeed, in the murmured, 'just-sounding-you-out-you-know', repellent English manner, an approach had even been made while he was still a mere senior lecturer at Leicester, to find out whether he would be interested in being a candidate for Vice-Chancellor of the new University of Essex at Colchester. Many years later, the admirable Edward Boyle, former Conservative Secretary of State, told him that the suggestion had been discreetly quashed by Cabinet ministers: 'Chap not quite sound, you know; remember Pilkington.'

There were plenty more such approaches to come. He so rarely said no. One wonders whether, not having yet found a new theme for a book to match *The Uses of Literacy*, he pledged himself to public offices by way of using his talents as consistently as possible for the common good. However this may be, he accepted big administrative commissions, just as he had at the Youth Service College at Leicester. He joined the trustees at the Birmingham Repertory Theatre, a large and flourishing enterprise in the very middle of

Birmingham's hideously rebuilt and soul-crushing city centre, and he became, *honoris causa*, a governor of the Royal Shakespeare Company whose famous theatre was spanking new when he had gone there as a schoolboy, paid for by his teachers. For sure, he tolerated high demands on his time partly out of his sense of public duty, partly because he found the extended, often dreary practice of public administration so absorbing.

In 1969 Britain had a Labour government, and those in the know said that the Education Minister between 1965 and 1967, Anthony Crosland (with Edward Boyle, one of the only two secretaries of state for education for the past forty years with the cultivation, the wits, and the sense of vocation adequate to the job) greatly admired *The Uses of Literacy* and had mentioned Hoggart's name as suitable to be nominated as Britain's candidate for a soon-to-be-vacant top post at UNESCO, the United Nations Educational, Social and Cultural Organization, no less.

UNESCO. One draws one's breath. Most people in the Anglophone world know almost nothing of its work and care little to correct their ignorance. The organization itself trundles on with, at present, some two-thirds of a billion dollars to pay its way, a third of that provided by the USA, currently threatening its withdrawal. In 1986, coerced by Mrs Thatcher's raucous chauvinism, Britain withdrew in a huff, only restoring itself to membership when the Labour Party returned to power in 1997.[18] And yet were there to be no such thing, the world would lack institutional expression of its unbelievably variegated culture, lack a collective and transnational location for the protection, extension, the making good and the making available to all its peoples the manifold cultures of – no less – its manifold humanness.

The big words come naturally, but they are not empty. UNESCO was conceived out of the remorse of world war; those who first imagined its purpose and possibilities in 1945 included some of the most unaffectedly highminded, idealistic and consequential intellectuals of the moment, Europeans and Americans mostly: the theologian Reinhold Niebuhr, the English biologist Julian Huxley, the French philosopher Jacques Maritain, the American poet Archibald MacLeish, the Scandinavian economist Gunnar Myrdal.

Together they conceived a world-collaborative institution which would not only direct aid of an 'educational, social and cultural'

---

[18] These and many more precious details supplied by a kindly official of the Organization, Deyola Adekunle, during my formal visit in April 2012. See also *UNESCO: The Seeds of Peace*, Paris: UNESCO Publishing, 2009.

kind where it was most needed, it would found schools and colleges, turn the world's millions of illiterates into readers and writers, bring the wonderful new technology of radio and television to all those living without news or learning and in desperate dereliction. More than that, it would recruit and deploy scientists intent upon the most urgent and eternal puzzles of human provision – the distribution of water, the sacking of the globe's resources, the preservation of its beauties, the tending of its species. It would seek out aspects of the world's cultures in pressing need of record or of guarding against war and pillage.

To rehearse these early imaginings, to check the history which gave them the realized life they achieved is, nearly seventy years later, to find your eyes filled with incredulous tears – tears of admiration, wistfulness, amazement. In the dreadful aftermath of war, so much of the world still blitzed, all this hopefulness and practical helpfulness was brimming over.

It couldn't and didn't last, or not in the image of these high ideals. Rancour and rivalry had their say, the Cold War began to freeze up, and the overdue disintegration of empires brought large numbers of new nations with confused and contentious accounts of what was done to their cultures to jostle together in the big conference hall at UNESCO headquarters.

The Charter for the Organization was first drafted at the opening conference on 16 November 1945 in Church House, a large dull building in Dean's Yard, Westminster, just across the square from the Houses of Parliament. It was rewritten twenty times but, even allowing for officialese, wind and generality, the constitution retains a certain nobility:

> That a peace based exclusively upon the political and economic arrangements of governments would not be a peace which could secure the unanimous, lasting and sincere support of the peoples of the world, and that the peace must therefore be founded, if it is not to fail, upon the intellectual and moral solidarity of mankind.
>
> For these reasons, the States Parties to this Constitution, believing in full and equal opportunities for education for all, in the unrestricted pursuit of objective truth, and in the free exchange of ideas and knowledge, are agreed and determined to develop and to increase the means of communication between their peoples and to employ these means for the purposes of mutual understanding and a truer and more perfect knowledge of each other's lives.[19]

[19] UNESCO Constitution in *The Seeds of Peace* (2009).

It was not, however, this worthy platform rhetoric which caught Hoggart's attention. Since in Britain he had become 'Dr Culture', the man who knew what the elusive, often vacuous concept meant, he had become member of the new Ministry for Overseas Development's sub-committee on culture. The Ministry was a timely innovation of Anthony Crosland's, and Hoggart took the job on, as usual, out of a sense that this was a public duty.

He was dispatched to UNESCO's Biennial Conferences in 1966 and 1968 in order to attend the Culture Commission which decided on programmes, ranging across the globe, of support for world arts and world anthropological inquiry. It so happened that the Francophone delegate from Mali, a hero of his country's struggle for independence, spoke of the tiny amount of time left for the collection of his nation's oral, unrecorded past. Its history, he said, was held in the memories of the old; the young were leaving the villages. Then he said, 'When an old man dies in one of our villages a whole library disappears.' Hoggart wrote later, 'That sentence more than any other took me to UNESCO.'[20]

When Hoggart was canvassed for the nomination he was in no state of readiness to move to a new job. The Centre had only been established for six years, its frameworks of inquiry were far from complete, there were still plenty of opponents in the university maliciously disposed, there were also other, quite juicy offers of jobs coming through, as in those days they did, on the phone: one in Australia, another in New York.

Most weighty of all, Mary's mother had, characteristically, advised her beloved daughter and son-in-law, by way of a plain postcard in August, that she had to go into hospital 'for tests', and asked Mary to go with her. Mrs France had been, without saying so, tending a lump in and then on her breast with antiseptic cream for twelve months; naturally, she stayed often at the house in Edgbaston, but Stalybridge was her home and she well able at eighty to look after herself.

Hospital, however, was another matter, and Mary left at once. Her mother took radical mastectomy stoically but the thing was, it soon turned out, far advanced and her earnest insistence on her not influencing her family against another career move obviously to be set aside.

But the elderly radical from Mali stalked Hoggart's imagination like a ghost. Shortly before the bad news about Mrs France's health

---

[20] Richard Hoggart, *An Idea and its Servants: UNESCO from within*, London: Chatto and Windus, 1978, p. 17.

arrived, and when the discreet murmuring about the nomination for the post of Assistant Director-General at UNESCO first became audible, Richard and Mary had taken, as they did, one of their long decision-making walks. They had gone out in the car from Edgbaston, a few miles along the A38 beyond the car works at Longbridge and into the gentle countryside of Worcestershire where the Lickey Hills at Cofton Hackett show off so sweetly and modestly some of the loveliest landscape in England. There they went over the prospect of three years in Paris – the job would be a secondment from Birmingham – with Simon finishing at Cambridge and starting work at the *Guardian*, Nicola studying at York, Paul preparing for university and for a spell in India at an arts centre in Mumbai. It was settled between the two of them in the sunshine that afternoon, that they would go. The call was, so to say, to join the international civil service. It was to put aside the small, endearing purview of even a grand university, to try out the premises of cultural studies in every life and hard up against the sheer variety of the world, to struggle for understanding the otherness of others, their lore and language, as these impinged upon the deep allegiances and the shallow caprices of innumerable quiddity. The fearful task would then be for this shadowy figure, the international civil servant, to find and live certain transcendent principles of impartiality and universal justice, of transcultural judgement and placeless humanism. The test would be that success in such a task merited either equivalent obloquy or equal acclaim from all parties. You are doing your human duty if you can bring that off. Plenty of people warned him of the sheer tormentedness of the job, among them Andrew Shonfield, and in particular Lord Ritchie-Calder, who was in a position to know, and who wrote (with candid admiration for Hoggart's gifts) of 'the arrogance of Maheu' and 'the extreme difficulty of working at UNESCO'.[21]

The pay was good – huge by British academic standards, untaxed as well and ample expenses provided to travel home. The two of them decided that they would hold the long bonds of family together by paying for the children to visit whenever they wanted to; in the event, about every six weeks one or two turned up. It is a delightful anecdote to add that one year, a short time before Christmas, no visit was expected, and the Hoggarts were returning from a gruelling trip to Indonesia (they went away together whenever they could, the ADG renouncing his first class airline ticket so that they both travelled economy). They got back to the massive apartment block at

[21] Hoggart papers, 3/6/694–7.

127 Boulevard Haussmann to a darkened flat; when they opened the door, the lights came blindingly on, and their two boys greeted them with noisy glee, come for a surprise visit.

From the Lickey Hills, things looked manageable. There were regular flights from Paris to Manchester near Stalybridge. Hoggart was sure he could count on Hall to maintain the Centre equably. Hoggart himself spoke fluent French, Mary pretty well. He had picked up sufficient Italian in Naples; English all through, he recoiled from 'little Englandism'. Earlier in 1969, he had been asked by the Organization for Economic Cooperation and Development, a well-funded research instrument of the wealthy West, to help write a report for the French, advising on what they might do to accommodate the angry reproaches and acid criticisms of their university students during the colossal upheavals of May 1968. 'Le chienlit,' as the President had called them, had brought about de Gaulle's resignation. It was a far cry from Birmingham's little spat.

There again, the English UNESCO nomination was thought to be long odds. They heard nothing for a long time. The Director-General, who mostly got his way, thought the post was due to go to an Asian. Suddenly, Mrs France's condition worsened, she came to live with the family in Birmingham, they would have to temporize if the job were offered, she died in January, the job offer came imperiously; late in the month, on a bitter cold day, the three Hoggarts (Paul went with them) flew from Birmingham to Paris.

IV

The UNESCO headquarters, in the Place de Fontenoy, at the other end of the rectilinear park which culminates in the Eiffel Tower, was built on land donated by the French government. On the approach side it presents a bland, curving exterior of modernist normality and little presence. Once you are inside, it opens at the rear into a wide, flat park punctuated by Henry Moore, Alexander Calder, and Erik Reitzel's big, fretted sphere lit from below. The lecture and conference halls are each subtly roofed in wavy concrete planes and beautifully lit in roseate and cerulean shades. The gigantic walls have been adorned by the greatest figures of modernism – vast graffiti by Joan Miro, just as vast a mural by Victor Vasarely depicting 'the unitary constant of the universe', legible as either concave or convex, a lean, solitary Giacometti, *L'homme qui marche*, a monumentally sombre Picasso.

Modernism dominates all right, but all the nations have donated their artworks, and a seventeenth-century Flemish conversation piece is hung beside Chinese rice paper paintings of a music lesson and a Cambodian goddess from the twelfth century. Those great architects, Breuer and Nervi, spread themselves with a fine show of intricate fenestration and a cast-concrete *porte-cochère* opening into the park. In the high, wide and handsome entrance hall, you will see pass you by world-celebrated scientists, artists and intellectuals, and not a few of their political bosses, as well as troops of the beautiful women functionaries, all just like Dante's vision of the gates of Paradise.

British academics knew, then as now, very little about UNESCO. Indeed one vice-chancellor murmured in the ineffable English way to Hoggart, on his return home five and a half years later, 'I wouldn't call myself a Hoggart-watcher, but some of us did wonder what possessed you to go to that place.'

For a while the Hoggarts wondered the same. Paris was very cold and not very welcoming. The apartment was central, hired from the French ambassador to Dublin and Prague, who was called, inevitably, Emmanuel d'Harcourt. It cost 1,480 francs per month, was on the fourth floor, and its high spaces were a bit overpowering and sparsely furnished with a few comfortless French pieces; but its splendid full-length windows opened onto wrought-iron balconies and the furniture from Edgbaston brought enough of homely familiarity with it even if the biggest carpet they had shrank to the size of a rug in the vastness of the reception room.

Then there was the difficulty of the boss. René Maheu had been Director-General since 1962. The DG had a deputy and five assistant DGs. Hoggart was ADG for culture and communications (which then meant broadcasting). Maheu, even today, is remembered as the most formidable, passionate, faithful and frightening director-general to have held the post. It is a measure of general ignorance about UNESCO that he was never popularly known for the towering figure he was.

Towering? Yes but, while certainly dedicated to the highest ideals of the Organization, he allowed his ardour to disfigure his service with sudden rage, arbitrary cruelty, lethal condescension. He was, naturally, product of the most élite of the *Écoles Normales Supérieures*, familiar of the philosophers, acolyte of Claude Lévi-Strauss who then dominated the human sciences with his extraordinary blend of Saussure's linguistics and anthropology's kinship structures. (When Lévi-Strauss expressed his admiration to Hoggart for *The Uses of Literacy*, by letter and in conversation, Maheu fairly reeled.)

Maheu's ferocious authoritarianism, the depth and variety as well as the Gascon predictability of his cultivation (he loved Verdi, rugby football, Inuit soapstone carvings, Javanese puppet plays, Renoir, *poulet de Bresse*) jarred and blended with a sexual heat which emanated from him like a radiator. Simone de Beauvoir had early been his mistress, he was known to promote good-looking women beyond their talents. His rages, never arbitrary, were ungovernable; not infrequently he reduced quite senior officials to tears.

Not Hoggart. But even he kept in his desk for the first twelve months a letter of resignation setting out to the Director-General, Maheu's own intolerable defects. They were not so much chalk and cheese as black and white, impossible to compound but tensely counterposed. Hoggart stuck to his own immense rectitude, however much it angered Maheu. Maheu, no less principled in his devotion to the Organization, demanded always his own way, and could not count on getting it. He wanted once to send home a Czech official who was adequate but not exceptional. This was after the collapse of the 'Prague Spring' and the Krushchevite purges which followed. Hoggart stood by the man, who was on his staff. Maheu, enraged, dismissed the Czech and ignored his ADG's opposition. The Czech took Maheu to court, won damages, got a job at the Pompidou Centre and Maheu looked out for his revenge.

The tales abound of his ferocity and of his geniality. He became monarch of UNESCO. By the time he retired, mortally ill with leukaemia in 1974, he had been director for thirteen of UNESCO's twenty-eight years in existence. The post itself was as riven, as contradictory, as the man who dominated it for so long. Hoggart remarks that its holder

> ... has at one and the same time too much power – vastly too much power – and too little power, so little that for some main aspects of his role he is rendered ineffective.

What dismays a sympathetic world citizen all these years later is how little one knows of the momentousness and frustration of this great office of world government. The job is too much for any one person.

> He signs too many things, too many documents go out in his name, too much directly flows from him, too much patronage depends on him.[22]

---

[22] Hoggart (1978), p. 138, p. 143.

175

The exceptional oddity as well as the punitive isolation of the job could only exacerbate those tough, parallel oddities of character its incumbents must possess. In Maheu's case, he had to keep a kind of autocratic faith with Hoggart, the only one of his juniors senior and brave enough to defy him, the one man whose integrity he always trusted even when at odds. Not that he would ever forego retribution.

He was fired, Hoggart thought, by a powerful yearning which provided the obverse of his hard ruthlessness and bullying egoism. He was touched with the vision of the moral philosophy which certainly inspired UNESCO's founders with their postwar and pacific idealism. Maheu had read philosophy at 'Sciences-Po'; he longed for the making of a secular ethics which would correspond upliftingly with the Organization's ideals of manifold cultural beauty, collective scientific reason, educational emancipation and fulfilment. Hoggart, formed intellectually by the sceptical practicalities of the English novelists, would have none of such vapourings. Idealism had no doubt drawn him to the Place de Fontenoy, but it was an ideal of unselfinterested devotion to justice, to fairness, and to reverence also, as manifested in protection of this particular country's art and that country's access to science or to new schools. Hoggart may not have been a universal humanist, but all the same he could hear the distant strains of the music in Maheu's ears.

In both senses of the verb, the Director commanded respect and didn't always merit it. He was a frightful snob when confronting any old French nobility. He was arrogant and wilful in the way he made appointments, and had opposed Hoggart's all the way only to concede, with his sudden generosity which was like a blow in the chest, how good an ADG Hoggart was, and that he had been wrong to oppose him. That said, he regularly threatened his ADG, detested any implied criticism on his part (especially when taking a junior's side against the Director: 'if he cannot work with me, he had better leave'), showed him respect, affection and fury in equal proportions.

There can be no doubt that he was an extraordinary statesman, that he built up UNESCO during his director-generalship into the far more scientifically powerful, geographically penetrative, culturally influential body that it had become on the world stage by 1974. His fearsome faults resembled those of any strong, vehement, self-righteous monarch whose subordinates dare not answer him back and whose word in the immediate corridors of power is law. As to his own ability to stand up to the man, Hoggart said drily,

176

Hoggart at UNESCO, reproduced with the authorization of UNESCO photographer Dominique Roger.

It took no particular courage for me to speak up. Whatever the inadequacies of British professional practice, we do not usually indulge in or tolerate public scorn and sarcasm towards subordinates. And I was a free man, ready and able to go back to my home country at any time.[23]

Glancingly, Hoggart once invoked those universal principles which he would not permit Maheu to flout without a fight as being 'intellectual objectivity, the rights of the international civic service, the just dues of a human being'. All the same, when Maheu asked him as a personal favour to stay on beyond his three-year secondment in order to see him, Maheu, out (he knew by this date that his illness was fatal and left him with very little time) and to help the next man in, Hoggart agreed. He turned, as always, to Mary and she, who had in the early days and for quite a long while after found it very hard to 'settle' in Paris let alone to settle for the very hard rhythms of work and overwork, proved sure he should say yes. Then the new Director, Amadou-Mahtar M'Bow from Senegal, asked him for another six months of his life, which would have taken him up to July 1975, five and a half years after leaving Birmingham. But things did not quite work out straightforwardly.

[23] Hoggart (1978), p. 153.

Richard and Mary at 127 Boulevard Haussmann.

V

The timetables were very exacting, the political pressures unremitting. Every new proposal, every programme – the key word – was
disputed and wrangled over for national advantage. To some countries, the principles of disinterested public service which the officers
were enjoined by the ideals of UNESCO to embody, were either
unintelligible or unrealizable, simply to be scrapped in the everyday
tussle for advantage. In the 1970s the Cold War kept its bitter sub-
zero temperature, and when Hoggart was compelled by the downright incompetence of a senior Russian on his staff not to renew his
contract, the fellow kept himself out of trouble when he returned to
Moscow by saying that Hoggart was an agent of the Foreign Office
and doing its bidding.

Such a tale characterized the trembling uncertainty of many
wretches, at the time and still, rapturously happy in the easiness
and plenitude of Parisian life, permanently tense with anxiety at the
brevity of their stay, the likelihood that switches of power in their
home country would mean some kind of bureaucratic exile or worse
when they went back.

If these stresses measured only the ambient weight of the job, its
everyday duties far exceeded those of normal academic life, even a

178

professor's at Birmingham with, say, the usual twelve to sixteen hours of committee work per week, two or three lectures to give, two seminars to conduct, and face-to-face tutorials in-between, all this before turning to one's own scholarship, with luck, on Friday.

But that is the way, the truth and the life chosen by anybody called to academic life, and each activity meshes with some proper part of the vocation. That is the ideal at least, and it still binds its spell even in the corporate university of today. UNESCO had no such tradition, and its stirring ideals were confounded and confused continuously. Its staff were not diplomats, but they had to be diplomatic; they were indeed bureaucrats, but normal life in the Place de Fontenoy flouted Weber's best principles of bureaucracy – anonymity of treatment, mastery of the files, perfect impartiality – at every turn.

Hoggart took home a heavy briefcase every night and the same monster accompanied their weekend trips out into the countryside beyond Fontainebleau, or into Normandy. Simon later recalled his beloved Dad becoming something of a bore at home on the subject of UNESCO politics, urgently needing to unload frustration at the abominable conduct of the boss, or the calm assumption of this diplomat or that politician that simple bribery would always get its way. The frightfulness of British official conduct was always closely observed by Hoggart, but non-lethally confined to casual racism and insolent snobbery. Details of these horrors he had been keeping for years in notebooks, along with a kinder collection of those linguistic and mannerly turns in social behaviour intended not to put down or put off but to connect and affect.

What could easily have been a killingly heavy schedule at head-quarters was regularly punctuated by necessary journeys worldwide to see what had been or might be done by a UNESCO programme or a proposal for research, to pay homage to a little display of local dancers, actors, puppeteers, or to admire a new school or college and the progress of the literacy plans which went with them. Beside reporting and checking up therefore, duty required the necessity of passive presence, which is to say, the emblematic figure of the Assistant Director-General conveying, by his attendance thousands of miles from his desk, his approval and his sanction.

In August 1970, seven months into the job, the long-noticed degeneration of the massive log piles which held up all the most beautiful, the most irreplaceable buildings of Venice, finally broke into world awareness. At the UNESCO conference convened to initiate drastic action – action which, it should be added, was swift, comprehensive and, however much argued over by the Italians, pretty effective – Hoggart wrote 'une declaration d'intention' for the Organization.

> Deux des choses les plus importantes au monde sont le pouvoir et l'indépendance ... d'une conscience capable de mettre en question ce que la société, ce que d'autres individus, lui presentent comme une vie digne d'être vécue.

It was a statement to which Maheu could give ready assent, and the more telling for acting as preamble to the planning of the mighty task of salvage and restoration. Saving san Giorgio Maggiore is not undertaken in order to help out the tourist industry; it is action on behalf of a life worth living because there are buildings like san Giorgio in it. The occasion was in his mind when, a little later, he wrote in the French house journal of schoolteachers, of certain 'réalisations les plus spectaculaires ..., c'est à dire, la sauvegarde de certains monuments ... exprime une conscience mondiale'.[24]

That was it. He was working for the world's conscience, and in his first year the work took him down the Nile to see the preservation being done on the temples at Abu Simbel, to Venice, to Mali to visit the hero of the independence whose remark about the death of oral libraries had so caught his imagination four years previously, to Kerala in India to see more temple remnants, to Rome, to Antwerp, to Strasbourg to ask for EEC money and support. In his first year report Maheu wrote, 'un bon début, plein de promesse'.[25] Hoggart was fifty-two.

It had been a hell of a year and, as we noted, Hoggart had kept a letter of resignation at the ready in his drawer throughout. Just after the Venice conference, Allen Lane had died, full of years and achievement. Hoggart was asked to give the oration at a thanksgiving ceremony for Lane's life. Maheu refused permission to release him. It was a big issue. Letters came from the Penguin Chairman, J. L. Beales, but it took a telegram from Edward, by then Lord Boyle, to hit Maheu in the solar plexus of his snobbery and win permission. Yet Maheu, punitive and perverse as ever, knew well enough what Penguin publishing meant, wrote his ADG an emotional letter afterwards, quoting back at Hoggart his own phrase about Penguins as being 'the citizens' university'. Hoggart had said at the thanksgiving,

> Penguins trusted a far wider range of people than had commonly been trusted before in these areas of activity, trusted them to choose the better when they saw it ... Penguins have stood for the idea that our

[24] L'Education, 28 October 1971, Hoggart papers, 4/7/246.
[25] Note dated 18 September 1970, Hoggart papers, 4/7/287.

potentialities are greater than the pressures of our time ... When you look at the whole Penguin achievement, you know that it constitutes one of the great democratic achievements of our recent social history.[26]

That was Hoggart's imperial theme as well as his fond and personal tribute to Lane and Bill Williams. It was typical that he fought out his disagreement with Maheu on the matter, because he had a lot of writing to do, as well as the endless memoranda, recommendations, references, evaluations which had to be kept flowing from his desk, let alone the succession of requests for articles, rarely declined, about the work of UNESCO.

There had been, however, another invitation, this one from the BBC, and no slight matter either. It was to give the BBC's own Reith Lectures in 1971. This was a more momentous affair forty years ago than it is now, though the Reith Lectures still recur annually, are never trivial, and represent the Corporation's recognition that half-an-hour a week for six weeks given over to a well-known scholar or intellectual thinking aloud about serious matters of whatever kind is proper expression of Lord Reith's own purpose in 1928 to give his audiences something meaty to think about. Talk radio remains a serious pleasure for millions, though the fact is overlooked in all the prating about television police thrillers. In 1971, the Reith Lectures were in any case more of an event in the schedules, and were reprinted in *The Listener*, the BBC's house and national journal.

Hoggart was surely an ideal choice. *The Uses of Literacy*, as its success showed, demonstrated his gifts for addressing a much-wider-than-academic audience. He spoke to and for everyday life. His Reith Lectures – announced and published under the title *Only Connect* [27] – would transpire as meditations not only on the themes of his classic work of fifteen years previously, but also on the thought that went into Pilkington as well as his efforts in Birmingham to vindicate an intellectual method for the analysis and evaluation of everyday life, both private and public.

It looked a winner: man, subject and moment would coincide. He had to hand his notebooks and observations of several years intended for just such a topic. He had already encountered, with delighted loathing, in UNESCO the new, repellent language of what was not yet called 'managerialism', and this would provide the occasion for warning as lies and scummy froth in so much of the language of daily

---

[26] Hoggart papers, 4/4/5.
[27] Richard Hoggart, *Only Connect: On Culture and Communication*, London: Chatto and Windus, 1972.

administration and by the powers wielding it threatened to swamp the conversations of politics and civil life. The year already spent in France would finally permit a bit of the international comparisons which the Birmingham Centre had so far failed to develop.

Billy Mayfield from Hull and Dennis Lawrence from the Pilkington days lent a hand and many words, and the amazing cinematic omniscient, Philip French, then talks producer for BBC's intellectual wavelength, Radio 3, weighed in with broadcasting counsel. The title, 'Only Connect', comes of course from E. M. Forster, and it has about it what a very bright spark of that day and this, Christopher Ricks, called, reviewing the lectures, 'A wise old owlishness' which the lectures themselves never, alas, quite dispel.

He begins by talking about one of his key concepts, 'tone', itself central to I. A. Richards' classic primer of the 1920s, *Practical Criticism*. He sketches a number of faces and voices, especially those so immediately characteristic of the English ruling class – full and glossy features, silver wings of hair, still-school-prefects at fifty – but without launching a class war, giving credit where it is due, for forty years ago the Tory Party had not lapsed into virulent and obtuse chauvinism and its phobia of the welfare state. But Hoggart's whole treatment, his moral stance and his easy-going vocabulary lack specificity, lack salt and savour and living detail. He speaks so kindlily his examples cannot take on exemplary tone. They need some satirical bite. When he celebrates the best of Sunday morning outdoor suburban life – the flower garden, a quiet radio, a car being washed, warm sun – the writing doesn't rise to the occasion nor prick the throat in the way the subject deserves.

It's a bold thing to say of one of the prose masters of the epoch, but Hoggart's Reith Lectures are not well enough written; not, that is, keen and sharp enough, nor moving nor funny enough for its elephantine, shapeless subject, a subject which is nonetheless coterminous with the meaning of life.

The book which emerged is only 111 pages long, a small thing in the life's work. But one feels slightly tearful at the chance missed, given the stature of the occasion, a receptive public waiting to be called both to the democratic colours and to the conversation of a culture daily diminished by the raucous bullying of its press, the tumbling sequences of its television programmes, and the mutual indifference of its social classes.

He urges his listeners to think about their own writing, much as he must have in Saltburn and Helmsley, but again he gives them nothing to go on, only generalized bromides about 'a direct relationship to experience'. But that's something you find in all great writing; what it is that is in common in such a relation as caught and held by as unalike a trio as, say, Dr Johnson, Ernest Hemingway and Iris Murdoch, needs to be fixed in the ear of the Reith audience.

Truth to feeling and in the idiom is the answer, but maybe feeling in these lectures runs a bit too shallowly, maybe – this is most likely – the demands of the work in Paris were just too heavy to permit the writing and rewriting one's hopes for the occasion demand. Even when Hoggart tackles the unspeakable but widely spoken gibberish of bureaucratic jargon, he doesn't give his attack the sort of cheerful, clean-fighting vividness which Orwell brings off so perfectly in his essay 'Politics and the English Language', much in Hoggart's mind.

It's all too vague. Even when drawing a linguistic moral from his day job, he declines, perhaps out of diplomatic necessity, to name place or person, or even to give solid physical actuality to his anecdote. Then, most disappointing of all, when he concludes on 'a common ground' he doesn't reach for some of the splendid prose in the Pilkington report, and reaffirm what public communication in varied, colourful, multi-toned and responsible broadcasting could do both to embody and direct the culture of the country.[28] For what is a country if not a nation?

One mustn't make too much of three hours of lectures. The book on UNESCO is so much better, however, and so little known, mostly because its topic is unknown or disregarded in the Anglophone world. Perhaps I haven't sufficiently brought out or don't know enough to do so the back-and-spirit-breaking load of work at UNESCO in the 1970s. Even those long journeys to beautiful destinations – one can't call them 'trips', the word is too unencumbered – were in the company of the laden briefcase, often joined to a second such load for twelve-hour flights to, say, Indonesia. Mary went, as we saw, as frequently as possible, but her husband was often poorish company.

The journeys were purposeful, not jaunts. Once they were visiting one of UNESCO's proudest preservations, the Buddhist temple at Borobudur in Southern Java. They were travelling with Maheu then almost at the end of his long service and, although weakened by the pitiless cancer in his blood, still fiercely dedicated and ruthless in his daily business. The Hoggarts had visited Borobudur before, and Mary

---

[28] Hoggart filled in this blank in 1973 with 'A Broadcasting Charter for Britain'. Hoggart papers, 5/11/73.

... remarked on how lucky the two of us felt in having seen Borobudur twice, set into its soft hills with all the smells and sounds of that lush but humanized landscape around it.[29]

Maheu had tears in his eyes as he turned towards her, away from the sumptuous building, and said, without any self-dramatization, 'I now feel an added pleasure and poignancy. I look at all such things as if I may be seeing them for the last time.' For a moment, he and his two juniors were indeed joined in the deep friendship of a common ideal.

By this date, in early 1974, he had asked Hoggart to stay on an extra couple of years after 1973, up to his own retirement and in order to play in the new director-general, the Senegalese career diplomat. Hoggart's acceptance meant that, out of a decent concern for Stuart Hall's welfare as well as for the future of his very own Centre, he would have to end his appointment at Birmingham as well as ensure that Hall got the post of Director. That was obviously only right, and Hoggart was pretty confident he could get a job for himself back home when the time came. (He was later amused to discover how often people supposed he was angling on the fringes of UNESCO for another post. But that was and is how, he had discovered, the international bureaucracy recruits itself.)

In his last year, two tasks filled his time. The first, one of the best examples of what the Organization could do, was set in Katmandu, and he and Mary were often there. The project (I can't avoid the word) was no less than to rescue a beautiful Nepalese valley from the horrors of untrammelled international development, already begun by a monstrous Marriott hotel. Hoggart's Sisyphean boulder was to assemble the team of environmentalists, wildlife consultants (a very practical as well as earnest tribe), town-planners, architects, public health and medical officers ... and, having screwed out of this barmy army a plan which kept faith with natural beauty and human habitation, then to ward off the strong hot stink of bribery which floated out of the foyer of the Marriott.

In the end, he was driven out of his post a few months early. He had kept up his fight against the dreadful jargon of official documents throughout, even going so far as to circulate a little pastiche of the worst kind of official obfuscation for the entertainment and improvement of his colleagues. He called his little guide, 'bafflegab', and it went like this:

[29] Hoggart (1978), p. 150.

... Project to implement research within the fields of UNESCO's competence on the importance of the human factor, its behavioural motivation and innovative patterns, its strategies of public policy, in seeking developmental goals in different societal settings, and the overall implications of UNESCO's interdisciplinary action in the field.[30]

It's just verbal sewage. We all know its repellent likeness. Hoggart was carrying on Orwell's struggle against all such gibberish, aiming as it does 'to give the appearance of solidity to pure wind'.

The new Director-General, however, Mahtar M'Bow, moved with a menace of which this venal language was fairly innocent. He was political all through, where 'political' is a dark word, and indicates that every decision he took was with a keen alertness to what Senegal's allies would want to win, whether financial advantage or the high gloss of ideological sanctimony. There was a report hit Hoggart's desk about the practice of archaeologists at work in Palestinian Jerusalem. The Israeli archaeologists were accused by some of UNESCO's official delegates of doing a poor job. Hoggart went to Jerusalem. Quite the contrary transpired. The fact was that it was Arab work which was poor, Israeli archaeology beyond reproach.

The anti-Israeli formations of Arab and African sympathizers flounced up, and passed a resolution docking Israel of $25,000 for the work (much less than she had paid in). Hoggart expostulated to the Director-General, pointing out that UNESCO must retain the support of 135 states, as well as of the scientists and intellectuals who work for it. Resolutions against racism in South Africa and Portugal had been proved, against Israel not so.

M'Bow replied to the memo in a manner at once touchy and chilly. In his own formal and icy letter of reply, indeed of resignation, Hoggart regretted the Director-General's 'sanctioning partisan letters' about the Israeli business, reminding him bluntly of his duties vis-à-vis disinterestedness and politicization. He ended, 'I feel wholly rebuffed, and conclude it would be best to leave the Organization.'[31] M'Bow responded coolly and courteously. In October the following year Hoggart wrote an *Observer*[32] article describing the affair, noting that the attack on Israel was launched by states with dreadful records, pointing out also that the Netherlands were duly punished for speaking out rightly and bluntly by the Arab states' withholding oil from them.

---

[30] Hoggart papers, 694/7/201.
[31] The whole exchange is in Hoggart papers.
[32] *Observer*, 1 October 1975.

Things have got much worse since. Not only has Israel indeed joined the hideous tyrants of the Middle East in oppressiveness and injustice, but UNESCO's director-generals have slid into the practice of blatant partiality towards national preference, never more so than during the reign of the Japanese, Koichiro Matsuura, between 1999 and 2009.[33]

So, bristling more than a little, the Hoggarts came back to Birmingham. He ambled into the senior common room after nearly six years and was met with passing friendliness by an acquaintance who said, in that strange, swallowed mewing of the English upper classes, 'Hello. Not seen you for a bit. All right?'

He supposed so, yes. He had been invited to spend a six-month fellowship at the University of Sussex by its magnificent Vice-Chancellor, Asa Briggs, ex-adult education also, and there he would write most of his book on UNESCO. Stuart Hall had taken the work of the Centre in strongly theoretic directions. Hoggart's signature had become much less legible in its workings, especially as both the *marxisant* Left and feminism had cut such a dash after 1968.

Although the university had offered Hoggart another two years' secondment when Maheu asked him to stay on in Paris, that would obviously have been unfair to Hall. There was a protracted hoo-ha at Birmingham, when those several members of staff hostile to the Centre leaked into the urinals of the press to the effect that Birmingham was cooking up a hot Red cell. There was a fuss, a special committee formed from all over England, a report criticizing Centrist jargon, applauding nonetheless its intellectual distinction; finally Stuart Hall became its official Director.

About time, too. Yet the career of social thought and method at the Centre remains a historic disappointment, a strong vein of energy which never hardened into ore, but dried out in the sandy wastes of Anglophone wanderings in search of the good oasis where theory runs pure and practice is clean.

Maybe Stuart Hall takes some of the blame for this. He had *such* talent: charm, fluency, dazzling intelligence, charisma. He had such good fortune in his formation also: the Caribbean origins, part white part black, his excellent schooling in the West Indies, his class position, his Rhodes scholarship, his friends at Oxford, great Canadian philosopher Charles Taylor among them. His sister had had a love affair at seventeen with a student doctor, middle class but black. Her

---

[33] See Yudhishthir Raj Isar, 'Richard Hoggart and UNESCO', in *Richard Hoggart: Culture and Critique*, M. Bailey and M. Eagleton, eds, Nottingham: CCCP, 2011.

parents forbade it. She suffered a breakdown. 'It broke down forever, for me, the distinction between the public and the private self.'[34]

That intense family anguish taught Hall, as he gradually acquired the concepts, that culture is lived deep in the subjectivity, but lived as a social structure. This truth he turned into the subject-matter of the Centre, and it chimed with the bell of the 1970s. What then happened was that the graduate students, some of them the cleverest in the country, seized with the liveliest pleasure on structural theory, and lost all their grasp on what they called 'the specificities', which is to say the facts of life, the living of them, the language of horror, boredom and glory.

Hall, infinitely wise but trying, it may be, to conduct too many conversations at once, saw all this but couldn't ride it. Feminism drove him out, finally.

> ... being targeted as the enemy, as the senior patriarchal figure, placed me in an impossibly contradictory position. Of course they had to do it. They were absolutely right to do it. They had to shut me up ... It wasn't a personal thing. It was a structural thing. I couldn't any longer do any useful work, from that position. It was time to go.[35]

He went – praise be but where else? – to the Open University, and was by then one of the best-known social theorists in the world. Intelligence, however, had been silenced by structuralism. It is a regular but lethal event. The structuralists rose and flourished and expired. What the bitter Red feminists at the Centre had rejected as 'the Matthew Arnoldian liberal humanist line of Hoggart' turned out, in its mild way, to have the greater stamina. Structuralism is become a tiny enough creature today, but old Hoggart still looms pretty large.

---

[34] Interview in *Stuart Hall: Critical Dialogues*, ed. D. Morley and Kuan Chen, London: Routledge, 1996, p. 488.
[35] Morley and Eagleton (2011), p. 500.

8

GOLDSMITHS AND GOLD
STANDARDS

I

Departure from UNESCO was a rather shuffling, ambiguous business, for word got out that there had been stiff communication between Hoggart and the Director-General. Some of his windier colleagues looked the other way as he left, some – especially juniors and receptionists and porters – pressed forward with little gifts and letters of farewell.

He and Mary had had in any case to leave 127 Boulevard Haussmann a little earlier, when the Ambassador was recalled from Dublin, and saw their time out in an apartment near the Sorbonne. When he resigned, Hoggart had no job to go to in Britain but Asa Briggs, in the way of things in 1975, had, with a vice-chancellor's authority, arranged a visiting fellowship at his own University of Sussex for six months, so that his old friend and ally could write his book about UNESCO. Two of the three children lived within the London ellipsis (Nicola in Norwich) and Hoggart knew, with no mock modesty, that there would be offers on hand of a suitable post.

There were indeed. As before, All-English murmurings on the phone – 'nothing official at this stage, my dear fellow, but might you possibly be interested in …?' – had implied, in that non-committal way, that his name was high on a list of two possible vice-chancellorian appointments, a research Chair was on offer in Boston Massachusetts, Hoggart at fifty-eight remained much in demand in a way which nowadays would seem peculiar. Choosing a vice-chancellor strictly on his intellectual prowess and achievements would be, after the year 1990 or so, a rare move. Such men and the

188

occasional woman were thereafter much more certainly checked out for their knowledge of a spreadsheet, for their propinquity to government and to the cheque books of rich Asians and Americans, for – as they say – their networking skills, for their gifts as recruiting sergeants in the Far East.

Hoggart, however, was captured by that extraordinary institution, the Goldsmiths' College, and the happiness of fit between his intellectual disposition, his lifelong allegiance to the education of the people, especially poorer people, and his staunch adherence to the best principles of social democracy, and all that Goldsmiths, in its kindly, rambling way, stood for, is a golden mark upon the epoch. The college deserves a more honoured place than it has in the Pantheon of British democracy and such constitutive intellectual virtues as that democracy possesses. To describe its busy life faithfully is to remind ourselves that the best parts of British academic life are far from being confined to the old class enemies in Oxford and Cambridge, Bristol and Edinburgh, but may just as well be found in New Cross SE14, and down the Mile End Road.

The rich and marshy pastures between Rotherhithe and Lewisham filled up rapidly after 1840 with a dense tangle of railway lines moving south-east on either side of the Old Kent Road; the small spaces in between were packed with the brick-and-boilerworks and choking smoke of high Victorian industrial production. New Cross, taking its name from an old inn and staging post, was eventually tidied into Deptford, which then equipped itself with a small but magnificent Town Hall of all-white Edwardian rococo, pillared, pedimented and oriel-windowed, later the college headquarters, while in 1891 the Worshipful Company of Goldsmiths bought the handsome premises of the Royal Naval School founded for the sons of naval officers.[1]

The Goldsmiths, along with other of the grand Livery Companies in the capital, were in a state of agitation about the extent to which the new, seething economy of Germany was steaming up behind the British, and resolved to improve the condition of technical education in the nation. Hence the Goldsmiths' Institute established itself in John Shaw's fine Georgian school buildings.

The Goldsmiths thought big. There were sports grounds, gyms, any number of societies providing chess, rowing, rugby, tennis, literary discussion for men and women (separately), and superb miniature

---

[1] This local history taken from A. E. Firth's excellent *Goldsmiths' College: A Centenary Account*, London: Athlone Press, 1991.

swimming and washing baths in Laurie Grove, also in the high rococo of the day, redbrick, white pillaring, deep lintels. After spending handsomely for a decade, the Goldsmiths handed over the whole enterprise to the University of London which, as we shall see, didn't know what to do with it, and sorely offended the old London County Council in the process.

The history of that polymorphous, young, idealistic enterprise may easily be read in the grounds, the buildings, the student member-ship and the curriculum of the present-day college. To begin with, the university established the college under a delegacy as a teacher training institution. The LCC kept its finger in the pie by paying for a school of art; assorted reports over a period of half a century recom-mended, first, that the college become the London headquarters of R. H. Tawney's Workers' Educational Association, second and third and fourth that the place be kept underfunded (one warden telling the university delegates that the students were too well fed in the refec-tory), such that for its whole history up to Hoggart's arrival in 1976 the constitutional and financial position of the college was queasy and precarious.

That history also gave rise to a busy jumble of courses, of stu-dents living in what became, even before the arrival of the *Empire Windrush*, the first truly multicultural district in the country. If, that is, 'district' is the right word for an area taking in a twenty-mile-long sprawling, sock-shaped zone of dockland, with sometimes wide, often narrow main roads thronged with heavy trucks on the way to the river and the Channel, streets of terracing still today speckled with the shops of a dozen distinct cuisines – Greek, Italian, Indian, Caribbean, Ethiopian, Polish, Jewish – a dozen and a half languages audible in the street, and huge numbers of people doubling as students, full-time, part-time, evening only, of the multitudinous Goldsmiths curriculum.

Over the twentieth century, its cheques always in peril of bouncing, Goldsmiths expanded its School of Art, acquiring an imposing head-quarters in palatial and conservative style from the royal architect, Sir Reginald Blomfield, assorted houses in the side roads being scooped into its boundaries, new buildings squeezed into the gradually dimin-ishing areas of spare space, the desacralized local church, St James's Hatcham, captured for student use, each acquisition or novelty duti-fully commemorating in its name the many august figures who had, over its hundred and twenty years, gone out from the college to do battle on its behalf – A. N. Whitehead, great philosopher; Graham Wallas, founding father of the Fabian Society; Rachel McMillan, educationalist; George Wood, the college's own and best registrar; Ben Pimlott, one of Hoggart's successors. After his retirement as Warden, Richard Hoggart's name was in turn given to the main building overlooking the college's very own green, a tranquil, tree-ringed little agora the size of a cricket field at the heart of the college.

This crowded and contradictory history mirrors with rare aesthetic propriety Hoggart's own complicated formation. I don't suppose there is a destiny that shapes our ends, but those who try to believe in such a thing should find it reassuring that Hoggart's official career was completed by the Warden's office at Goldsmiths. He was foreign enough for a start, Hunslet-born, now among Poles, Greeks, Cockneys, Italians, Pakistanis, West Indians; he had done what he could for world harmony and the preservation of a world's multifarious culture; he had worked the crazy, needful, all-day timetables of adult education, and he had battled all his life on behalf of the millions excluded by poverty, indifference and hard old English class barriers from the deep fulfilments and discoveries of education.

He had another fight on his hands when he arrived from his fellowship at Sussex at the terrace house in St Donatt's Road, which was his home during the week. Every day in 1976, beginning soon after eight in the morning, the last of them going home at half nine or so at night, more than seven thousand students arrived and departed every term-time day. With so much traffic the place always looked a bit worn-out, the refectory untidy, the toasted sandwiches half-eaten and anyway awful, the old brick walls in the main building hastily emulsioned; yet the purposeful activity, the sheer busyness, the clamour of conversation on its paths and in its corridors bears unselfconscious witness to the lived meaning of its life.

These things confirmed the Warden in his most settled convictions. These thousands of people – academics, students, administrators, cleaners, porters, technicians, security men and women, mailmen, decorators, plumbers (the college had begun teaching courses for plumbers in 1907), nurses, gardeners, glaziers, TV cameramen, refuse handlers . . . all these and more came under the Warden's careful authority, required that he be visible at suitable times, counted on him and his adjutants to keep the college solvent and at peace with the university's senior officers, only half-aware of Goldsmiths' existence, a few miles and two social classes' distance in their ghastly Kremlinate Senate House in Malet Street, WC1.

George Wood, the long-lasting Registrar, was Hoggart's best help in these dealings to begin with, for he had old and sympathetic friends at the Department of Education which held the college's money even

191

though the university was its official authority, and in spite of the fact that all universities were paid by the University Grants Committee, as they had been since 1920. This anomaly was more than an accident of history; it expressed the reluctance of the university (grand enough in its way although itself an accidental collocation of its constituent colleges, not even getting a full-time vice-chancellor of its own until the 1960s) to admit to full membership such a strange, piebald cross-breed as Goldsmiths.

This irked Hoggart and in any case made him apprehensive that one day the university might push the college further away; he was well aware that, as universities became at once more prominent in the national economy and therefore more vulnerable to changes of government and policy, then the more massed their defences by sheer numbers and plant, the better. There was of course great satisfaction to be had when the Department, as it did when anxious not to return unspent funds to the Treasury at the end of the financial year, phoned George Wood to ask if he could spend, very fast, several hundred thousand quid. He and Hoggart always could, even when they had once to pile vast heaps of new books, bought at top speed, in empty tutorial rooms, until they could be catalogued.

As is plain, Goldsmiths' College was a peculiar amalgamation of institutions and their intellectual and practical traditions – many of them at odds with the habits and categories of British academic life. According to the reluctant parent, for instance, the academic study of art must be critical and historical. But the Goldsmith School of Art, in Blomfield's resplendent building, trained painters to paint, two of the alumni, Graham Sutherland and Robin Tanner, being about as distinguished a painter and a printmaker of landscape as they get. The university recoiled from such artisanal labourers. By the same token, the college's music department was much more concentrated on performance than on the history of music, and this too ran up against the university presumption of the superiority of cultivated appraisal over practical music-making. Last and most substantial of the university's mute objections to Goldsmiths' way of doing things was to the college's large commitment to the study of education and the training of teachers.

This latter, as the foregoing history relates, had always been a main part of college activity, right from its origins teaching the two-year Certificate of Education course. By contrast, the University of London taught a one-year training course (the PGCE) to graduates only. From the early 1960s, however, Tory and Labour governments worked hand-in-hand to create an all-graduate profession for teachers, and the two-year Certificate was enlarged to three, with an extra year of academic study and the award of an honours Bachelor of Education at the end to those who came up to scratch.

This last was an intelligently conceived degree, much of its structure across the country the work of three men: a remarkable psychologist, Ben Morris, rare in having been both head of the Tavistock Institute (psychoanalytic in orientation) and the National Foundation of Education Research (solidly statistical), Roy Niblett, an educationist and historian of justified eminence, and Richard Peters, a philosopher strenuous in the effort to attach the abstruse difficulties of his subject to a practical ethics of some use to schoolteachers. The form of the degree was, quite properly, influenced by contemporary arguments about interdisciplinarity and the permeability of boundaries between intellectual subjects, and the new degree, with its four foundation stones in its education components of psychology, sociology, history and philosophy, invited a student whose special subject was, say, English, to follow Hoggart in the reading of literature as a means of studying society. To the gimlet-eyed scholars at headquarters, defenders of the absolutism of the disciplines, the new degree was further token of the fishiness of things down at Goldsmiths.

Hoggart cared little for such objections when they boiled over from what he took to be class-based objections made from a position of social superiority towards the paltry strivings of improperly trained people polluting the pure waters of truth with the messy business of everyday life. But he was hard and sharp with anybody who slackly maintained, as plenty did, that intellectual (and moral) discriminations in art were mere expressions of emotion. As the Oxford philosopher, A. J. Ayer, had notoriously contended as early as 1936[2] in his quick, witty and heartless way, 'moral judgements are like saying "Boo"'. For Hoggart, all inquiry was moral inquiry, and making accurate judgements as to value the point, meaning and significance of the study of human activity, whether as sociologist, historian, philosopher or reader of poetry and novels.

The years in Paris, beset not only by the warriors of political self-importance and their often desperate juniors, but also faced daily with utterly incommensurable moral attitudes, had hardened and toughened him, not necessarily for the better, his daughter sometimes thought.[3] Certainly, he was blunter, more terse and uncompromising in his decisions as Warden than ever he would have been in Leicester

[2] In his *Language, Truth and Logic*, Oxford: Clarendon Press, 1936.
[3] Long conversation with me, 5 July 2012.

or Birmingham. Maybe that was the merest consequence both of his much-increased power, the necessity in so vast and sprawling an institution as Goldsmiths for a swift and sound decisiveness, but others as well as Nicola noted a new severity and unbendingness about his judgements, especially as to the worth of the very uneven expressions of artistic-cultural life which passed before him for review.

He noted in himself, in his discerning way, a tendency to hot anger when his most cherished bywords – the idea of a university, the accuracy of literary standards – were slighted or betrayed on his watch; he recoiled, as well he might, from the sanctimonious and puffed-up play of pieties put on display by a group of fierce feminists offended by a drawing, part of the artist's exhibition in the senior common room, of big and beautiful female pudenda (belonging to the artist's wife). The Warden condemned in the college newsletter the objectors' 'crass failure to respond to the beauty of line in the drawing, let alone its tender subject'.[4]

II

The protracted test, however, of the Warden's temper, his powers of patient diplomacy and his ardour and loyalty towards the jumbled, untidy but inviolable principles of the common good enshrined in Goldsmiths' everyday life, was to be found in the interminably slow movement of the college into full membership of the university.

This was a saga of leaden tedium, about which all his children, on their frequent visits, recall their father as being frequently a bore, and their mother as bearing up with her usual stamina as well as her keen powers of criticism, under the weight of detail and committee confabulation.

The old, hateful story of university condescensions towards practical study (music, art, dance), towards training courses rather than (as they say) 'pure inquiry' and therefore all the doubts about teacher training, towards the sheer propinquity of academic scholarship next to such oil-stained and overalled activities as plumbing, central heating and the care of internal combustion engines, all these suppressed hostilities came to the committee tables. Alongside, they were accompanied by the contradictory tangle of different provisions for Goldsmiths' money, the incorporation of assorted colleges in the neighbourhood, in particular two colleges of education, St Gabriel's

[4] *Goldsmiths' College Bulletin*, June 1978.

and Rachel McMillan, and the always uncertain career of the Laban School of Dance.

Just about the moment at which Hoggart took over, the Labour government's minister, Shirley Williams, was advised that the country was training far too many teachers, so the student allocation to the college was changed substantially from education to any number of students for non-educational degrees. Anomaly abounded; this was a large university institution not subject to the (then) University Grants Committee, nor to London's own University Court.

It's not a tale to hold us gripped for very long. But perforce it lay atop of Hoggart's business for all his time at New Cross. Bit by bit, the university edged towards the college, and the assumption of full parental responsibility. In an indicative anecdote, when Hoggart was invited by another London anomaly, Chelsea College, to help in its submission of a postgraduate programme of cultural studies for degree status, the onlie begetter of the discipline itself came up against the old chestnut, stuck to with all the old vehemence, that graduates of a single discipline simply cannot pursue 'truly' advanced work across several disciplines. All this as though English, sociology, history, philosophy (let alone physics or medicine), were not all of them a medley of conflicting concepts, fluid method, and changeable idioms.

There was also a perhaps larger and related matter – related, that is, to the touchy question of university snobbery. To teach for a London degree at Goldsmiths, a member of staff had to become a 'recognized teacher of the university'. Elsewhere in the university recognition came automatically at the end of a two-year proba-tion. At Goldsmiths, those seeking recognition had to submit their curriculum vitae and publications, and were judged accordingly. Hoggart determined to embarrass the university and to show solidar-ity with his staff by making such application himself. Embarrassment duly followed, and he was asked not to pursue the application. The university's senior administrator caught him on the Senate House stairs for one of those candid but swallowing sorts of encounters, fresh-faced innocence on one side, murmured confidentiality on the other: '. . . puts us in a rather difficult position. You're a Head of School after all [he wasn't] . . . be very grateful if you'd withdraw your name . . .' Diplomatically, he obliged, although the business of teacher recognition was only one of the many routine ways in which Goldsmiths was put down – as part-time, non-academic, practical and applied not pure and disinterested, rejected once more for School status only a year or two before Hoggart arrived. The college had

195

only been permitted to appoint its own professors bit by bit and in slow step with the process of full admission to the university which Hoggart began again in 1977.

Things ground gratingly along. In 1980 yet another report concluded, on pitiful grounds, shoddy argument and inaccurate statistics, that School status should be refused. Once more, institutional malice was in evidence. Hoggart took a couple of weeks to prepare a careful, unpolemical rebuttal, recruited four colleagues, and presented himself and them at the door of the new, courteous and sympathetic Vice-Chancellor, linguist Randolph Quirk.

Quirk had read their objections and was wholly convinced by them. The author of the shoddy report was present for the Vice-Chancellor's humiliating opening, 'This report is to be considered withdrawn, is it?' Thereafter the university protested its goodwill but was saved from having to do anything by the then Secretary of State, Sir Keith Joseph, staring-eyed convert to the doctrines of Chicago's economic sado-monetarism, who had decided in 1981 that since universities 'were not wealth-creating institutions', whatever Keynes would have said, he would abruptly slice off 16 per cent of their money.

So everything stalled again, and it was not until four years after Hoggart's retirement, as then statutorily required at the age of sixty-five, that at last Goldsmiths was admitted to full membership of the university as a 'school'. It remains as such, but remains also, as Hoggart and his successors very much wanted, a multitudinously *local* institution, compounded of many unalike activities, motley, variegated, multicultural indeed in the many cultures of its staff and students, as well as in the varieties of its intellectual experience, the happy, sometimes quarrelsome blending of its disciplines.

These qualities, of variegation and the strains it causes, come out noisily from Hoggart's personal commitment to the establishment of serious media studies at the college. Obviously this came close to his heart and had, after all, been a lifelong and absolute preoccupation of all his thought. When he arrived there was only something called the Department of Visual Communication which taught graphics for a certificate award and was headed by a commercial artist.

Hoggart sought a new degree in media studies, one which might and should have its practical elements, should naturally teach its students to handle the technology, quick-changing as it was, but which would be built on a stout theoretical and historical foundation the principles of which would be those of a powerful and discriminatory criticism such as he had propounded all his life.

One aspect of Goldsmiths' ethos had irked Hoggart from the start. It was what his first (and continuing) head of media studies called 'the excessive decency and gentleness of the college',[5] by which he meant, with his own decent gentleness, a certain mushiness and sentimental tendency at the time in the intellectual climate at Goldsmiths. This might manifest itself in a, to Hoggart, intolerable readiness not to pass judgement on well-meaning, hopefully aspirant but nonetheless awful performances, whether of music or drama or weekly essays. The Warden had to speak diplomatically, of course, but he *would not* accept the debile or slack-jawed responses of those who, like indulgent parents at the primary school's Christmas show, applaud with enthusiasm dismal, inaudible, badly directed Nativities.

Least of all was he going to permit the media degree any slackness. Seeking to sidestep the usual academic reluctance to admit a new discipline, Hoggart had wangled an agreement with London's Institute of Education (a huge organization and one traditionally tolerant of newcomer disciplines) to validate, but only for a year or two, joint degrees in communications and sociology, and communications and education. His ally in this venture was Basil Bernstein, Professor of Sociology at the Institute and supreme theorist[6] of how disciplinary structures defend their boundaries and repel novelty, reproducing as they do so the class distinctions bedded deep in the structures of knowledge.

This arrangement was only intended to hold for two or three years. Goldsmiths' application for a media studies degree was first refused on the grounds that the staff were not qualified to teach such a degree. This blow broke the spirit of the commercial artist in charge of the department who was escorted from the building in a state of breakdown. By 1982 Hoggart had fixed on a candidate to take on the headship of a new kind of department of media studies, James Curran, a former member of the famously pioneering media department at Westminster Polytechnic (as it was), and successful editor of the weekly *New Socialist* set up by the Labour Party in the 1970s as a source of new ideas.

Back at the ranch, the Visual Communication Department favoured its own house candidate, Ros Coward, an advocate of cultural studies and later author of very well-known studies in feminist criticism as well as a prominent journalist. Passion and loyalty worked their usual ferment, but Curran was appointed to the post he still holds. His

---

[5] James Curran, letter to me, 19 June 2012.
[6] In his canonical paper, 'On the Classification and Framing of Educational Knowledge', collected in Bernstein, *Class, Codes and Control*, vol. 3, London: Routledge and Kegan Paul, 1975.

task was to build the new degree, along with a department capable of teaching it. He went to the college bookshop, bought a copy of Dick Hebdige's *Subculture*,[7] not long published and a miniature and instant classic study of punk and other forms of dissident pop and rock music. Hoggart, who one might have thought would be hostile to such subject-matter, saw its force at once, and wrote to Curran saying Hebdige should be recruited. The quite new kind of department for Goldsmiths was on its way.

There was a to-do, certainly. Curran had to bear some obloquy from the members of the old department who lied about him to the local paper, while uninformed, partisan students took to their spray-guns and college walls. Curran bore up with exemplary calm with the Warden beside him, while the rest of the staff, in a moving display of solidarity, made it clear they repudiated the nocturnals and their scurrilous methods. Under Curran's leadership and with Hoggart's early support, the department advanced to the point where now, nearly thirty years later and Curran still in charge, it has fifty-odd doctoral students, two hundred postgraduates and five hundred undergraduates, as well as all the prizes for research publications.

On the way, some of the old stagers had to be fired. Long afterwards, when Curran and Hoggart had become fast friends, Curran asked why he had not been told that staff would be sacked, since had he known he would never have taken the job. Hoggart said, 'I did not know at the time.' This, one fears, is impossible to believe. Hoggart's whole purpose was to create a new department of all the talents, one which would embody – as indeed it came to do – the highest standards of intellectual ability to be found in the subject. To achieve this, some staff would have to go. Effecting such decisions is inseparable from such an office, and Hoggart had learned the necessary toughness in Paris. But while he would know his man and keep these necessities from him until the contract was signed, he should have admitted his tactical reticence later.

III

Such are, no doubt, the commonplace scars carried by anyone who wields executive power. Running an outfit like Goldsmiths demands

---

[7] Dick Hebdige, *Subculture: The Meaning of Style*, London: Routledge, 1981. All these details provided directly by James Curran, during and after an interview on 18 June 2012 and in a subsequent careful letter.

very quick thinking and the sort of flexibility your enemies will describe as serpentine exactly because the reckless variety of life in such a place poses insistently different problems every day. The parable of the Laban Institute of Dance and the short happy life of Marion North brings this out.

Marion North was self-appointed monarch of modern dance, 'fiercely independent and also incredibly ambitious'.[8] Dance had long figured on the Goldsmiths' curriculum for teachers in training, and of course Laban himself, along with such other pioneers of young children's self-expression as Maria Montessori and Rudolf Steiner had inscribed art, dance, music, 'exploration of the self' on the foundation stones of childhood education back in the 1920s.

At the time of Marion North's appointment (at Hoggart's invitation) and in Goldsmiths' dreamy way, the Laban Art of Movement Studio moved, as a consequence of God knows what machinations, to New Cross. So there was a strong presence of the ideologues of dance with a fierce and determined leader gifted with redoubtable powers of persuasion. Having got Ms North on the premises however – hers was the biggest name in dance education in the late 1970s – Hoggart wasn't going to pledge her her independence. He wouldn't concede that dance provision at Goldsmiths would never be dissolved into the broad curriculum of teacher education. To a true follower of Laban any such dissolution meant pollution of the pure waters of Laban's doctrine. That would be, in Basil Bernstein's language, to cause the destruction of the frames and classification of the subject.

The argument went to and fro, but Marion North would not agree to yield the autonomy of the discipline and its redemptive force. She refused time and again to leave her beloved dance and its purity vulnerable to raids by the regiment of the cherry-pickers in early childhood education.

Finally, she wore Hoggart down. She proposed that the Laban Institute be formally separated from Goldsmiths while retaining its choice premises in an old church on the crowded acreage of the New Cross townscape which is the campus. 'She got the building, the staff and the courses,' her later successor, Gregory Sporton, said incredulously. She raised money, plenty of it, to extend the buildings, and Laban throve accordingly, a mini-state in the sprawling territory of the college.

It was a crazy arrangement, quite impossible according to the

---

[8] Phrases used by her successor as Director of Research at Laban, Gregory Sporton, in conversation with me, 22 June 2012, and a detailed letter.

corporate rationality of today. Hoggart remained wry about it, but if
the tale reveals anything significant, it can only be that the Warden of
such a contradictory, jumbled, madly independent place is besieged
by the sheer necessity to take decisions on the hoof, quick, before the
next supplicant is at the door or catching you crossing the grass while
round about you the students take their ease. All the same North and
Hoggart retained a good deal of respect for one another, for all that
retrospective rage drove her, when it suited her, to call him 'a misogy-
nistic little shit'. The same high style on North's part was rewarded by
her keeping the Laban Institute independent indeed, for all the later
plotting by subsequent Wardens to reincorporate dance back into the
body politic, and thereby to snaffle its precious buildings. A maternal
ferocity was her ruling passion; she thought him nonetheless the best
Warden she had had to do battle with.[9]

His was, it still is, such a strange office, closer in the nature of its
face-to-face variety, its duty of arbitration now over the future of
some essential buildings, now over the drawing of a woman's bottom
in the common room, now over the safety of women students late at
night on local streets, closer in all such matters to the daily work of
his brother Tom, Head of a secondary modern school near Grantham,
than to the usual knightly labours of a vice-chancellor visible only on
a short walk to the official limousine.

If, as Hoggart always said, 'tone' is the key to understanding and
valuing human utterances accurately, then the tone of the Warden's
farewell to his treasured Registrar, George Wood, who died in office,
tells us much about the full, rich life of the Goldsmiths' College.
Wood died in harness only a couple of years into Hoggart's time as
his boss, but the boss knew what he was, and at his memorial service
began by saying:

> One of the porters standing at that busy axis where the stairs come
> down near the refectory door, said to me, 'How are you going to
> manage without him?'[10]

Wood had spent years in Africa building up Higher Education institutions, and as Hoggart said and understood, 'Institutions whose purposes are more than material, which have intellectual and imaginative
ends, attract such men and then tempt them to commit themselves
without stint.'

---

[9] As Sporton puts it, there is a 'sanitized' account of this long-running drama in Glenn
Wilson, *In Just Order Move*, London: Athlone Press, 1997.
[10] Hoggart papers, 4/9.21, 1978.

We say that valedictory addresses such as this one are 'generous-hearted' and are right to say so. Say rather, however, that this is the true tone of someone finding in a dear friend and colleague those qualities of humankind he most admires and which he feels coursing strongly in his own being, even as he tries to pull himself back sharply from the errors into which they might lead.

> He took to himself too many problems, he saw none as insoluble, so that is why he was so rarely alone in his office – never offputting, no dispiriting litany of the case against – considerate, sympathetic, responsive, unassuming, large and generous in spirit.

As the Warden approaches his coda, he eases the tone of his elegy, as one must, with a touch of admiring amusement, so that his audience may smile as well as swallow hard at the openness of feeling.

> We remember too with awestruck amazement his penchant for buying new property for the College, his fundraising phone calls, his gay foresight – his unshakable conviction of the uniqueness of Goldsmiths', the rightness of expanding Higher Education – trying always to reach a just consensus.[11]

A just consensus. That is the goal of the good and diplomatic ruler-bureaucrat, and it is a depressing measure of the poverty of popular political speech – never more so than, say, in the pages of the *Daily Mail* – that 'bureaucrat' is only used as a swear word and that no one since Max Weber officially recognizes the indispensable needfulness of a sane, rational, competent, virtuous bureaucracy.

One sometimes tart lesson of Hoggart's life-and-work is the visibility, in so many public places, of his struggle for just consensus in all circumstances. This was not to say that that same consensus and its justice were together arrived at without his own allegiances being part of the agreement. Indeed, there were plenty of people who took resentful umbrage at the firmness with which, for instance, he administered cuts in the Arts Council budget when in 1976 on his return to Britain, he accepted an invitation from Kenneth Robinson, then Labour Minister for the Arts, to join the Council, and in 1980 to become its vice-chairman.

We have seen plenty already of Hoggart's readiness to accept public office in addition to already demanding forms of employment. Adding the Arts Council to the Wardenship was, well, self-punishing as well as so plainly civic-minded. He went into these activities with

---

[11] Hoggart papers, 4/9.21.

so little self-protection that one's natural instinct to warn him against overwork on such a scale – he lived well into his nineties, so what the hell? – is silenced. He could do it, somewhere in himself he *wanted* to, somebody had to, just as well it was him.

John Maynard Keynes was the mighty figure who, in between rescuing the European economies from devastation in 1945, persuaded the Labour government to allocate a hefty sum from a beleaguered Treasury to helping the arts to struggle on in the midst of bomb-damaged cities and universal rationing. The Arts Council was created, and regional orchestras, local repertory theatres, penurious city art galleries, ballet dancers in warehouses, movie-makers in railway carriages, and sculptors in beachside cabins, were variously helped to keep art in its traditional forms alive, even vigorous, at a time of undoubted privation and, it may be, of dulled imagination and beaten-down morale.

By 1976, when Hoggart, a nationally known figure as well as a Labour sympathizer, was invited to join the Council's main committee, the Arts Council, with offices at 105 Piccadilly, had grown enormously in influence, in prestige, and in its taken-for-granted national importance and permanence as paymaster to all the arts, by then a good deal more numerous in form and variety than in 1945. Indeed, one might risk saying, as Hoggart a bit too bluntly did, that various arts organizations, especially theatrical ones (always liable to narcissism in the nature of the trade itself), supposed themselves entitled to financial support as of right.

This settled graspingness, from – of course – always hard-pressed and whoreson players – corresponded at times to something both slack and sanctimonious in the Council's assessors which riled Hoggart badly. All his intellectual life he had insisted on the necessity of judgement, never more so than in relation to art. Judgement for Hoggart, as for Leavis from whom he took his lead, was little to do with a sentencing and bewigged authority sitting above the tribunals of life; it was the natural wakeful life of any human being, sorting as each of us must between – Charles Taylor's phrase – 'the distinctions of worth' which direct our lives.

So when an officer of the Council corrected him for asking how it was decided whom to help with grants – '*we* don't judge, we respond to the needs of the grass roots' – he was hard put to it, as a newcomer, not to burst out angrily against this abrogation of mind. This intransigence was, however, exactly why he had been invited aboard. His lifelong friend, Roy Shaw, was newly appointed Secretary-General of the Council – fellow-soldier in uniform, fellow-soldier also in adult education, Roy Shaw who had written with such affection to Hoggart back in 1957 of how much their friendship meant to him, written also of the patriotic shame he felt at the time of the disgraceful Suez sortie – Shaw welcomed Hoggart onto the Council precisely because his skilfulness in committees ('just consensus') was given steel and stamina by his principles of judgement.

There was plenty of occasion for both. It may be that a certain hardening in his disposition as a consequence of the rugged, sometimes scurrilous combat at UNESCO, let alone impatience with the sheer goofiness of one or two colleagues at Goldsmiths, combined to make him more terse, even harsh with some of the queue of supplicants. He said himself, there is no intrinsic case for a society to reserve money to pay for the arts.

> No society need give a penny to the arts unless it chooses to do so. No one can prove it should, as one may prove pure water and effective sanitation are necessary to healthy physical life for a community. To give public money to the arts has to be based on a particular value-judgement, on beliefs, not on determinable facts.[12]

It's worth saying that he had got himself hung up once again on the wholly misleading and unnecessary commandment that 'you can't get an ought from an is'. The Wittgenstein he never read would have reassured him that to demand something called proof for everything one believes is to sentence oneself to sterility. The very creation of a state, from its early inceptions in sixteenth-century Italy, was token of the desire on the part of a society for an authority above and external to the sovereign power, which would act as 'the moral agent of the people'.[13] Such an agent would, in a necessary fiction, tend the health of a society, guarantee its debts, declare its wars, and provide for its wellbeing, whether physical, intellectual or spiritual, according to those forms of life which pertain to such matters. Insofar as moral progress itself can be said to be a guiding ideal of a society, then only a State is capable of directing the collective activity towards such a thing – once, that is, Church and State have been split apart by the march of modernity.

What Hoggart was arguing for was the benign officiating of the State itself and, as he wrote only a decade or so after his service on the Arts Council as its Vice-Chair,

---

[12] Hoggart (1992), p. 218.
[13] The formula is Quentin Skinner's, in various works, beginning with *The Foundations of Modern Political Thought*, Cambridge: Cambridge University Press, 1978, vol. II *passim*.

The arts are to be kept up because they are the most profound expression of our nature and experience. Without the constant and free practice of the arts, without people aware of the arts and free to come to them, however awkward they often are, a society is the poorer.[14]

No doubting the sincerity and excellent simplicity of this voice. There was, there is, however, a particular timeliness to these commonplaces. When he joined Roy Shaw at the Council the relevant Education Minister of the then Labour government was a worthy herbivore called Shirley Williams, lifelong Fabian and daughter of a Party heroine of feminist Leftism called Vera Brittain. This friendly creature, not somebody much possessed of stomach for a fight when, as happened a little later, a fight was called for, endorsed all the Arts Council was doing and made decent shift to find it the money. She also invited Hoggart to chair an advisory council on adult education, a post which, for all its dull-sounding title and certain-to-be-tedious-and-lengthy labours, his whole career had directed him towards and which his compelling sense of public duty obliged him to accept.

But the deep tides of historical change were on the move, pushing the heavy sandbanks of political sentiment into new shapes. The two surfers riding these waves were Ronald Reagan and Margaret Thatcher, and the crude and mindless slogan with which they carried off their daring swoops was 'roll back the State'. Anti-*étatisme* became the new government's chorus, and it caught and channelled one powerful response in popular sentiment.

In Britain, at least, such changes are rarely absolute; political fervour in the USA is different and far more sentimental as well as nationalist. Thatcherism only gradually became fully aware of itself as a doctrine across about ten years, and remained replete with ignorance and incoherence. Insofar as its guiding idea was to oppose and reduce the expense and effectiveness of the State, however, the uneven, inexpressive character of a docile, even (as George Orwell said) somnambulist people gave its assent.

Which returns us to our hero. For Hoggart's life's work was to bend the good offices of the State to the service of all those millions whom exploitation, accident and sheer, damnable meanness on the part of their society had kept without succour for their sensibility or cultivation for their minds.

Hoggart chaired his little committee according to his own best commitments. He was no vulgar Leftist; he sought the 'just consensus'; he had to carry with him others of a different colour and their

[14] Hoggart (1992), p. 218.

own strong allegiances. He was known, as you'd expect, as no friend of the government, and it transpired that Mrs Thatcher took his enmity, as she often did, quite personally. In one particular instance, however, his fellows on the committee and the Chair were joined in a gratifying unison.

They had commissioned a survey, mentioned in a previous chapter, of the demand for the kind of adult education in which Hoggart had spent thirteen postwar years. The survey helped the advisory committee screw a bit more money out of government. What thrilled Hoggart and, even now, brings a lump to one's throat was the way so many respondents to the survey[15] gave as the reasons they wanted their part-time, evening education not for vocational training of various kinds, but out of the old, beautiful longing for 'wholeness', for 'fulfilment', for 'enriching' experiences, for 'broadening their minds', for becoming, even, 'a better person'. The gentle clichés stood up and walked off the page, back into everyday living and Hoggart cheered them on with a favourite quotation from Coleridge, 'Men, I think, are to be weighed not counted.'

IV

His committee did its bit towards keeping 'the moral agent of the people' up to the mark, ensuring that the State do its duty by the education of the people. Back at the Arts Council, the arguments were much cruder because closer to policy and politics. The Council's cheques were to be drastically reduced because ... because why? Because in a Tory world the realm of the State *must* be reduced, nor is it the State's obligation to ensure that not-very-well-off people can afford to attend *Cosi Fan Tutte* at the Royal Opera House.

Hoggart was in any case more than a little torn in himself. Quite apart from the fact that the Council could only dispense the funds allocated by government – it had no resources of its own and must, obviously, do as it was told – there were clear decisions in terms of natural justice to be made. Where professional livelihoods were in danger – repertory companies in provincial theatres threatened with closure – it was plain that they took precedence over strictly amateur organizations who had been given a helping hand when the account book was flush. In addition to these contentious but straightforward decisions, Hoggart himself was torn as to the worthwhileness of some

---

[15] Published as *From Policies to Practice*, London: HMSO, 1982.

*The National Adult and Continuing Education Committee, meeting at
Goldsmiths in 1978.*

arts organizations whose cheques were being stopped. The judgements had to be made as to whether this barmy street theatre group
peddling its piffling drama round hospitable primary schools or that
folksong quartet in ill-judged straw hats and Worzel Gummidge trousers tied with string below the knee, merited public support. Would
the health of the culture be impaired by their disappearance?

Hoggart, however unwilling a junior of the new government, was
pretty sure that it wouldn't. Astonishing amounts of sanctimony
were punctually on display outside the Arts Council headquarters.
Hoggart himself, in the absence of the chairman on sick leave, had
to announce, in 1981, the first round of cuts in funding its depend-
ants. In the way of such antics, protest was ferociously personal.
Arts activists renounce the habitual docility of the British. They fight
dirty and punch low and, all things considered, probably retain more
financial support than they would have won without streetfighting.
So the three per cent of Council clients affected (the figure is correct)
marched and countermarched in Piccadilly and the banners and
effigies were adorned with slogans reading 'Hang Hoggart high'. It
was rare for Hoggart to be publicly maligned, and without rational
and informed debate. Rarer still for a man unmistakably faithful to
the principles of open democratic debate to be noisily accused of

undemocratic obduracy. When invited to appear, with Roy Shaw, on a Channel Four debate about the cuts, Shaw and Hoggart on the platform, the audience out for blood, the two public figures declined. Rational debate hadn't a chance in such theatre.

It was, however, a stiff test for a man who had spent so much of his life working on behalf of the highest standards of public broadcasting. Hoggart chaired the Broadcasting Research Unit, based at the British Film Institute, almost from its inception at the hands of Kenneth Lamb from the BBC in 1980, and remained in office until 1990. Still feeling stung by the reckless abuse of the protesters (who turned up again at Goldsmiths for his retirement farewell in 1984), he set himself to write on behalf of the Research Unit a Broadcasting Charter for Britain.[16] Its roots were, naturally, deep in the Pilkington Report. It set out the rights and corresponding duties of audiences, of programme-makers, and of legislators. Audiences should have rights of access wherever they lived, the right 'to be approached as adults', the right 'not to be got at politically, commercially, piously' (typical of Hoggart to put things like that). They should be justified in expecting broadcasting to speak 'as the voice of the community', justified that is in finding a common identity shaping itself out of the jumbled discourse of a week's television and emerging as something sane, intelligent, understanding, spirited, kindly, stern, delighted ... the adjectives might stretch out forever, but the hope of such a thing is presently extinguished. There are still fine programmes made, of course, but as the cables and satellite dishes cluttered the country and as the vast, all-swallowing empire of Sky filled the skies, the chance of nations speaking peace unto nations (as the BBC news banner in the 1950s read) according to their singular national voices faded into the babel of the airwaves.

It goes without saying that Hoggart never gave up, and as the long reign of Mrs Thatcher's governments stretched into the 1990s (and after her fall were carried on, more feebly but so far as social democracy went just as malevolently under John Major), Hoggart's public tones and private resolution became harder and more intransigent. It became known to civil servants and junior ministers that, though he never met her, his was a name to which she was swiftly hostile, and when her creatures in junior posts ran up against it in the network of committees in the arts and broadcasting worlds they followed suit.

At times this toadying made Hoggart angry, at times resigned. The temper of the country – if one can ever catch certain hold of

---

[16] Drafts in Hoggart papers, 5/11/75. The Charter was finally published in 1989.

such a thing – seemed to be on the move. Where once the ruling parties had not only shared many assumptions – about moral limitations on wealth, for example, as well as the importance of decent opportunity – but also tolerated cross-Party plain speaking, they now drew apart, one side openly gloating over the money to be made, the other hapless, resentful, forced into a crouching almost-mimicry of attitudes their forebears would have detested.

So Hoggart was impelled to bear his witness. Often to be seen in television discussion, he saw it as a duty to accept such invitations as long as the conversation would be open and its ends unfixed. There were home truths still to be spoken. When Melvyn Bragg, himself a public figure in the Hoggart mould and much in debt, as he acknowledges, to *The Uses of Literacy*, invited him onto *Second House*, a BBC talkshow, to discuss class in Britain, Hoggart could be as firm and sharp as he wanted. And he wanted to be heard, he liked his fame, as one would, but quite without hammering in his points, told a listening audience about itself.

Bragg played a sequence of television clips to display British social class manners in action. Clive James was at the time the completely admirable television critic at the *Observer*.

> A week after the event at least one viewer is still chuckling at the sublime outrage with which Richard Hoggart, in an absorbing *Second House* on Class (BBC2), reacted to an old clip of John Betjeman (as he then was), Nevill Coghill, A. L. Rowse and Lord David Cecil sitting around in Oxford congratulating themselves on their own degree of civilization . . .
>
> Hoggart started to point out what was plainly a fact – that the claims these men were making for the intellectual productivity of Oxford were absurd – but there was no time to pursue the argument in the full richness of its potential. It really was marvellous to watch A. L. Rowse talking about the disinterested quest for Truth while his friends lolled about nodding wisely, forgetting to add or else never having noticed that for A. L. Rowse the Truth had usually been any foolish notion that happened to pop into his head.
>
> You could say Betjeman had distinction, and all four men had undoubtedly seized the opportunities offered by Oxford to cultivate their eccentricities to the full, but that was about it. What we were looking at was not a concentration of mental power but a mutual admiration society – a club. And it was surely the knowledge that such clubs are still with us that led Hoggart ever so slightly to blow his cool.[17]

[17] Clive James, *On Television: Criticism from The Observer 1972–1982*, London: Picador, 1991, pp. 147–78.

Hoggart was there to tell us that class was as blunt and horrible a fact about Britain as ever. James, however, the unaccommodating Australian, pointed out that Bragg and Hoggart themselves, by their very presence on the screen, changed the voice of the community as it spoke to itself. In a splendid aphorism – 'anaemic high art is less worth having than low art with guts'[18] – James himself summarized the best of Hoggart's own argument about culture and its popularity.

I think it probable that he accepted so many public duties and television appearances in part out of a sense of gratified and sheer amazement at his own success and recognition. It had been like this in miniature at Cockburn High School, when he arrived as Herbert and at once became Richard, and when his quick wits and sunny disposition brought him popularity among other pupils, and the regard of his teachers. When, at the peak of his career, all these dramatic and glossy-seeming invitations to join, to have his say, to give himself, his time and energy to so many enterprises – let alone the twelve-hour day at Goldsmiths – they confirmed, surely, to his still apprehensive and longing self that he was who he was because so many others wanted him to be so.

Nothing wrong with that, and in any case for such a man duty is less, in Milton's terrible words, 'stern daughter of the voice of God', than the very ground of action in a godless universe. In any case, what is a motive? Is it the quavering of the inner self, or the straight summons of an ethics? Mary might have wished – in Paris she did wish – that the ethics were less imperious. But when in 1978 the trustees of the *New Statesman*, Britain's always ailing, always necessary Left-Labour weekly, invited Hoggart to chair its board of management, of course he said yes. He had known it well in its heyday, when every adult education tutor read its every word; he liked Phillip Whitehead, the Labour MP and trustee who had proposed his name, the need was pressing ... what else could he do? The excellent editor at the time, Tony Howard, resigned because, as he bravely and candidly said, he couldn't hold the slide in circulation and had better find a new job before it was too late. Riven by disagreements over the kind of journal the *Statesman* should be, the board made the unhappy decision to appoint an investigative journalist, Bruce Page, who promptly sacked the journals' house humourist, Arthur Marshall, whose weekly full-page article was immensely popular with the readership, and the decline in circulation deepened. Hoggart quit quietly.

[18] James (1991), p. 206.

He had one other public office, one of muffled comedy as well as legislative weight. After the Williams report on the laws controlling obscene publications came out in 1977,[19] the official instrument of control, the British Board of Censors, was wound up. The Chatterley trial may have released one single work of serious moral purpose onto the open plains of literature but its main consequence was to permit a torrent of routine, trivial and more or less revolting pornography to flow into a new kind of sex shop, flourishing just off the High Street, and selling dozens of cheap and lowering movies available in the new domestic form of the video.

There was a handful of tightly strained militants protesting against this new latitude, and objecting to bare breasts and bouncing buttocks sometimes visible on late night TV, but by and large the common attitude of calm tolerance seemed about right. Hoggart's own plain speaking on the witness stand in 1960 had come to be generally shared even if, in 1980, no one foresaw the almost infinite multiplication of television channels, and the dismal tedium of gormless girls with enormous bosoms fondling themselves sexlessly onscreen in order to sell access to the dreary films in which they make their living.

Even if they had, and however severe one's Hoggartian judgement might be on that nauseating little corner of the culture, the moral premise would probably still hold that these things should be officially tolerated in the name, no doubt, of freedom, as well as in the conviction that the undergrowth of culture, except where it conduces to vilenesses or cruelty, is best kept legal. Limits must be set to the access of children to such stuff, naturally, and offensive materials should be prevented from causing too much offence, sewage belongs underground in the sewers, but the authorities are responsible for keeping them cleaned up and safe from the plague.

To effect hygienic labours the new British Board of Film Classification (not, therefore, of censorship but of the degrees of public visibility) appointed, in 1985, the Video Appeals Committee, to which videos proving difficult to – well – classify were referred and, as any reader who has followed me this far will have anticipated, Hoggart was asked to serve, and did so for eleven years.

He was joined in the task by Laurie Taylor, sometime Professor of Sociology in the heyday of the University of York, subsequently for forty years a dead serious, wonderfully funny satirist of academic absurdities in the house weekly, *The Times Higher Education*, and

---

[19] *Report of the Committee on Obscenity and Film Censorship*, London: HMSO, 1977.

a gunslinging broadcaster of high repute. Both men knew well and respected each other greatly.

They turned, in a spirit mingled of serious attention and necessary hilarity, to a quarterly immersion in the cesspit, along with *Sex Dens of Bangkok*, *Once Upon a Girl* and *Slavs and Slaves*.[20] They, and a few others (the Committee was quorate with five members) sat through those dire movies which had been refused permission even to be sold in sex shops and whose makers had appealed for a hearing. Hoggart always had, as we know, a lively, monogamous interest in sex, a keen eye for well-formed women's bodies, and unsparing aesthetic standards of judgement. What he couldn't stand were badly made films as well as male performers with long unwashed hair, straggling beards and, as both officers noted frequently, spotty bottoms.

One day he burst out at the maker of one such wretched video, who was required to be present, asking him just *why* the film technique was so awful, moving in and out of focus, the camera swinging about all over the place, the narrative line, such as it was, broken, incoherent and banal. The film-maker, gobbling, desperately eager to please, said he quite understood the criticisms, but the badness was quite deliberate since then the audience believed that the film wasn't just acted but was real life in action, and consequently more erotic in its effect.

V

Hoggart occupied the post of Warden of Goldsmiths for eight years, carrying on alongside his position at the Arts Council, the Broadcasting Research Unit, European Museum of the Year Award, the *New Statesman*, the Advisory Committee on adult education, the classifying of porn movies, keeping in regular touch with the training of youth workers he began in Leicester in 1969. With many of his fellows in such work, he was also looking out fearfully (after 1979) for the Tory government's much-bruited cull of the 'quangos', the acronym which designated all those benignly intended organizations commissioned to keep the common weal more or less smooth in operation.

The content and schedule of such a life was at once punishing and fulfilling, worthy and benevolent in its effects, or hapless and

---

[20] This anecdote reported to me by Laurie Taylor in one of several conversations and letters in 2012.

superficial, according to your age, your politics, or the degree of tired-
ness brought on by overwork. Not that the Hoggarts ever complained
of overwork, and Mary was ever stern in ensuring that their strong
lifeline to the North of England was kept in good repair. Simon
and family, Paul and his family were both in London and often in
Farnham; Nicola, a bit further off teaching in Norwich where her
husband Richard was an administrator at the University of East
Anglia, was no less tightly bound into the family redoubt. Between
times, Richard and Mary made their way to see the Aunts and sister
Molly in Yorkshire, and brother Tom near Grantham.

It was, in his own adjectives much-quoted here, a 'full, rich life' as
well as a good one. Yet Hoggart was fretted by the sense that the one
true vocation to which he had always knelt was consistently sidelined
by the contingency of every day. As he wrote, with some self-distaste,
in the preface to a new collection of papers and lectures which Chatto
brought out in 1982 (the publishers always knew that any Hoggart
collection was good for a few thousand hardback sales),

> I now realize that I've been practising the long essay, which sometimes
> starts life as a formal lecture, for almost a quarter of a century. It's a
> teasing form and more demanding than is generally recognized. I like
> some of its disciplines. But it is also constricting and constraining. My
> next book will start at page 1 and go right on to the end.[21]

That would only be possible with the oceans of time beckoning on
the horizon of retirement. The constraints, moreover, of the official
lecture or solicited publication from someone in his position, are
frequently plain to see upon the page. Too often this particular
'smiling, public man' (as Yeats put it) is obliged to let go of his most
powerful gift (in Clive James's tribute): 'combining general argument
with specific detail'.[22] Instead, he allows his argument, perhaps
perforce, to be carried along on the cushions of official rhythms and
formal diction. Not that he lapses ever into UNESCO 'bafflegab', but
that these are not occasions for 'the elegant and beautiful sight of a
solitary human being putting himself to the test through language'.[23]

The sight of such a testing however, in his book or his life at this
time, is not absent by any means. Taking his thrice-weekly swim in
the public baths in Laurie Grove on Goldsmiths' perimeter (at a time
before their noble restoration in the 1990s), he was,

---

[21] Hoggart, *An English Temper: Essays on Education, Culture and Communications*,
London: Chatto and Windus, 1982, p. xi.
[22] James (1991), p. 149.
[23] Hoggart (1982), p. 55.

... not all that long ago, in a public baths, built *circa* the turn of the century, lavatorially tiled, smelling of chlorine, very bleak-looking, very shabby. I had been there often, so was beginning to be known. This particular morning the attendant on duty was a man of, I suppose, just over twenty. He was far too heavy for the good of his health. He sat in the dreary cabin provided at the side of the pool for the use of the attendants, smoking a good deal, brewing a succession of cups of tea and leafing through the day's issue of one of the popular newspapers ... That day, as I was getting dressed and we were alone in the place (it was about 8.30 in the morning) he walked over to me, looked up at the great glass roof held up by its Edwardian wrought ironwork and asked: (I will not try to reproduce his speech): 'Have you ever noticed all that iron stuff? It's pretty, isn't it? The other day I found in a cupboard at the back a lot of them old kind of photos – you know, all browns. But they were really pretty.' His vocabulary was massively inadequate to what he was trying to say. His conscious sense of the amazing thing that was happening inside him was almost non-existent, and I guess he may soon pass the point at which he can be moved to utter such obscure intimations to a near-stranger (though perhaps it was easier because I *am* a near-stranger, and because he'd guessed that I am connected with an artistic institution, the College up the road).

The manner of this parable was to be his aspiration when, with all the time in the world, he would turn to his autobiography. Until then, there was the glacial, interminable labour of preparing Goldsmiths' 'humble petition', in the anachronistic jargon of such documents, 'to the Queen's Most Excellent Majesty in Council'.[24] In the event that preparation ground on until 1988, four years after Hoggart retired. Before that there were the indicative little campaigns of media studies and Laban dance to conduct, a death threat to ignore (Hoggart and the Queen herself as targets in Brussels) at the Museum of the Year award ceremony, while all the time the skies darkened under the vast cloud of what he called in the *Observer*, 'Mrs Thatcher's bigoted egoism'.[25]

Even as he left office, the bitter, unsorted divisions of a society losing its gentility and coherence, losing hold of the political narrative which gave it these qualities, broke into Goldsmiths' busy forum. In June 1984, as preparations were made for his farewell occasion, the victims of the Arts Council cuts dusted off their banners reading 'Hangman Hoggart', quite unable to heed either his courage or his honesty in explaining the necessity of those decisions. A leaflet was

[24] *Goldsmiths' Petition*, nd, kindly provided by Pat Loughrey, present Warden.
[25] *Observer*, 29 December 1986.

circulated by the National Association of Teachers in Further and Higher Education (the more raucous of the two relevant trade unions) demanding (as it's always put) a boycott of members at the official farewell reception.

The whole staff, I am happy to say, ignored the injunction. The students, much-affronted, (also in the jargon) mandated their representatives to attend. On 12 July 1984, 350 people piled into the biggest of the college's halls. Hoggart found a note on his desk from his faithful secretary – called, of course, Pat – reading:

> Thank you for your reassuring note about the new Warden. There are many good men, however, but very few of them bring poetry into our everyday lives. That is what I shall miss, I think.[26]

Randolph Quirk, London's Vice-Chancellor, who had, we recall, rejected the shoddy report from a group of his professors once more excluding Goldsmiths from full membership of the university, declared to the applauding crowd his esteem for the departing Warden:

> May I in turn say how impressed I have been by the untiring efforts and intellectual drive you have selflessly contributed to the present and future of Goldsmiths' . . .

Hoggart, as is proper on such occasions, turned the occasion into an act of fealty to the institution: 'Goldsmiths' belongs to its district.' He commended its hospitality, he spoke of the college's crossbred pedigree – 'the mongrel must be female from the way she takes new babies under her' – and he gracefully praised 'the change in atmosphere' at the university after the new Vice-Chancellor's arrival. He concluded by wishing the college well in its desperately slow advance towards full membership of the university.

> We'd all like to help, though some of us are inhibited by our relations with the Prime Minister. If I threw my hat in the ring, the lady, who is the fastest gun in the West, would drill it full of holes.
> So good luck. Barkis is willing. The toast is 'Goldsmiths".[27]

He left, as he would, on a genial, fighting note. There were twenty years of writing still to be done in Farnham. So he passed over into retirement and all the trumpets sounded for him on the other side of his sixty-fifth birthday.

---

[26] Hoggart papers, 4/9/91.
[27] Hoggart papers, 4/9/15.

9

TIRING THE SUN

I

Retirement brings a reckoning. The farewell dinner, the much-meant tributes, closing down the little terrace house in St Donatt's Road, the slightly mumbled expressions of good wishes from staff, from cleaners, secretaries, porters, from students old and new, surely marked the end of something, not of a career nor a working life, but something. What was it? It was the end of institutional membership, of being part, part of the hurrying crowds of the Goldsmiths' population about him, part of the vast, indifferent University of London, part of New Cross, the further East End, part of the recently and, all things considered, happily multicultural neighbourhood (the word was hard-earned). Goodbye to all that except as a visitor or elderly relative come to see how things were getting on. But Hoggart, untearful mostly, relieved also of heavy duty and, so to say, of the sweat of social engineering, could not conceivably count himself out of productive society. Far more than the natural wakeful life of committee chairmanship, which he had become so firm and good at, far more than the world of negotiation, deliberation, execution, evaluation which had been at the middle of his life since leaving Leicester twenty years earlier, far more even than the teaching which was his trade, his art, and his avocation, productive life was, for Hoggart, writing. For years now he had battled against the deathly evasions, lies and obesity of managerial English, struggling to find among the polysyllables the sane, affirmative speech which Auden named. Now he could write not for himself (as people say) but (as D. H. Lawrence put it) 'for the race, as it were'.

The form or genre to hand would be that kind of not-quite-autobiography but of cultural history which he had made his own in *The Uses of Literacy*, a history attracting naturally the description 'personal' but far more than personal, quite without the pious sanctimony with which the adjective is commonly invested, personal emphasis going well beyond autobiography into that realm of experience the poet seeks when an individual takes on a sort of historical radioactivity, when one man or woman's life glows in the future with the energy it draws from its culture, energy which charges a biography – this one too, I hope – with more than local life.

Such energy is laid down by a living tradition where tradition is far from being the authoritarian and punitive command of the past. The writer of this kind of autobiography is searching, as Eliot's wonderful essay on tradition puts it[1] – an essay known pretty well by heart to Hoggart – for the *im*personal in a personal history, for the force of circumstance pressing on a life and directing it, in spite of itself, towards the finest life it can imagine for the present, 'The awakened, lips parted, the hope, the new ships.'

Tradition, a painter once said, you have always beside you, and when you lose your way, you can stretch out your hand and steady yourself on its durability and companionship, finding your way once more. Hoggart's tradition was that irregular, ununiformed army of writers in 'the condition of England debate', where 'England' to his generation took in, perhaps annoyingly, the then united, now disputatious kingdom. Its many unharmonious voices included the self-made English-American, T. S. Eliot, for sure, the great Orcadian poet Edwin Muir and *his* autobiography, his 'Welsh-European' comrade in adult education, Raymond Williams, the Irish poet and Nobel laureate Seamus Heaney, Yorkshireman poet quoted earlier, Tony Harrison, these five names among dozens as indicating that his ecumenical subject-matter embraced all the Anglophone archipelago, its intense localness and domestic rivalry.

The tradition stretched back, as we have seen, to the beginning of the Romantic-democratic movement, which still shapes the essential self of Britain, for better and worse. Its members, like William Cobbett, say, or Mary Wollstonecraft; like Wordsworth early *and* late; like Shelley and Keats; like Dickens and Mary Ann Evans, the Brontë sisters in darkest Yorkshire; like noble-hearted but slightly dotty John Ruskin; had no common politics nor a shared picture of a good life. Thomas Carlyle yearned wistfully for what he believed was

---

[1] T. S. Eliot, 'Tradition and the Individual Talent', in *The Sacred Wood* (1921), London: Dent, 1960.

the good society of medieval St Albans; William Morris brought the improbable *News from Nowhere* of an England perfected by socialism, such that healthy and handsome young men and women worked harmoniously at time-sanctioned crafts and husbandry, free of old England's awful old class system and its inequalities.

These figures, 'united in the strife which divided them' (Eliot's famous words) in all the variety of their writing, were Hoggart's Canterbury pilgrims, following their erratic route into the future, telling anyone who would listen the stories which measured off the miles.

If those were his ancestors, his own century provided as numerous and as good a band and a familiar roll already called: Leavis, Orwell, Gertrude Bell, R. H. Tawney, Richard Titmuss, E. M. Forster, D. H. Lawrence, Learie Constantine, Nikolaus Pevsner . . . the list stretches out to the crack of doom and was, for Hoggart and many others, transformed from a list into a historical tradition by the American-Englishman's great, imagination-shaping poem, *Little Gidding.*

Hoggart himself said on several occasions that he wished he had had the talent to be a poet or a novelist. Simon recalled his father saying that he thought his books were of little account; but *all* writers think that from time to time, *must* think it for mere modesty's sake, must also think what Keats said (thus quoted, moreover, by Hoggart), 'I shall be among the English poets after my death.' The tradition in which Hoggart takes his natural place, however, gathers up all literary forms in a common endeavour to see the local world straight and to make of it a life worth living, out of its bits and pieces to build a safe home.

It sounds a bit corny, but then Hoggart himself was never afraid of doing so. Joining a tradition isn't exactly a voluntary business. It chooses you, and if it transpires that you belong to it, you move into the ranks quite naturally. So the writing which awaited him would be in the form he did best, but a form well known to his 'familiar compound ghost', the 'brown baked features' of F. R. Leavis, T. S. Eliot in the pale grey suit and panama hat which he wore to testify to the Pilkington committee, D. H. Lawrence, fierce, cross, passionate, speaking his curse over 'Nottingham and the mining countryside'.

These names come naturally in Hoggart's company. But an unignorable feature of his writing is the facility with which he appends timely epigraphs to most chapters, as well as the frequency with which certain of his favourite quotations recur. All his life, in a habit nowadays, I think, largely disappeared from bookish lives, he kept commonplace books in which he wrote out telling quotations wherever he found them. Sometimes he retained them on scraps of torn-off paper, mostly he copied them into notebooks, sometimes – for he had an excellent memory for such things – he simply knew them by heart and repeated them many times. I don't know how often he quoted Chekhov saying to his own people, 'You live badly, my friends, it is shameful to live like that', but he took it, rightly, as licensing his own severe admonitions to his own people. The anger of a good man comes upon him righteously all right; it is the necessary obverse of love. His people should not act shamefully, and when they do, they should be told.

The reiteration of these sampler texts is more than just a survival from the nineteenth century, and far more than just a habit. It is the very ground of being in a man for whom the love of literature goes as deep as he can reach. Moreover, 'literature' is too blank a word here. Rather, from the countless books on the shelf, the person who loves them selects for him- or herself those voices which summon the reader with rightful authority. Their discovery may be accidental, as it was when Hoggart found Swinburne in Hunslet library. Or it may be directed, as when Bonamy Dobrée directed him to Henry Adams.

Either way, the telling voice or the single observation moves into the field of force of individual being – that vivifying interplay and ceaseless bombardment of the countless cognitive particles which together compound our thought and feeling, the two as being insepa-rable, mutually formative. It is hard to fix the metaphors for any such account of the formation of a character, the synonymity of life and work, the course set for a person's selfhood by the presences who move his or her life this way rather than that. For a man like Hoggart, his test for authoritativeness in those whose influence counted for most was, in the first place, their powers of loving kindness and the fidelity bound into it: Grandmother, Mary, his children, his dearest friends – his brother Tom and Roy Shaw above all, Michael Orrom the film-maker, David Lodge, Arthur and Jean Humphreys, Stuart Hall, Michael Shaw his agent, Charles Frankel and many more. The second moral quality he looked out for was the refusal of class, of any taint of that dreadful kind of English class arrogance, that calm, closed-minded presumption of superiority against which Hoggart always had to brace his natural good manners. Thirdly, his moral compass – no, the deep ontology of his nature – flickered magnetically towards the steady building of true because dependable judgements of value and distinctions of worth. He liked very much this definition of Charles Taylor's:

To be a full human agent, to be a person or self in the ordinary meaning, is to exist in a space defined by distinctions of worth.[2]

Taylor, a fine man and a generous hero of the early New Left, as well as founder of the Canadian New Democratic Party, retrieved for himself a version of Catholicism miles away from Hoggart's refusal of Christianity. But Taylor insisted on a moral philosophy rooted in judgements of the right and the good,[3] and Hoggart was pledged to the same cause.

Hence the likeness to music – their ring and cadence – in the beautifully chosen, unexpected epigraphs in so many of his books. These, as I insist, are far more than adornments on the exterior of each work. They have their own strong patterning, they have deeply patterned our man. Consider the first four from *The Uses of Literacy*; the second four from *The Way We Live Now*.

The Uses of Literacy

By this means, a kind of virtuous materialism may ultimately be established in the world, which would not corrupt, but enervate the soul, and noiselessly unbend its springs of action. (De Tocqueville)

Toleration is not the *opposite* of intolerance, but is the *counterfeit* of it. Both are despotisms. The one assumes to itself the right of withholding liberty of conscience, and the other of granting it. (Tom Paine)

Reflecting upon the magnitude of the general evil, I should be oppressed with a dishonourable melancholy, had I not a deep impression of certain inherent and indestructible qualities of the human mind. (Wordsworth)

. . . One would have said beyond a doubt
That was the very end of the hour,
But that the creature would not die. (Edwin Muir)

The Way We Live Now

Two nations; between whom there is no intercourse and no sympathy; who are as ignorant of each other's habits, thoughts and feelings, as if they were dwellers in different zones, or inhabitants of different planets; who are formed by a different breeding, are fed by a different food, are ordered by different manners, and are not governed by the same laws. (Benjamin Disraeli, *Sybil*, 1845)

Here was a medium of great power, of potentially wondrous delights, that could help to emancipate us from many of the stifling tyrannies of

---

[2] Charles Taylor, *Philosophy and the Human Sciences*, Cambridge: Cambridge University Press, vol. 2, 1985, p. 3.

[3] The title of a forgotten, worthy essay Taylor himself appreciated at Oxford. See David Ross, *The Right and the Good*, Oxford: Clarendon Press, 1938.

class and status and gutter-press ignorance. (Dennis Potter, the 1993 MacTaggart Lecture)

Who is the Tolstoy of the Zulus? The Proust of the Papuans? I'd be glad to read them. (Saul Bellow)

Not the great nor well-bespoke,
But the mere uncounted folk.
Of whose life and death is none
Report or lamentation. (Rudyard Kipling, 'A Charm')

These are not all writers one could have predicted would appear in Hoggart's commonplace book. They are products of prodigious reading, but that's the job. More to the point, they illustrate the formation of a character and the disposition of a spirit. They tell us, as good writing should, what it would be like to know the man, how he would act in certain situations, how, above all, he conceived of his own life as a unity and therefore how we might judge it as a success.

In 1981, while he was at Goldsmiths, another old ally from the early days of the New Left in the 1950s, Alasdair MacIntyre, published his classic of didactic moral theory addressed to his times, *After Virtue*.[4] Hoggart gulped it down. MacIntyre, it may be recalled, had written appreciatively, in a personal letter, about *The Uses of Literacy*. He had then been a member of the legendary department of extra-mural studies under Tom Hollins at Leeds, and one editor, with E. P. Thompson, of the combative little journal of the Left, the *New Reasoner*. He subsequently made more and more despairing and determined efforts to hold together the ideals of Scottish Catholicism and the local community life in which he was raised by his doctor parents, until he resolved his difficulty by moving to Notre Dame University in the American South.

Nonetheless, his magnificent book was immediately recognizable to Hoggart. In his crucial chapter 15 entitled 'The Virtues, the Unity of a Human Life and the Concept of a Tradition', he cuts the moral key to living a life one may be proud of in the scattered, pathless landscape of modern morality. A person's life, he writes, gains its unity by being lived according to those virtues the individual discovers as truly part of his or her disposition. Such a unity will only be discoverable as such at the end of a life; a single or a collective life is good insofar as its author shapes it over a long time into as fine a work of art – true, beautiful, good – as the life in question permits.

---

[4] Alasdair MacIntyre, *After Virtue: A Study in Moral Theory*, London: Duckworth, 1981.

Virtues are not values. MacIntyre gives the book its title exactly because ours is a world unapt to speak, with Aristotle, of the virtues as given. 'Values', much on the tongue of sanctimonious demagogues and staring-eyed newspaper editors, may mean something or nothing. A value may indeed denote a fierce little concentration of significance which irradiates life with purpose, or it may be nothing more than a glinting shard of meaning – 'Loyalty', say, 'evidence' even, 'sincerity' (ha!) – picked up from the moral litter of modernism and flashed about for purpose.

While 'values' cannot shape themselves into an ethic, there is nonetheless common recognition of the durable virtues, and these remain findable in the life of a person or a nation. Hoggart responded to MacIntyre's argument as to a noble poem; he saw it as something he had thought and felt since becoming a man; since, indeed, recognizing his grandmother's loving goodness of heart and responding to Mr Harrison's unselfinterested seeing of a little boy's intelligence.

II

So the first, enormous task he set himself after returning to the now permanent home on Beavers Hill, Farnham, as a newly retired old professor was to write his three-volume account of his life, in part straight autobiography, secondly an extended moral judgement on the times which made the life what it was, and thirdly, naturally part of such a venture, an extended meditation on his people and on their rulers.

He had retained various of his public offices, and remained in the limelight of his fame, still writing for the Sunday papers, lecturing in Paris, Berlin, New York, being asked to act as anchorman on television programmes, one of these – entitled 'Why Culture' (as well it might be) a succinct, easygoing reply to the question which had beset him since he first found the word. Produced by his friend Michael Orrom, it began by putting side by side assorted shots of two weddings, one in Leeds, one in Tunis. The attractive likenesses of both, their proprieties and their exuberance, as well as the obvious contrasts made instantaneous that meaning of culture which connotes a way of life; a piercing extract from a play by Samuel Beckett which ended the programme did all that was necessary to remind viewers of the force of art. In between, Hoggart spoke as always, his respectful, arresting, direct and honest prose doing all that he said good broadcasting ought to do.

But the giant task, not without its intrinsic egoism, was the autobiography. For it required massive self-confidence as well as stamina. He began as soon as he was home for good. He put files and records and notes together for a while, he and Mary took a holiday in Provence soon after his birthday in the autumn of 1984, he began writing in the new year, and finished, 700 pages and three volumes later, in the summer of 1991, just after Mrs Thatcher was so satisfactorily ejected from number 10 by her own henchmen.

The Uses of Literacy took him five years. The autobiography – to disobey Hoggart himself and call it that – took less than seven, a time also filled with extensive work for the Broadcasting Research Unit (an offshoot of the British Film Institute) for whom he co-authored a full report in 1989. Simon recollected[5] from childhood that his father was always sidling off to his study, even on Christmas Day, to bash away at, first, his inevitably battered old typewriter, then his PC, though he adds, 'You could always pop in for a chat, help, money or advice.'

The autobiography is chronological, as it must be. (Even postmodernists must agree that selves are constituted by time's arrow.) It is also as garrulous as its author, by the same token self-aware, self-critical, and expansive on those subjects to which he gave his life. It would be invidious solemnly to pass through its pages with commentary and exposition, for this biography is already tied tightly to Hoggart's version of himself in those 700 pages. A biographer must take an *auto*biographical record on trust, take it, salt and sweeten it, put it at a distance from its original, turn it in the light, make a face or two at it, as well as add all that time has done to thin it out or thicken it up, with rare significance.

Make no mistake, however. Hoggart saw these three volumes as wholly different from his celebrated classic. It was to be a *magnum opus*, all right; his ambition was to build and sail his heavy craft, to arm and armour-plate her, and to steer her against the strong tides of her day. The books teach a detailed moral lesson about the history of his country over the seventy-odd years of his life, retrieving what he saw as the best that had been thought and said, in his hearing anyway, and setting that against all that had been done, both pitifully and disgracefully, to others' harm.

So *A Local Habitation*, which was published by Chatto in 1988, took him from childhood to the summons to war. For the first time,

---

[5] Preface to *Re-Reading Richard Hoggart*, Sue Owen, ed. Newcastle: Cambridge Scholars Publishing, 2008, p. xiv.

he had to write directly about finding his mother stricken on the rag rug, recall the mute anguish of separation from sister Molly, six years old, and brother Tom who, as bigger brother (by two years), had in a fatherless household always assumed more than a trace of parental authority, sort among his recollections of the riven household in Hunslet, Aunt Clara's rages, Uncle Herbert's fuddled evenings, Grandmother's silent and loving courage.

It is nonetheless a calm and cheerful book. In all his intellectual inquiries, as we know, Hoggart had made much of 'tone', of reading in such a way as to capture and describe faithfully the right tone of voice in which a piece of writing is truly pitched. In his Reith lectures, carefully written to sound not careless but carefree, he had had this to say about tone:

> It is easy to see that tone is more important than the dictionary-meanings of the words we use. Properly described, tone is a complicated matter of pitch, stress, timbre and the like. But I am using the word as a shorthand way of referring to those qualities in speech or writing which carry our sense of a relationship to another person. I want to get away from any remnant of the idea that tone is a dead carrier of live substance. Tone is part of substance; it can make the same words carry wholly opposed meanings. If you know your contexts it's simple to make 'Goodbye' mean '. . . and I hope I never see you again' or '. . . and I can't wait to get back to you' or many points between.[6]

So he was at pains in this first volume to sustain tones of unselfpitying plainness, non-rancorous but respectful descriptions of the facts of poverty and those of neighbourliness, loving-kindness, one little boy's observant ease before the world. He had been much put out by those criticisms of *The Uses of Literacy* which accused him of 'nostalgia',[7] of a wistful looking-back at the good old days of working-class propinquity. Such criticisms ignored Hoggart's own, fond irony when he designated one section in the original book, 'the full, rich life', precisely recreating the brief but splendid jollity of communal singing at the Club, the social affirmation made by a full table once a week.

The feelings in that part of the book ran two ways, one athwart the other. So, too, in *A Local Habitation*, he sought to bring out the shortness of the moral horizon of his class, its stolid acquiescence in such dull pleasures, its agreement with the social contract that it could be permitted little access to the huge fulfilments of art and education.

---

[6] Hoggart (1972), p. 14.

[7] Most symptomatically and, it must be said, gratuitously (good book though hers is) by Carolyn Steedman in *Landscape for a Good Woman*, London: Virago, 1986.

The figure braced against this tired indifference was Hoggart's own and the most dramatic moment – of which I have made much here – in the story left barely acknowledged. It was when arriving as a new boy at Cockburn High School, he decided, without consultation at home (they would have paid little attention in any case), to shed 'Bert' and become 'Richard'. One wonders if, in so rejecting a monosyllable heavy with class echoes, he was slightly ashamed of himself? Certainly he makes little of it, autobiographically. It is the determination it took, at eleven years old, which is the principal character in the story. Hoggart once remarked that the present day offered a cultural moment at which biography was more accessible – more *usable* – than the novel. Stefan Collini noted in him 'the presence of a strong writerly urge that has only found partial satisfaction in conventional academic genres'.[8] (Hoggart, we know, had always regarded it as a failure on his part not to have become a novelist or poet.) Shaping a biography ('finding the form in the stone') is as exacting and far-reaching an art as that of the novel. Form itself may be less of a difficulty in biography but not significance ('why does this person matter'?), nor detail and observation (a favourite quotation of Hoggart's was Henry James's injunction to the novelist, 'try to be one of those on whom nothing is lost').

So volume 1 progresses, by way of Messrs Harrison and Norden, the Salem bicycle club, the bed bugs of Harwich, and the fateful moment on the library steps when the invitation to see *Green Pastures* was made. Honour is done to Bonamy Dobrée, war breaks out and cheerfulness breaks in on every page. Also on every page there are the tones of a man holding stoutly to the idea of *progress*: progress of his own life towards the work of art it would constitute and of which he could be proud, progress of a class towards imaginable emancipation, and of the fighting temerity which such progress demanded of him.

This was not the fight of old politics, of Labour unions and industrial action. It was the fight of one good man to act on behalf of those like him and in the name of all that education can do for happiness, for freedom and fulfilment; for equality also.

Hoggart was nationally admired to stand for these great words; his career, known – it transpired – to many more thousands than he realized, was taken as emblem of the continuity of those values and of the tradition in which they arranged themselves as livable. So when the book was published, reviewers spoke with one accord of, in the

---

[8] Stefan Collini, *English Pasts: Essays in History and Culture*, Oxford: Oxford University Press, 1999, p. 220.

words of Keith Waterhouse (himself a leading figure in the rise of the working-class novel in the 1960s):

> Hoggart being Hoggart this is much more than a nostalgic stroll down Memory Lane . . . his purpose is to catapult us from the small world of his boyhood into the larger history beyond . . .[9]

'Hoggart being Hoggart'. People knew what that meant. So dozens of them wrote to him directly;[10] he always replied. As people will – they brought a lump to his throat, they bring a lump to mine – they registered their deep affect and recognition of his reminiscence by adding their own. Freddie Moss, from Cockburn days, recalled two-penny haircuts, penny baths in Joseph Street; Harry Elridge, Hunslet neighbour, wrote 'I wept. Silently. As I have while writing to you' (a closely written four-page letter); Muriel Guyver, one of the teachers at Jack Lane Elementary, recalled the ten-year-old's jokes; Edna Paul, the blind Sunday School teacher, wrote also; Joan Halloway wrote to say how her father, now dead, contemporary at Jack Lane, 'studiously followed your career'; Stanley Walker wrote to say that '*A Local Habitation* showed my daughter, now a GP, what her father's early life was like'; Hugh Phillips, his 'radical student' friend,[11] wrote in praise of the book's 'vivid, effortless recall of Leeds University life fifty years ago' (but of course it wasn't effortless. That is the point). All these, and many more, wrote, their eyes bright with recognition, at the just representation of their own lives, the only possession many of them had ever held tight.

Volume 2 followed swiftly, in 1990. The title is taken from Philip Larkin's much-honoured poem much honouring seaside holidays. It's one of Larkin's best, undisfigured by any sudden rush of coarseness as many of even his finest poems are. It's set in a lovingly recalled Scarborough, in the days when you might have seen Len Hutton on the beach during the cricket festival, in the background 'the small hushed waves' repeated fresh collapse', in the middle of the picture the men 'sort of clowning' – playing a deeply traditional, self-aware sort of fool – but 'helping the old, too, as they ought'. Out on the horizon of the North Sea, 'A white steamer stuck in the afternoon . . .'

The life-story is brought up to 1959 and Hoggart's departure from Hull. As he becomes more mature and reflective, so does the story. I fear that it is likely that this biography fails, in spite of efforts to

---

[9] *Sunday Telegraph*, 27 April 1988.
[10] Hoggart papers, 4/2/245–287.
[11] Hoggart (1988), pp. 192–3.

correct such a grievous fault, to bring out just how full, happy and congenial a family life the Hoggarts created for themselves. One way of writing the social history of domestic Britain after 1960 or so is by way of the fracturing of domestic life, the porousness of marriage, the radical alteration in sexual permissions and then, as the commination picks up speed, the broken homes, the single parents, the bitter recriminations, the desolate childhoods ... it's a dirge everyone can sing, it contains many truths. But not *the* truth, testified to by the strongest currents of popular culture, which Hoggart gave his intellectual life to plumbing and sampling. For the truth is that almost everybody cherishes marriage of a more or less loving sort, a safe home, children probably, the love that lasts a lifetime, a steady, interesting enough job, as the essential materials of the sufficient work of art they will have made of their lives. Recreating the necessarily private magnificence of the Hoggarts' family life is impossible to me: I don't know enough and I haven't the talent. But its actuality cannot be doubted, and the doughty second volume has as its counterpoint to warfare, almost-fatal injury, the shed for writing in Marske, the long dark journeys in unreliable automobiles to evening classes, it has the solid presences of the three children and of Mary, to whom so many of the books are dedicated. One of the only two Hoggart houses I visited often was Mortonsfield in Farnham, and it was eloquent of the joint achievement of this family-life-as-a-work-of-art, the steps down from the front door gathering you into its warmth and safety and comfort, the big landscape paintings on the walls confirming that same sure feeling for homeliness, the kitchen putting, for all its up-to-dateness, this sentimentalist in mind of the most famous kitchen in English literature, which is the Badger's in *The Wind in the Willows*.

It's risky, writing like this. You have to stay wide open, to use the clichés, even if they might kill the prose. These things must be set down, however. They are a life's work, and goodness knows (as you might say) they are the artwork of popular culture.

That domestic life provided the bulwark of Hoggart's politics. He once said of himself that he was 'much less sorted out, politically, than Edward Thompson and Raymond Williams'. In certain important ways, he opposed Williams. In a review of Williams's programmatic *The Long Revolution*,[12] Hoggart was at odds with Williams's rejection of the, as Williams saw it, middle-class and servile ideal of 'service'. One might say that Hoggart's book on UNESCO, *An Idea*

[12] Published by Chatto in 1961, Hoggart's review appeared in *New Left Review* 7, 1962.

and its Servants, was his riposte to Williams. Certainly, Hoggart put himself, in a wholly 'sorted-out' way, at the service of all those who longed for the freedoms of imaginative literature, film, television, all those narratives which tell of how the world is and how it ought to be.

Hoggart turns several times in the three volumes to the nature of his socialism. It is the socialism of Tawney's *The Acquisitive Society* and *Equality*, but is also that of Richard Titmuss's *The Gift Relationship*.[13] That book only came out in 1970 but Hoggart pounced on it. It is a study of the conventions and institutions of blood donation. In the USA blood is sold and bought which, as you'd expect, means that reserves of blood are provided by the poor and poorly. In Britain, blood is given; the symbol and the material of life is given to strangers. No need to labour the moral and political point.

So Hoggart's was never a revolutionary politics. Raymond Williams, like many on the Left, repudiated Fabianism ('the inevitability of gradualism') as the instrument of beneficent bureaucrats bringing improvement to their inferiors. Hoggart admired and endorsed the best old Fabians, led by Tawney, Sandy Lindsay, Bill Williams of Penguin, the beautiful Beatrice Webb. Their programme of education, of the provision of universal utilities (medicine, fuel, clean water, home sanitation, gas and electricity), of common and equal access to the staff of life, was his own. While he could see and feel the force of one-nation Conservatism as embodied in, say, Harold Macmillan, he could never have joined it, and in its commonplace behaviour, its ludicrous snobberies and arrogant assumption of privilege, found it laughable and hateful.

In any case, as he was writing in the 1980s, a new and much more monstrous Leviathan was taking shape in the murk of daily politics. When *A Sort of Clowning* came out in 1990, the reviewer in *The Listener*[14] described it as 'a fine and engrossing book, against which all other annals of the period will have to be measured'. The measure to be taken was that of the new Toryism which took its name, accurately enough, from Margaret Thatcher, but was energized by crazy doctrines of piratical finance supposedly dreamed up by laboratory economists in Chicago, and ratified by a dim, amiable lawyer called Geoffrey Howe, Mrs Thatcher's chancellor.

When Hoggart was describing, in volume 2, the quiet assiduity

---

[13] Richard Titmuss, *The Gift Relationship, from Human Blood to Social Policy*, London: Allen and Unwin, 1970.
[14] Philip Oakes, *Listener*, 12 October 1990.

of Arthur Humphreys' English department, he had been necessarily unaware of the menace that would threaten it twelve years later. When, in volume 3, he welcomed that amazing university expansion presaged by Lionel Robbins's great report, he had to do so while making his readers aware of the gathering of the Gradgrinds and the Mr Dombeys twenty-odd years later at the end of the road. In the 'annals of the period', as his reviewer had put it, Hoggart took the measure of a fearful weakening in his own tradition of social democracy, and the concomitant rise of a dark power always lurking in the British body politic, a mean, vengeful, grasping power, most at home, it is to be feared, in the home counties, and sanctimoniously certain that the Welfare State cosseted the inadequate, that private provision always trumped public service, that money talks louder than anything else, that trade unions were in the pay of the Communists. Above all, this creature believed only in utilitarian principles to decide on public policy. There was no common good, only usefulness, applicability and, in a new, popular travesty of a once-sacred word, vocationalism, the deathly contention that all education provided was training for the job three million people didn't have.

An Imagined Life measured all that for the coffin. But the monster still walks abroad even though its throat was cut by the world crash of 2008. So volume 3 is in part a threnody. It wasn't, however, that when he came back from Paris, things looked as glistening and hopeful as they had ten years before.

> In the late seventies Britain seemed, to a returning migrant, like a punch-drunk boxer in a dingy fairground; unions and bosses more than normally at odds with each other, the government tattered and torn – all in all a much less attractive place than we had left at the beginning of the decade.[15]

He used just these words in a talk for Granada TV. It is not often that Hoggart writes so badly, so casually, the sort of thing old buffers say as they switch off the ten o'clock news. Everyone did it, still does. It's all there in Andrew Marr's awful, dashed-off tour of the 1970s, also a BBC series.[16] But some such angry mournfulness was usual at the time among the influential classes, and it brought Mrs Thatcher to Downing Street, where her bankrupting policies were paid for by the amazingly lucky strike of oil in the North Sea.

This isn't the tone of the book. The first line of the first volume

---

[15] Hoggart (1992), p. 176.
[16] Andrew Marr, *A History of Modern Britain*, London: Pan Books, 2009.

reads, 'My Aunt Annie is dying in St James's Hospital';[17] the same line provides the close of the third volume. On her death in September 1983, he wrote to the hospital to thank its staff for their care of Aunt Lil, and to add 'we were reinforced in our belief that the NHS is one of the finest recent achievements of this country'.[18] The theme of this final volume is political, surely, for he had lived the years it describes, from 1959 to 1991, in the eye of – so to say – second order politics, that is, in the middle echelons of public life whose officers receive their orders directly from the power élite, and must do the best they can with them.

Hence his teasing title. It is taken from Logan Pearsall Smith, a minor man of letters in the 1920s, who wrote, in an augury of 'the coming of celebrity', 'People before the public live an imagined life in the thought of others, and flourish and feel faint as their self outside themselves grows bright or dwindles in that mirror.' Hoggart, taking as his subject that most public period of his life, wanted to repudiate this 'dire thought' (his words). His riposte, in his last paragraph, is that in truth his subject, 'above all else', is 'the continuity of love'. Not many intellectuals end their books like that, and that he unself-consciously could is one reason he had so many readers who would not count themselves in the intelligentsia. He says at one point[19] that 'thirty years after Michael Young coined the word, a sort of "meritoc-racy" can be seen moving into position. To which, yes, I belong, and probably you, since you are reading this book.' Well, *An Imagined Life* deals with his years in the public eye, years of membership of a minor élite and its distribution of powers. But many more readers followed him than were familiars of such a life, followed him from the United States also, where all three volumes were published as one, under the subtitle *The Times and Places of an Orphaned Intellectual*.[20] Maybe that surprising designation (his own choice) indicated his sense of lost-ness, the feeling, present in the book, that his tradition of combative, low-key socialism was fading, that the family of his comrades was either ancient or dead, and their heirs scattered and uncertain.

Yet there is no hint in the book of defeat or failure. Andrew Motion, Poet Laureate (and biographer of Larkin), wrote of it in the *Observer*,[21]

---

[17] Hoggart adopted the old-fashioned convention of *noms-de-plume* for the older genera-tion of his relatives. I have restored their proper names, 'Lil' for 'Annie', as he did in a later memoir: Hoggart (2001), pp. 211ff.
[18] Letter dated 26 September 1983, Hoggart papers.
[19] Hoggart (1992), p. 266.
[20] *A Measured Life*, Rutgers: Transaction Publishers, 1994.
[21] *Observer*, 3 January 1992.

Honorary doctorate (one of more than a dozen such awards to Richard Hoggart) at the University of Hull. The Vice-Chancellor, Sir William Taylor, is on Hoggart's left. Reproduced with the kind permission of the University of Hull.

> His anger about unfairness still burns ... his good heart remains robust and his devout absorption in a certain kind of Englishness is unequivocal.

The tone of that is representative. 'Good old Hoggart, still going on, still going on.' And in truth, he was increasingly alone. His great tradition was indeed lapsing. Traditions, of public feeling and political action, of moral direction also, fade, even disappear, until picked up and their flame blown back to life by a later generation.

The work in hand for the elders is therefore to keep going ('I can't go on. I'll go on,' Beckett makes one character say) and as far as Hoggart was concerned – to the relief of his thousands of senior readers – there was no question of his stopping. Jean Humphreys, Arthur's widow, wrote, we know, affectingly when she received her copy; it is worth quoting her again: 'Volume three arrived this morning and I have spent this morning crying like a child ...'[22] and she continued in a

---

[22] Letters dated 5 March and 17 March 1992, Hoggart papers.

second letter two weeks later, 'You have laid it on the line so clearly and trenchantly that the Thatcher years have damaged us all.' It is only the most vicious and unpleasant frame of feeling latent in British culture which would still take offence at that judgement, but that same feeling is strong and unkillable. Moreover, the continuing docility and obedience of the British people causes even hopeful politicians to acquiesce in the damage done to the nation's best parts.

III

So there was, God knows, plenty of work for Hoggart, now seventy-four, to do. He had been much encouraged in the November of 1991 by a lecture-with-readings from volume 3 which he gave at the University of Warwick. Old pupils turned out – Richard Dyer from Birmingham, David Howe from Leicester – and so did three hundred others. Hoggart's eye was caught by a bright, eagerly smiling, attractive face halfway back in the audience and, as he told her afterwards, he gave his lecture to her. The occasion was typical of several. No other such figure (I think of, say, Denis Healey, whose autobiography came out in 1989, or of Edward Thompson, whose stirring polemics so caught the anti-Thatcher mood in the partisan pages of the *Guardian*) was held in such direct public affection as well as esteem. He had been appointed spontaneously the prose-poet of dissenting politics.

This circumstance called for a quite new kind of book. He and Mary had been more or less settled on Beavers Hill by now since 1975, allowing for weekday living in the little terrace house in St Donatt's Road next to Goldsmiths. The choice of Farnham had startled some friends, deep in Tory Surrey as it was, unindustrial, sometime farmers' town, well-off, thickly populated by well-fed, well-upholstered public-school members of the Institute of Directors, crowding the railway stations each morning in their pinstripes and British warms.

Hoggart addressed himself to this massive continuity, rapidly discovering that this new class dominance was only eighty or so years old, that beforehand Farnham had been tougher, restless, jammed with itinerant workers come to pick the hops once piled in Mortonsfield itself and then to drink, in vast quantities, the beer the hops became.

Two writers are commemorated from old Farnham; Hoggart went well with them. The first was William Cobbett, now with a statue to his name, an ornate tomb, a pub called after him. That's the way of things. But it was Cobbett, in the very early nineteenth century, who named the ancestors of the portly, silver-haired exquisites on Farnham station platform 'Old Corruption', and put them in his pillory. It was Cobbett who, at the age of fifty-six, wrote the thundering condemnation of the government's responsibility for the deaths of nineteen protesters at the hands of the militia on St Peter's Fields, Manchester, in 1819.

Cobbett was, in his day, the towering journalist of the people, as well as their teacher. He wrote textbooks on good husbandry and on the right way to keep a poor home from starvation and disaster. He adjured young farm labourers to renounce 'the supple crouch of servility'.

The second writer from old Farnham was George Sturt, who had run, for his livelihood, a wheelwright's shop in Farnham from 1880 or so, and later written two classics of rural memoir, *The Wheelwright's Shop* itself and, under the *nom-de-plume* of George Bourne, *Change in the Village*.[23] These beautiful histories had been picked up by F. R. Leavis as rich, compelling evidence of the living civilization which was the achievement of the English folk before the advent of commercial culture, a civilization evident in the poetic dignity of their speech and the wonderful subtlety of their craft.

Hoggart set himself the task of seeing and judging the present civilization of Farnham, testing Leavis's theory of deturpation, seeking out the continuity of popular artistry – if it could be found – and the quality of the people's speech.

He tried out Farnham first for its built identity. Much has been written since Thomas Sharp's[24] pioneering work in the 1940s about the loss of shapeliness and of the sense of place in urban development. Hoggart took with him Kevin Lynch's splendid little textbook, *The Image of the City*,[25] and deploying its vocabulary of 'nodes, edges, landmarks, paths', finds Farnham still *there*, shapely, identity-bestowing, home to its people, but . . . but disfigured by the horrible 1960s and its mindless fashions – a vast roundabout, the dreadful 'Woolmead' edifice and the blasted vacancy around it.

Compiling a sort of personal ethnography – 'observer-participation' – Hoggart greeted the abandoned old pensioners who had made the bench and the blank space of the Argos entrance into their village

[23] The first published by Cambridge University Press, 1923, the second by Duckworth: London, 1925.
[24] See Thomas Sharp, *Oxford Replanned*, London: Architectural Press, 1948.
[25] Kevin Lynch, *The Image of the City*, Cambridge MA: MIT Press, 1960.

green, relished the breezy, archetypical young men who ran the greengrocer's stall in Castle Street, the best bit of the town, spotted any number of those stuffed-looking, over-lipsticked, blue-rinsed Tory matrons with voices that cut like arc-welders when they address offending passers-by, and who invariably shook him out of any anthropological neutrality.

He is back at his best spotting the tiny class variations in provisions which distinguish Spar from Tesco and both from Sainsbury's (where pious *Guardian* readers mostly belong, apart from treats in Waitrose), before turning to compare the many private schools and one sound Comprehensive, making all the still accurate, much-rehearsed arguments for the civic duty of the well-off to use the same schools all the other townsfolk use. Then, relevantly enough, he opens the diapason to play the full chords of political-martial music:

> We are still a badly under-educated nation; we waste the brains to be found in large parts of society as though they grew on untended trees, and we need only leave aside the masses of windfalls.[26]

The fault, he thinks – setting aside the insolent class contempt of the Ministers then on the job – is in the tight knot tied between the intellectual populism of broadcasters and the thick-skinned complacency of a still-philistine populace. His consistent refrain – he knows it is his refrain, but is compelled to restate it – is that so many people recline on the smelly sofa of bad habits while their favourite programmes feed them fat with the greasy fast-food of infantile quiz shows, talentless talent-shows, profit-spinning vacancy. *The Royle Family* told painful truths.

He finds threads of the good life in Farnham as he and Mary patrolled its pavements – at the hospitals where his cartilage was replaced; then he sings a short hymn in praise of the Women's Institute and, his longest such eulogy, lists joyfully the innumerable clubs, societies and less official gatherings, which bear continued witness to the pleasures of archery, fishing, ballroom dancing, old people's ballet, swimming (excellent to learn that our hero regularly took his antique breaststroke to the huge new sports centre-with-pool-plus-aquatic-supertechnology), birdwatching, thespians (big amateur productions six times yearly), music-making, gun club, model railways ... and in this throng, still vigorous and still far larger in its hopes than can be glossed as 'training' or 'recreation', the evening classes of

---

[26] Richard Hoggart, *Townscape with Figures: Farnham – Portrait of an English Town*, London: Chatto and Windus, 1994, p. 85.

Richard Hoggart while filming An Idea of Europe in 1987. Reproduced with the kind permission of Channel 4.

WEA and 'Lifelong Learning' (not a bad phrase) in literature, music, philosophy, the history of ideas, of viniculture, of painting.

All this, as I said earlier rebuking Orwell, is not *private* life; it is communal, mutual, neighbourly, cultivated, all Hoggart's best words. Then again,

> As I write, the latest Tory government is doing its best to wreck this lovely, complex, delicate but sinewy fabric – by its characteristic insistence that any adult educational provision from public funds should have a clearly defined vocational purpose; the rest is, belittlingly, 'recreational'.[27]

Cheerfulness keeps breaking in. Around Farnham there still stretches the lovely Surrey countryside, ample, undiminished, lushly green, the blackbirds, wrens, robins and tits still loud in birdsong even if the nightingales and cuckoos have gone.[28] Hoggart still pines

[27] Hoggart (1994), p. 161.
[28] Not everywhere, but in Surrey and Somerset, as Jeremy Mynott tells us in *Birdscapes*, Princeton: Princeton University Press, 2009.

for Wharfedale and Wensleydale, but there is much to love along the Hog's Back.

One figure stands out in the townscape: a postman in his mid-forties who paused at the front door one day to say to Hoggart that he 'was sorry to be missing some of your television programmes on Europe' ... 'but they overlap with Bryan Magee's series on philosophy and I've been following these from the beginning'.[29]

The postman, for Hoggart, stood beside Jude the Obscure and Forster's Leonard Bast. He is unlike them in that far more opportunity for education was available to him than to them, but that in his time and in order to follow the philosophers, he must ignore the advertisers, the cheap columnists, the footling TV programmes all telling him that philosophy is just a matter of 'dusty tomes' (a very usual cliché), that fun is where the heart is, let nobody tell you that the trivial is trivial. Who are they to say?

IV

The postman set Hoggart off on the next book. *Townscape with Figures* remained in hardback, it sold a few thousand, enough to keep his editor at Chatto happy. Topographical literature has always been a strong and living genre off to the edge of English literature, as the shelves of any secondhand bookshop testify. They aren't so visible in France or Italy, and the vast American distances make the pledge to place in the USA hard to avow. The Farnham book is Hoggart's pledge, even from a divided heart, half of which always longed for the Dales. He lived where he was. Belonging was his nature.

Farnham or Wharfedale, both were in England, and England, stuffy, 'snobby' (his adjective), split across its middle, England 'the family with the wrong members in charge', faded as to power, still stouthearted on its good days, she was still his subject of choice. So at top speed, he wrote *The Way We Live Now*,[30] the title taken from a scathing novel of Trollope's about just that.

It was a bold thing to do, and the report is not cheering. A lot turned for him on the moral propensity he found in his times towards 'relativism' – the book was published in the States under the title *The Tyranny of Relativism*[31] – by which he meant a refusal to judge

[29] These became (with Douglas Johnson) *An Idea of Europe*. See also Bryan Magee, *Men of Ideas*, London: BBC, 1978.
[30] Richard Hoggart, *The Way We Live Now*, London: Chatto and Windus, 1995.
[31] By Transaction Publishers, New Brunswick.

anything about the culture, a sort of moral laxity which evaded judgement (rejected as 'judgemental') for being punitive or snooty or undemocratic or in innumerable ways unconducive to just getting along mindlessly and fine.[32]

Hoggart was right to detect this quite strong strand in popular sentiment, especially as it transpired on television or in the tabloid press. To blame something called 'relativism' quite so loosely will not quite do. Relativism as a term in moral philosophy is surely the product of a world-change which has come about as peoples recognize just how immitigably various are the world's ways of thinking and feeling, as to its customs, cultures and ethics. In a classic essay on the topic called, with deliberate periphrasis, 'anti anti-relativism', Clifford Geertz, with years of comparative fieldwork in anthropology behind him, wrote:

> A scholar can hardly be better employed than in destroying a fear. The one I want to go after is cultural relativism. Not the thing itself, which I think merely there, like Transylvania, but the dread of it, which I think unfounded. It is unfounded because the moral and intellectual consequences that are commonly supposed to flow from relativism – subjectivism, nihilism, incoherence, Machiavellianism, ethical idiocy, esthetic blindness, and so on – do not in fact do so and the promised rewards of escaping its clutches, mostly having to do with pasteurized knowledge, are illusory.[33]

Geertz wrote his essay a little time before Hoggart wrote his book, and when there broke out a rash of academic studies all declaring the menace of something called relativism which its fevered opponents identified with nihilism.[34] Those serious people who suggested that neither rock-bottom foundations for aesthetic nor moral judgements, nor ultimate proofs for scientific ones, are, three and more centuries after Galileo and Spinoza, to be disinterred or built up, found themselves 'accused of disbelieving in the existence of the physical world, thinking pushpin as good as poetry, and regarding Hitler as just a fellow with nonstandard tastes.[35]

The poetry/pushpin contention was the one which preoccupied Hoggart. The cast of mind, or view of the world with which

---

[32] In a review of the book written at the time, I characterized his use of 'relativism' as meaning 'moral gutlessness'. I still think that's right – see *THES*, November 1995.

[33] Clifford Geertz, *Available Light: Anthropological Reflections on Philosophical Topics*, Princeton: Princeton University Press, 2000, pp. 42–67.

[34] Geertz (2000), p. 44.

[35] Among these works, the most balanced (which Hoggart read) was probably Hollis and S. Lukes, eds., *Rationality and Relativism*, Cambridge MA: MIT Press, 1982.

'relativism' was associated, however, is something more momentous than an academic tale of a tub or than a wild exaggeration about the-end-of-civilization-as-we-know-it. It is no more and no less than a change of mind brought about by the fact of increased propinquity in the world, the unignorability of other countries with other cultures and categories. The horror-struck anti-relativists ran terrified from the dangers that human meaning and collective significance would go down in a welter of opinion, and the good, the true and the beautiful be drowned by the vulgar horde, all unaware that eating people is wrong.

The Way We Live Now is damaged by this scary ghost come to tell us that Shakespeare doesn't matter, that – even worse – there is no such thing as evil. The answer, some prominent writers thought, was to rediscover and reground a theory of human nature, to restore rule to a fixed concept of the 'natural'.[36]

The new and queasy condition of certainty caused angst and exasperation, not least in Hoggart. As usual, fear and loathing damaged both clear thought as well as good feeling. What had happened, both as a result of work in the human sciences, in particular anthropology, and also, as consequence of the upheavals of world war, globalized trade and happy holidaymakers, was the not-very-awful discovery that morality cannot be placed beyond culture nor knowledge beyond belief.

His encounters with some of the tougher eggs among sociologists who were still able to persuade themselves that their social science was a hard factual science like that of the grown-ups in physics had left Hoggart too sensitive about the necessity of proof and the status of evidence. He had been a pioneer in pointing to the uses of literature for the purpose of sociological enlightenment but he had never quite got over a diffidence about the epistemological validity of words and concepts like 'insight', 'intuition', imaginative truth', let alone 'value' and its purported separation from 'fact', 'evidence' and its too-easy victory over 'example'. At just about that time, the last notes by Wittgenstein's students and the last fragments from his papers were being published, and in *On Certainty*[37] he says, 'If I had to give up my most basic assumptions I shouldn't be able to judge *anything*.' These are what another philosopher to whom Hoggart could have turned for polemic support, R. G. Collingwood, called 'absolute

---

[36] e.g. Mary Midgley in *Beast and Man: The Roots of Human Nature*, Ithaca: Cornell University Press, 1978.

[37] L. Wittgenstein, *On Certainty*, compiled from notes taken by Yorick Smythies and Rush Rhees, Oxford: Blackwell, 1971.

presuppositions',[38] and both proof and evidence, the sociologists' knockdown words, are just such.

So relativism was no synonym for nihilism, nor the scourge of standards in criticism. It was and remains merely a name for the discovery of the dissolution of certainties, of the huge energy of superstition, for the drunken disorientation which accompanies visits to the Orient; and *vice versa*. 'If we wanted home truths,' Geertz writes, 'we should have stayed at home.'[39]

Hoggart's arrows were certainly aimed at home, but he wanted urgently that they be true to the whole world. He places a marvellous and moving quotation from Václav Havel (another surprising source from his commonplace book) as epigraph to *The Way We Live Now*.

> I favour a politics not as the technology of power and manipulation, of cybernetic rule over humans, or as the art of the useful, but politics as practical morality, as service to the truth, as essentially human and humanly measured care for our fellow humans. It is an approach which, in this world, is extremely impractical and difficult to apply.[40]

Not a statement one can relativize much, nor one on which to act without becoming highly specific. Its application for Hoggart was simple and direct. His larger enemy remained commercial culture and those forces of production which, on television and in the yellow press, in the terrible tat and tattle of the supermarket magazines, demeaned human aspiration and hopefulness by their coarseness, flagrancy and confident assertion that price is value and success is money. His particular target was, however, that dreadful *trahison des clercs* whereby self-appointed spokespeople for the people, some of them academics, so betrayed their vocation as to say, as one did,[41] 'lavatorial graffiti are not to be distinguished in any qualitative way from the drawings of Rembrandt'. The loose-mouthed endorsement of this attitude generally came from the short-lived moment of academic Marxism fashionable in the nineteen seventies and eighties, whereby all culture once called 'high' (Tolstoy, Bach, Piero) was classified and condemned as bourgeois, and the earnest cowboys of prairie Marxism pronounced meaningless slogans such as 'culture does not (cannot) transcend the material forces and relations of production',[42] a dictum one can only translate by saying that novels

---

[38] R. G. Collingwood, *An Essay on Metaphysics*, Oxford: Clarendon Press, 1936, pp. 31ff.
[39] Geertz (2000), p. 65. His lecture was first given in 1983.
[40] Václav Havel, *Living in Truth*, London: Faber, 1987.
[41] Hoggart (1995), p. 55.
[42] Quoted in Hoggart (1995), p. 55. The remark made by one Anthony Easthope.

are produced on typewriters and sold in bookshops (at least until Kindle came along), a fact which needs no fancy diction.

What made Hoggart so angry about these vacuities – and he reined back his anger by writing the book – was the offence they perpetrated on all the evening classes he had ever taught. He had met the people holding to this vulgar populism during his years on the Arts Council – heaven knows what Keynes would have made of them – and what so roused him to scorn and rejection was their suppressed contempt both for great art and for those people innocently looking for and at it, millions of them in the libraries, art galleries, opera houses and tourist capitals of the world.

He traces these hostile, standardless attitudes in many places – in public libraries[43] buying innumerable copies of Jack Higgins and Barbara Cartland, in CD stands of 'easy listening' (why not 'hard listening but worth it', Hoggart says), and in Arts Council money going to fifth-rate street theatre groups and banal installations.

There's no doubt that there was, across the past twenty years or so, quite a strong movement at the aesthetic end of intellectual life to diminish the authority of established literature, 'firing the canon' as a good joke put it. The paradox was that contemporary cultural studies launched this venture, and picked up support from the brilliant goblins of deconstruction such as Roland Barthes on the death of the author,[44] and Derrida's work on the ultimate slipperiness of verbal meaning.[45] Hoggart's version of cultural studies started out, on quite another hand, from strongly affirmed standards of discrimination, themselves grounded on the evidence (needful word, here) of powers of expression, disinterestedness of judgement (important, as part of Hoggart's argument, to point out how 'disinterested' is now used to mean 'bored'; its prior, more important meaning, has almost vanished), compassionate attention . . . these are all qualities recognizable and honoured in our everyday interlocutors; it is just as straightforward to detect them in writers. Hoggart quotes George Eliot's last farewell to Dorothea Brooke in *Middlemarch*. I can't refrain from quoting it here.

> Her finely touched spirit had still its fine issues, though they were not widely visible. Her full nature, like that river of which Cyrus broke

---

[43] The historical repudiation of the Left populists is made in Jonathan Rose's splendid history, *The Intellectual Life of the English Working Class*, New Haven and London: Yale University Press, 2001.

[44] Roland Barthes, *Writing Degree Zero*, London: Jonathan Cape, 1967.

[45] Derrida (1967) as already cited.

the strength, spent itself in channels which had no great name on the earth. But the effect of her being on those around her was incalculably diffusive: for the growing good of the world is partly dependent on unhistoric acts; and that things are not so ill with you and me as they might have been, is half owing to the number who lived faithfully a hidden life, and rest in unvisited tombs.[46]

The tone and language are perfectly adjusted one to another; the delicate recognition of obscurity made in such a way as to demand not just our moral sympathy, but to name our own membership of such hidden lives; the long and lovely cadence of the paragraph sweeps us up in its music and opens us, involuntarily palpitating, to the facts of our common humanity. That is what such writing can, may do; not always and not to everybody – people have to learn to listen, hence classes in literature – but often enough for the sake of, well, proof.

Having unfurled his standard, he goes on, in 'aspects of the dominant mood' to put 'mass' and 'popular' beside and below George Eliot, D. H. Lawrence, George Herbert and all, in order to say, usefully, that there are 'good bad books' and films and television dramas which, poor though they may be, 'leave something bright on the imagination', that popular art may speak even from ill-made materials for corners of the human heart with much good in them. Hoggart has in mind Orwell's famous essay on seaside comic postcards, still the supreme instance of finding the best parts of mass-produced popularity. Those best parts lived on for years in the magnificent tradition of radio and television comics, the years of Al Read, Les Dawson, Eric Morecambe and Ernie Wise, Tommy Cooper, Victoria Wood, Julie Walters; they are not over yet. Hoggart's own working busily away, *not* at connecting high (or élite or bourgeois) art to popular (or folk) art, but at discovering wherever it is to be found the best, the most fully human 'culture of the feelings', is his great legacy. He worked at this grand topic in books and in life, as it is the whole point of this biography to affirm.

It's a rare affirmation to be able to make. Yet there is a fine convention in British life, available until recently to public-spirited academics, to pursue the preoccupations of their thought into the administration of public life. Men and women such as Michael Young, Peter Townsend, Richard Titmuss, Mary Warnock, Lady Plowden, the Runcimans, did so conspicuously with their work on education, welfare, poverty, drugs and disability. Hoggart, more unusually, did

---

[46] George Eliot, *Middlemarch*, Harmondsworth: Penguin, 1965, p. 896.

so with his work on culture, class, communications and capitalism. It may be that this career translation is now becoming neglected, as governments of both stripes no longer appoint Royal Commissions nor serious academic advisers. If so, followers of Hoggart will have a harder time applying his lessons.

Pondering this danger is a right response to the book in hand. For his concern is always with the public consequences of what he criticizes even while he insists that in matters of culture the separations between public and private, between citizen and subjectivity cannot, indeed must not, be made. This he affirms while repeating the truth that freedom lives in the quiddity of individual lives.

When he returns once more to the public language of our buying and selling, our everyday administering of our bodies and minds whether at the doctor's surgery, the parents' evening at school, or gaping at the sheer bloody self-assurance of the politicians on *Question Time*, then he is on his very own ground. Once more, he frolics, with a pungent gaiety, among all that fatuous phraseology, and in particular the language of 'scientific management' – those verbose evasions, grotesque neologisms, and that downright mendacity. It's a pleasure to see 'virement', 'tranche', 'matrix management', 'interact' (instead of 'talk to') done to death like this, see 'headcount reduction' (for sacking staff) or 'rationalizing compensation' (for cutting wages) lined up for the evasions they are, and to watch lies being called lies ('difficult choices but no alternative', 'sharing the pain', 'equitable rebalancing of the economy'). The trouble is that this zombie diction is no sooner shot through the heart than it gets up and walks again. Nearly twenty years after his book was published, the unspeakable language of managerialism is more widely spoken than ever. One has to put a lot of faith in that quotation from Matthew Arnold which concludes chapter 1 in these pages:

> . . . he has not won his political battles, he has not stopped his adversaries' advance . . . but he has told silently upon the mind of the country . . . he has kept up his communication with the future.

My word, I hope so.

There is no diminution in the energy with which he pursued the enemy. He uses his years with the Arts Council to illustrate and condemn cant on the part of sponsors and providers (in the jargon), to hunt down the innumerable quarries in government and official agencies which effect censorship on the sly, by way of official murmurings (England, my England) and by discreet threats of litigation or dismissal.

241

It must be said in fairness that years as a committee chairman – and he was acerbic as well as intransigent in that role – sometimes led even Hoggart into the phraseology of the upholsterer. That, however, is the necessity of the democrat, of the man who, searching for the just consensus, must in truth stretch out reconciling hands to irreconcilable opponents, the chairman who knows that at the last his committee must be allowed to go home.

V

He had ended, as so often, with a song in praise of the immortality of neighbourliness in Britain; not monumental stone to build on but it would have to do. Mrs Thatcher's years had done fearful damage, her aftershocks are hardly stilled in 2013. The public penetration of the deadly polysyllable 'privatization' reaches deep into private lives. So Hoggart being Hoggart, as the man said, he carried on writing.

There was an easy rhythm to it, a lifetime's rhythm, on Beavers Hill. The Hoggart children were by the end of the century citizens of standing: Simon, now in his mid-fifties, a much-respected and very funny journalist with the *Guardian*, let alone wine reviewer for the *Spectator*. His precocious gift for comedy, sometimes biting, served him well as parliamentary correspondent in Norman Shrapnel's old seat; Paul, lecturer in Further Education and television correspondent for *The Times* and elsewhere, as well as, later and a bit more precariously, freelancing; Nicola, long a primary schoolteacher in Norwich; plenty of grandchildren, plenty of welcome, boisterous visits to the roomy house in Farnham, all these happy seasons punctuated by regular short holidays in France, back to the Lubéron and a rented cottage Richard and Mary favoured near Gordes in the gorgeous lavender fields inland from Cassis.

The writing still insisted upon itself, mostly in the mornings, Mary always a very early bird, Hoggart not much slower and in front of the computer screen by 8.30. He had passed eighty in 1998 and received a new knee; Chatto had demurred at a new book proposal; Piers Burnett, his own boss at Aurum Press and a long-standing admirer, had said yes, and *First and Last Things*, begun as soon as he finished *The Way We Live Now*, appeared in 1999.

As one would expect, the book didn't lack nerve: it openly declared allegiance to and competition with Montaigne. Not many intellectuals are still writing at eighty-one, and they mostly remain on their small half-acre. Hoggart still sought to address his country, but especially some portion of those millions in it about to take their pensions and to look out warily for the last things they trust are still some way off.

He does so, as so many times before, standing on a thick rag rug of quotations, a magic carpet of commonplaces carrying him, never very far off the ground – 'Quick, thy tablets, memory' – to ruminate on love and self-love, on capitalism no less, and democracy and, with a greater ease than Montaigne, on the coming darkness.

> What are the roots that clutch, Son of Man,
> Out of this stony rubbish?

His answers to Eliot's terrible question are, as you'd expect, calm, sufficiently apprehensive, loving, tart. I could wish his chairmanly mien could be put off at times, that he could have *named*, for history's sake, Robert Macnamara as the very high official in the USA who had so strongly prosecuted the Vietnamese War, and years later wished he hadn't.[47] When he quotes his hero Richard Titmuss on 'the responsibility of the State . . . to reduce or eliminate or control the forces of market coercions', one can only cheer him on.

His memories carry him back into the past, he floats easily on them until the sudden moment when a cigarette lighter flashes tinily and he flinches again at the terrible yellow flash and roar of flaming petrol vapour rushing to consume him from the door of the hovel in Pantelleria.[48]

He once more floats past his family, not at all self-centredly, more a matter of prompting similar memories in the more-or-less elderly readers he imagines as his listeners. One good thing about one's children and grandchildren in the old age of those with enough money is that they are mostly somewhere else, mostly happy enough. He looks back to his brother Tom, who had died suddenly of cancer in 1990, and feels again the gentleness of Tom's great, protective strength, he comes across a photo of his sister Molly, aged twenty, slim and beautiful like her mother. He recalls Simon, at four, on a very happy day at the beach round the corner from their house in Marske, bringing a rush of loving tears to his mother's eyes by asking, 'Shall I be happy all the days?' Paul, then barely out of small childhood, disparages those friends who 'slag off' their parents. 'I don't do that. I love you two.'[49]

[47] Hoggart (1999), pp. 75, 76.
[48] Hoggart (1999), p. 145.
[49] Hoggart (1999), p. 167.

He reflects on sex, as often, and on food, also as often, and takes most readers along with him. He muses, with Trollope, on marriages less fortunate than his own, on a certain hardness in husbands where tenderness is called for.

> With people that are indifferent to him, no man is less exacting, but with those near to him in life he never bends, not an inch.[50]

I believe I am treating the book as he would have wished, catching hold of those many passages that are moving, storing up those quotations which hit the mark, matching his thoughts against like ones of my own. 'There can't be long to go.' He tots up the bodily weaknesses of age, the parts wearing out, and 'the hope, the new ships'. For after all,

> You need the time to finish the next book, which is always, nowadays, to be the last. But somehow you don't quite believe that. There is always another – one more – interesting job to attempt . . .[51]

Then he ends with George Herbert's loveliest lines:

> And now in age I bud again,
> After so many deaths I live and write,
> I once more smell the dew and rain,
> And relish versing.

Needless to say, but I say it, *First and Last Things* was by no means the last book. Aurum published a collection of essays called *Between two Worlds* in 2001. Mostly material published in the previous ten years, it included a fine essay written for a well-deserved *Festschrift* presented to Philip French, staunch defender at the BBC for almost forty years, of exactly those principles of intelligent democratic broadcasting Hoggart had expounded all his working life. As Hoggart said, French lost the battle. The war was and is still being fought.

Hoggart's is a grim threnody. Ever since *Broadcasting in the Nineties* it was obvious that the standards of public service broadcasting were disintegrating. The shameful assaults of the Murdochs' empire and its eponymous chief on the BBC, and their wholly self-interested campaign so to dominate British media that they could sell, at cut-throat prices, a media bundle of Sky TV and newspapers (as well as iPad access and all the other bits and pieces of electronic black magic), was allowed disgraceful latitude until the boiling scandal

---

[50] Hoggart (1999), p. 173.
[51] Hoggart (1999), p. 228.

of 2011 finally broke open, and the pus drained into public ears. Hoggart repeats once more that public service is a noble ideal, never more so than when shaping a nation's broadcast conversation with itself. Now, perhaps for a season, perhaps for ever, it is finished. It lives inaudibly on in corner studios like the World Service, but as a principled forum for a nation's innumerable narratives, it is done for.

At the end of the collection *Between two Worlds* (the two worlds in question being those of public and private life), he added a hundred pages of new autobiography, addressed to his grandchildren. They are beautifully done. In them he returns their proper names to his early family in Hunslet – Clara replacing 'Ethel', Lil replacing 'Annie', Bert replacing 'Walter', and 'Winnie' becoming Ivy, as she was. He does honour to his slightly stiff, always upright father-in-law, Harry France, and sees Harry's widow, Doris, through almost thirty years of widowhood, endlessly attentive to her grandchildren, teacherly and tolerant as she ought to be, in the end dying, like Harry, of cancer without fuss. The finest pages in this late memoir are given to big brother Tom, with a plain, unidealized tribute to the right feeling which led him to conscientious objection and service on the Normandy beaches with the RAMC and, singing an elegy to an uncelebrated, exemplary life, calls up Tom's headmastership of a Yorkshire secondary modern school and ushers us beside his deathbed in 1990 when, having ordered his family to bring champagne (ten of them in attendance) he bade them all a loving farewell. He died next day, 'a hidden life' revealed by his brother.

Apart from expressing appreciative astonishment at Hoggart's durability, it would be invidious to plod through the remaining books assigning ticks or crosses to different chapters, weighing their place in the oeuvre. What is important to the biography is, first, the continued centrality of writing to the order of his life and, second, the affectionate public esteem which ensured that enough people, perhaps mostly the elderly or at least those getting on a bit, would turn to Hoggart for sound advice and just reflection on how to view modern Britain. When Boyd Tonkin, literary editor at the *Independent*, sent his reviewer *Mass Media in a Mass Society* after it was published in 2004, he wrote 'I don't know how good it is, but we must do it because it's him.' The *Guardian* accorded him two full pages.[52]

These things said, *Everyday Language and Everyday Life*,[53]

[52] *Guardian*, 7 February 2004.
[53] Richard Hoggart, *Everyday Language and Everyday Life*, New Brunswick and London: Transaction Publishers, 2003.

while providing the vast subject-matter of his life's work once more, remains a cracking read and is both swiftly and firmly organized. He dedicated it to Molly, who had died at just eighty and after a tough life, the year before. It is another family book in that it is addressing the 'country with the wrong members in charge', but it is not so much reproachful of that country (Chekhov's 'it is shameful to live like that') as sombre and repelled. Cheerfulness just about breaks in, as he reckons up the continuity of parts of the old moral language of the working class and as he welcomes better clothes, better health, better equipment in the home.

But things are bad. He may be a little off-target in blaming everything on what he again calls relativism, but one cannot doubt the accuracy with which he analyses the disintegration of a shared moral vocabulary, nor fail to agree with his bitter condemnation of the revolting chaos punctually broadcast to mass audiences as 'reality TV'. However little one can be sure of in the argument on the effects of mass media, one needs no figures to support the judgement that, as Clive James used so splendidly to put it, these programmes win the award for 'bad sight of the week'.

Against these ruins, the narcissism, the greed for money, the vindictive envy and giddy worship of celebrity, he pieces together his fragments of hope: 'the traditional cant expressions which lubricate our daily life', the 'putting up',[54] the tolerance, then he cites this wonderful quotation from Tony Harrison (who else? Mind you make 'gas' rhyme with 'pass'):

> Though my mother was already two years dead,
> Dad kept her slippers warming by the gas,
> put water bottles her side of the bed,
> and still went to renew her transport pass.

It is important even if supererogatory to say that at no point does Hoggart sound like a columnist in the *Daily Mail*. Indeed, he blames its editor for so thoughtlessly doing much to dismantle a common moral vocabulary. Yet in ordinary life he finds wives and mothers still mostly at the centre of family, still retaining a moral authority larger than mere personality; marriage and children still shaped by canons of love and care and responsibility living on in gesture, phrases, in common expectancy that good and not evil will be done to all at home.

Hoggart is completely unafraid of charges of banality or obvious-

---

[54] Hoggart (2003), pp. xiii, 30, 42.

ness. If 'class' has yielded to 'status', if deference has declined and courtesy with it, it is still plain to him that our culture ratifies cruel inequality, strips youngsters of a fair chance, teaches in everyday ways which neither schools nor universities can correct, contempt for the life of the mind, the neglect of beauty, the queasiness of truth.

Here, in these living processes and growing pains, public and private lives meld into the heavy mud and swift waters of old culture. One thing Hoggart rarely mentions in all this is the system of the social recognition of achievement. Such systems tell one much about a nation, and the British system of the Queen's Honours list tells us that public recognition is made smelly and poisonous by the squirming and toadying in the queues of political preferment which lead to the sword tapping the shoulder. As one would expect, Hoggart twice declined a knighthood (once from each Party). It's good to know that he is joined by such other refusers and natural allies as R. H. Tawney ('what harm have I ever done the Labour Party?' Tawney asked), Richard Titmuss, the playwright Alan Bennett, the historian Quentin Skinner, the film-maker Ken Loach.

He looks at the adages, the slang and the readymade phrases for religion, for sex and food and takes his leave, not grim but severe enough, putting his faith in the secularized Methodism in which he was brought up, and placing at the heart of the best of his times, the moral necessity of decency.

Maybe it is hard to ward off charges of banality, cliché, sententiousness and the rest in the rush of books published after his eightieth birthday, though Hoggart sails blithely past them. In his very last book,[55] published when he was eighty-six, he rewrites *First and Last Things*, some of those things said again, he's a bit surprised to find himself still here, still finding them worth saying, enough people still in the audience.

He and Mary had moved from the big house in Farnham the year Molly died and while he was finishing his work on everyday language. Nicola had been particularly pressing that her parents were no longer able to handle the demands of Mortonsfield. Her mother's sight was become very poor and her father's memory at times uncertain. Her brothers joined her in urging that the parents should move near her in Norwich and, after twenty-six years, far and away the longest they had stayed in one place, they left Farnham. Nicola had sought out a smaller, suitable house at 19 Mount Pleasant in Norwich where she had long been resident with her family. The new house was only three

[55] Richard Hoggart, *Promises to Keep: Thoughts in Old Age*, London: Continuum, 2005.

hundred yards away and her parents' welfare, for all that they were still independent and self-propelling, readily and daily at hand for checking up.

It had been a fearful wrench leaving Farnham. They were solid homemakers, always confirming and thickening their presence in the house by way of a new painting, a piece of furniture, a small memento. The books and bits and pieces of grandchildren's visits were tucked noticeably away as part of the natural flora of the home. Moving all that, chucking away so many of the signs of gone times, is always painful and, at over eighty, exhausting. A part of a person who has had the good fortune to root him- or herself in a handsome house is torn off in such upheavals; the past which was part of one's self-possession drains away.

Much of Hoggart's library had to be stored in the garage on Mount Pleasant, and much more given away. As the elderly will, and as Mary's sight faded away, they kept knives and forks, cups and plates out on the open surfaces of the kitchen rather than put them away. But although Mary became pretty well housebound, Richard found a pub close at hand which served a fry-up to his satisfaction, and kept on writing. 'I could "bridle" (lovely word)' he wrote in the new book, 'at the assumption that you can have little to say at 80-odd',[56] and as always he gathered in defence against the coming darkness his book of quotations. Ulysses told him, in Tennyson's voice,

Death closes all: but something ere the end,
Some work of noble note may yet be done.

So off he went, treading the pavements of memory, some personal – a marvellous memoir of a State Visit by his two very elderly aunts, Clara and Lil, at last reconciled, to the family home in Birmingham ('me feet are killing me')[57] – some hugely historic (the Gulag). In all of them the same sound, reassuring, goodly voice comes through to its many listeners, repeating his old stories, telling us with all his old directness to keep faith with love, with charity, and with writing. A young man's voice underlines his point. John Keats says on Hoggart's behalf: 'I am convinced more and more and day by day that fine writing is, next to fine doing, the top thing in the world.'[58]

During his ruminations, he describes himself as 'a bit of a loner'. Surely this is wrong? In the summer of 2006, a group of his admirers,

---

[56] Hoggart (2005), p. 6.
[57] Hoggart (2005), pp. 44–6.
[58] Hoggart (2005), p. 103.

summoned to the University of Sheffield (which gave him an honorary doctorate a few years previously) by Sue Owen, custodian of his papers lodged in the university library, testified in a series of papers to their admiration for and indebtedness to him.[59] He was there in person, his memory a bit shaky, but cordial, accessible, friendly without fail, nothing of a loner. 'Modest and engaging' the reviewer said in the *Guardian* of his last book. There are adjectives in a major key to add: 'steely' perhaps, 'courageous' for sure, loving always, warmhearted towards anybody who came to talk with him in a spirit of common inquiry into the old trinity of truth, goodness, beauty, stern and uncompromising with any show of the arrogance of caste and the presumption of inequality.

VI

It is time to take leave of number 19 Mount Pleasant. The Hoggarts had to move again to a care home near Paul as Mary's muscular coordination and her very self failed, while Richard's memory and lucidity lapsed as well. But this biography concludes, as absolutely it should, by saluting those two lives at their most venerable.

Speaking a valediction, it is always difficult to avoid plangency, and especially so at a time when, as his last books bore witness, the civic virtues are in shaky repair and, for a time, when Hoggart's prime allegiances – to equality, to mutuality, to a vital democracy, to the possession by a nation of the common wealth of its culture – when these lights are darkened. Large portions of the rich world are having now to face up to radical and uncontrollable reductions in their acquisitions, especially of money, and Britain in particular will have to discover for herself how not to live solely off the gains of its financial buccaneers. Old Corruption, in Cobbett's still resonant phrase, must needs recall that the Kingdom stretches well beyond Watford, and if its culture is to prove as tough an integument as Hoggart thought, it will need to enfold and protect many more people than it does at present.

So eulogy of its nature turns mournful, and there is plenty for those of us Hoggart leaves behind to mourn. But as I have already said in these pages, a biography, if it is any good, illumines 'lines of force for transformation'. Those who share Hoggart's commitments and

---

[59] Published as *Re-Reading Richard Hoggart*, Newcastle: Cambridge Scholars Publishing, 2008.

share them because they have learned from his work and his life why these latter count for so much, pick up mass, energy and light from the lessons of a life, and put them to work for the future which is just emerging as the present.

It will be useful therefore to name a few such successors as hostages to our fortune, all of them members of the generation after Hoggart and therefore themselves beginning naturally to creak a little, serving here however to show that elusive concept 'influence' in action and therefore to indicate what it is to keep up the radical tradition.

The first such figure is the poet, Tony Harrison, several times cited in these pages, self-avowed admirer of Hoggart and his work, and a poet of great strength who has been determined to make his poetry out of his class and his origins in Leeds, and to reconnect its accents to the huge family of canonical poetry, the Latin masters and the school of eloquence. His fighting poem 'V' was written in Yorkshire out of the heart of the miners' strike of 1984–5, inevitable defeat in which announced the end, at the hands of the Thatcher government, of heavy industry in northern Britain. Yet at its close, the poet goes home to his woman and puts his faith for the future in a seat in front of a coal fire.

The second writer is Dennis Potter, who died of pancreatic cancer twenty years ago, then only in his fifties, but whose immense literary achievement spoke eloquently for the vision of public television Hoggart fought for from the Pilkington Report onwards. He made his debt to Hoggart explicit, saying of that great TV drama, *The Singing Detective*, that it was a parable contrived out of the story of 'the scholarship boy',[60] as well as the influence being clear as day in the rest of that splendid trilogy, *Pennies from Heaven* and *Lay Down Your Arms*. All three dramas are punctuated by performances of the most open-hearted popular songs of their day, songs which, as Potter said,[61] stood in an unbroken line 'from the Psalms of King David'; so, 'lay down your arms, and surrender to mine'.

The third writer declaring indebtedness to Hoggart's work and his friendship is Alan Bennett. His marvellous making of poetic drama for television out of forgotten lives and speechless individuals – Patricia Routledge dying with a little patience in and out of hospital ('Ee, we laffed'), Thora Hird dying puzzled and alone on the floor beside her sofa – perfectly enacts so much of the loving analysis in *The Uses of Literacy*. By the same token, the exemplary use made by

[60] TV interview with Alan Yentob, BBC2.
[61] In a famous final TV interview with Melvyn Bragg, BBC2.

Victoria Wood of the mass observation diaries of a dogged housewife during the Second World War puts Alan Bennett's recreation of the muffled poetry of class diction to fresh effect.

There are many more contenders jostling for a place in the queue of those directly influenced by Hoggart, and declaring that influence in the making of everyday and wholly serious culture. His friend David Lodge's solid novels, tenderly (and bitingly) remaking Mrs Gaskell's classic *North and South* into a contemporary corner of class and sexual struggle in Birmingham in *Nice Work*, is one such. He wrote many more, all of them serious and intelligent, all of them funny. Melvyn Bragg, who much acknowledges the directness of Hoggart's ideas as an influence on the television programmes he has made for well over thirty years, deserves a book on his own, chronicling all he has done to keep class and culture (the title of a 2012 three-part series he made) on speaking terms, and to keep television and radio culture, and the debate about it, serious, speakable, uncondescending, alive.

These are men and women nearing the end of their careers. But that is the point. They picked up Hoggart's tradition and ran with it. Their heirs will have a harder time of it. But those heirs won't be able to put up much of a fight unless they turn to the work, the thought and the life of our great original.

This is therefore merely the end of a biography, not of a tradition. That will renew itself. The life recounted in these pages remains however our subject. We honour the life, by telling of it truthfully, cheerfulness breaking in as it must, and because it plentifully did. We help the old up to their end, as we ought. Then, with a sort of clowning, await our turn.

The good life is given unity and meaning to the extent that the virtues exhibited in it are virtues in all possible circumstances – at home, at war, in intellectual composition, in a television interview, in the university or in UNESCO. Eminence itself inflects the enactment of the virtues. It is the importance of Richard Hoggart's life that it justifies by its mere existence the claim that the pre-modern conception of the virtues still lives and moves within its tradition. The damnable thing about the concept of a tradition is, as I have three times said in these pages, that it has become monopolized and disfigured by the Right. In urging that, in Leavis's phrase, Richard Hoggart's is a name that, in these days, we should peculiarly honour, I am intent upon the calm consistency with which he incarnates both domestic and intellectual virtues as these are livable in our time. Domestic love, the love of art, intellectual straightness and stubbornness, a vigorous egalitarianism, absolute hostility to what is shameful, corrupt and wicked in people's lives and the life of the times, unfailing and hospitable courtesy, a keen sense of the ridiculous . . . these qualities are very far from being fragments to shore against ruined lives, and modern Britain is far from being a wasteland. They are strong and active, as we have seen, and we had better keep them in as good repair as Hoggart has.

BIBLIOGRAPHY OF HOGGART'S WORKS

The following are the works of Richard Hoggart treated in the text.

Auden: An Introductory Essay. London: Chatto and Windus, 1951.

The Uses of Literacy: Aspects of Working-Class Life with Special Reference to Publications and Entertainments. London: Chatto and Windus, 1957; Harmondsworth: Penguin, 1958; followed by many editions, including New Brunswick: Transaction Publishers, with a postscript by John Corner, and most recently, Penguin 2009, with a new introduction by Lynsey Hanley. Published in French as *La Culture du Pauvre.* Paris: Editions de Minuit, 1970.

The Literary Imagination and the Study of Society. Birmingham: Centre for Contemporary Cultural Studies, 1967.

Contemporary Cultural Studies: An Approach to the Study of Literature and Society. Birmingham: Centre for Contemporary Cultural Studies, 1969.

Speaking to Each Other, volume 1: About Society. London: Chatto and Windus, 1970.

Speaking to Each Other, volume 2: About Literature. London: Chatto and Windus, 1970.

Only Connect: On Culture and Communication (the Reith lectures). London: Chatto and Windus, 1972.

An Idea and its Servants: UNESCO from Within. London: Chatto and Windus, 1978.

An English Temper: Essays on Education, Culture and Communications. London: Chatto and Windus, 1982.

An Idea of Europe. London: Chatto and Windus, 1987.

A Local Habitation: Life and Times 1918–1940. London: Chatto and Windus, 1988.

A Sort of Clowning: Life and Times 1940–1959. London: Chatto and Windus, 1990.

An Imagined Life: Life and Times 1959–1991. London: Chatto and Windus, 1992.

The three volumes of autobiography were then published in the USA as *A Measured Life: Times and Places of an Orphaned Intellectual.* New Brunswick: Transaction Publishers, 1994.

Townscape with Figures: Farnham – Portrait of an English Town. London: Chatto and Windus, 1994.

The Way We Live Now. London: Chatto and Windus, 1995. Subsequently published in the USA as *The Tyranny of Relativism: Culture and Politics in Contemporary English Society*. New Brunswick: Transaction Publishers, 1997.

First and Last Things. London: Aurum Press, 1999.

Between Two Worlds: Essays 1978–1999. London: Aurum Press, 2001. This collection was later published in the USA by Transaction Publishers, 2002.

Everyday Language and Everyday Life. New Brunswick: Transaction Publishers, 2003.

Mass Media in a Mass Society. London: Continuum, 2004.

Promises to Keep: Thoughts in Old Age. London: Continuum, 2005.

INDEX